lonely

LONDON

Hannah Ajala, Tharik Hussain, Linda Konde,
Travis Levius, Demi Perera, Qin Xie

Contents

GIORGIOGALANO/GETTY IMAGES ©
PEDESTRIAN ZONE
No vehicles Saturday 10 am - 4 pm
Except

Above Portobello Road Market (p160)

COSMOPOLITAN **CUISINE**

When the population of a city has more than 270 nationalities (and counting), is it any surprise the culinary offerings are as diverse as the people living in it? Whether it's fine dining or street food you love, London will have a Michelin-starred restaurant or a market stall dishing up your favourite cuisine.

→ A REAL CURRY

If you're tired of the menus offered in most of London's 'Indian' restaurants, try new eateries like Graam Bangla. which serves authentic Sylheti food, on Brick Lane (p128).

DI FANFO/SHUTTERSTOCK ©

Left Curries at Camden Market
Right Goru di Hatkora, a traditional Sylheti dish
Below Seafood at Da Terra (p136)

MICHELIN-STARRED EAST LONDON

Central London might be famous for its Michelin-starred restaurants but some of the most exciting are now in the East End. Go for micro-seasonal dishes at Lyle's near Brick Lane, or Behind in Hackney for a sustainable fish-focused tasting menu (p136).

RIGHT: SUPPLIED BY DA TERRA
LEFT: I WEI HUANG/SHUTTERSTOCK ©

↑ FUSION FUN

London has a long tradition of restaurants experimenting with cuisine; indulge in fusion food at the likes of Michelin-starred Da Terra, which plates up a set menu inspired by European and South American cuisines (p136).

Best Foodie Markets

▶ **Head south of the river for one of the best places for street food, Southbank Centre Food Market.** (p78-9)

▶ **Learn how to make your own bread and doughnuts at Borough Market, one of London's oldest food markets.** (p80-1)

▶ **Visit the underrated Exmouth Market in Clerkenwell for Indian and Mediterranean food stalls.** (p110)

▶ **Find the widest ethnic choices and the largest halal offerings of all the markets at Brick Lane's Sunday food market.** (p125)

STREET MARKETS

London's markets fall broadly into two categories. There are the local ones that still 'stack 'em high and sell 'em cheap', and those that are less about buying and more about the experience, whether that be browsing for vintage clothes as a busker plays jazz nearby, or tucking into a delicious Sri Lankan *sambal* as you eye up that handmade necklace.

Left Columbia Road Flower Market (p125)
Right Vintage clothes stalls in Spitalfields Market (p114)
Below Brick Lane Market (p125)

HAGGLING

Haggling is fine when buying anything but food at a market – just don't be too cheeky, and if you want the best deals, arrive towards closing time.

PAOLO PARADISO/SHUTTERSTOCK ©

↓ SUNDAY MARKET TRAIL

There are lots of Sunday market experiences in London, but few match Bethnal Green's Brick Lane and Hackney's Columbia Road Flower Market combo (p125).

RIGHT: ELENA ROSTUNOVA/SHUTTERSTOCK ©
LEFT: ELENACHAYKINAPHOTOGRAPHY/SHUTTERSTOCK ©

THE LOCALS

For delicious Asian street food like chana chaat or just to observe real local life in East London, visit markets such as Whitechapel Market (p136).

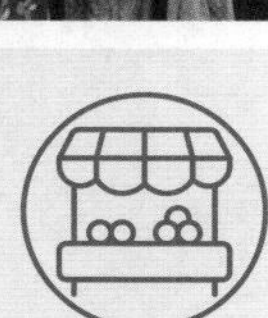

Memorable Market Experiences

- ▶ **Head under covers at Spitalfields Market, a handicraft haven, to escape rainy days.** (p114-5)
- ▶ **Browse authentic African clothing at Walworth's East Street Market.** (p187)
- ▶ **Spend a lazy Sunday afternoon at Herne Hill Market for artisan crafts and vintage finds.** (p187)
- ▶ **Indulge your green thumb at the Columbia Road Flower Market, a literal shopping jungle.** (p125)
- ▶ **Enjoy that clichéd but very much essential Notting Hill experience: Portobello Road Market.** (p160-1)

THE WORLD **IN LONDON**

London has always been an immigrants' city: Romans, Vikings, Anglo-Saxons, Huguenots, Jews, the Irish, African-Caribbeans, Asians and, more recently, Eastern Europeans have all called it home. It's what makes London such a spectacularly special place. Some of these communities arrived in larger numbers and established themselves in neighbourhoods where they today have their own markets, restaurants, places of worship and community centres. Wandering through them is like wandering across to another place.

Left Chinese New Year celebrations (p21)
Right Tara Arts Theatre (p186), Earlsfield
Below Boishakhi Mela festival (p23)

→ FRINGE THEATRE

Wandsworth's Tara Theatre (p186) stages plays produced by British South Asian communities, which explore the sociopolitical issues that these communities are facing.

ARCHITECTS: AEDAS. SIMON TURNER/ALAMY STOCK PHOTO ©

BLACK ARTS

London has some great galleries dedicated to diverse voices such as Brixton's 198 Contemporary Arts, which was once at the forefront of Britain's Black Arts Movement.

RIGHT: OLIVIER GUIBERTEAU/SHUTTERSTOCK ©
LEFT: JESSICAGIRVAN/SHUTTERSTOCK ©

↑ CARNIVALS

Notting Hill Carnival may be London's most famous, but other ethnic festivals like Boishakhi Mela, which celebrates the Bengali New Year, are also worth discovering.

Best Ethnic Neighbourhoods

- **Explore the neighbourhood around Brick Lane to glimpse life in London's Bangladeshi community.** (p128-9)
- **Meander from Shoreditch through Dalston and into Haringey for a distinctly Anatolian air.** (p132-5)
- **Take in a vibrant display of Chinese culture in Chinatown, albeit a commercial version, in central London close to Soho.** (p50-1)
- **Hit Walworth's East Street Market to experience the area's African-Caribbean heritage and culture.** (p187)

LONDON BY FOOT & PEDAL

London is the capital of a country that popularised the very notion of hiking, which is why it is an extremely walkable place with plenty of green spaces. Discover new waterways and explore fascinating wildlife on interesting walking and cycling trails that allow you to enjoy the city in different ways. London remains slightly behind when it comes to cycle friendliness, however, so be careful and cautious on your bike.

Left Skyline views from Primrose Hill
Right Santander Cycles
Below Westminster Bridge during the World Naked Bike Ride

→ HIRING BIKES

Bike hires are few and far between in London, as most people opt to just rent the ubiquitous Santander bicycles (p208).

APPY WALKS & CYCLES

Try these apps for routes: TfL Go, Footpath Route Planner, Cyclestreets and Cyclers. Also try the Sustrans *(sustrans.org.uk)* website.

↑ THE NAKED CYCLE

Fancy raising cycle safety awareness as you pedal in your birthday suit? Then join London's World Naked Bike Ride in June.

Best Walks & Bike Rides

▶ **Walk the River Wandle Trail and explore a secret 'bucolic' London river.** (p178-9)

▶ **Cycle the towpaths of the Lea Valley to experience a hidden rural London.** (p130-1)

▶ **Stroll through the magnificent Hampstead Heath and enjoy stunning views from Primrose Hill.** (p146-7)

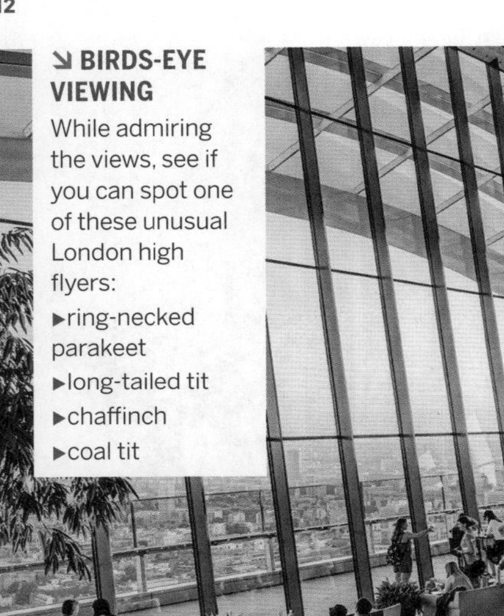

↘ BIRDS-EYE VIEWING

While admiring the views, see if you can spot one of these unusual London high flyers:

- ▸ring-necked parakeet
- ▸long-tailed tit
- ▸chaffinch
- ▸coal tit

VISTA VENTURES

Back in the '80s there was one skyscraper in all of London, the Natwest Tower, and the general public weren't allowed to enjoy the spectacular views it offered. Today Londoners are spoiled for choice; there are sky-high restaurants, cafes, viewing balconies and even public parks offering stunning vistas across the city.

Best Viewpoints

▸ **Grab breakfast at the Duck & Waffle as you watch the sunrise over the city.** (p72)

▸ **Visit London's public park in the sky, Sky Garden, for stunning city vistas.** (pictured; p65)

▸ **Sip a cocktail at GŎNG bar, located inside the city's iconic 'piece of glass', which looks upon London from south of the river.** (p88)

▸ **Enjoy a coffee while staring directly at London's impressive skyline from the Tate Modern's cafe.** (p87)

FB93/SHUTTERSTOCK ©

↘ THE SMALL ONES

There are a number of great small green spaces:

London Fields in Hackney

Victoria Park in East London

Coram's Fields in Russell Square

Southwark Park in Bermondsey

PARK LIFE

One of the greatest achievements of London's Victorian city planners was their success in integrating green parks into the otherwise heaving and overburdened city. Today London has more green spaces than most of the world's capital cities, with almost every neighbourhood featuring a green space of some sort. Some of the most iconic and famous make for a great day out.

The Big Ones

- ▶ **Enjoy pleasure boats on lakes and Shakespeare plays in the evenings during the summer at Regent's Park.** (p52)
- ▶ **Brace yourself for a dip in one of three swimming ponds at Hampstead Heath, one of the most popular green spaces in northwest London.** (p146-7)
- ▶ **Hang out with the peacocks at the wonderful Kyoto Garden in Holland Park.** (pictured; p163)

LONDON BREWING

London's always been obsessed with making its own 'poison' – remember the 18th-century gin craze? Today things are a bit more sensible. While local gin distilling has returned, the coolest thing to do is head to one of the many trendy microbreweries, where a local connoisseur will serve you the perfect craft beer.

LEFT: CAR PUBIMAGE/ALAMY STOCK PHOTO ©; BOTTOM: GEORGE FISHER/ALAMY STOCK PHOTO ©

★ DRINK IN A HISTORIC PUB

Down a pint in an ancient London pub like the Ye Olde Watling (p68); built by Sir Christopher Wren in 1668, this is where he reportedly drew up the plans for St Paul's Cathedral.

Best Microbreweries

- **The Kernel Brewery was the first to set up in Bermondsey and its brews remain ever popular.** (p183)
- **The Fourpure Brewing Co in Bermondsey promises unpretentious, full-flavoured craft beer.** (p183)
- **The Crate Brewery in Hackney Wick makes great craft beer along with tasty on-site pizza.** (p127)
- **The legendary Howling Hops Brewery & Tank Bar is famed for how generous they are with their hops.** (p127)

MAKE YOUR OWN

Make your own gin at the City of London Distillery or cider at London's only urban cidery, Hawkes Cidery & Taproom (p182).

Above Crate Brewery and Pizzeria (p127) **Left** Howling Hops Brewery & Tank Bar (p127)

FREE CULTURE

No other city in the world offers free access to as many world-class cultural institutes as London. Given how expensive the city can be, the fact that you can see a genuine Rembrandt or Monet and try to decode the Rosetta Stone for free is mind-bogglingly wonderful.

KIEV.VICTOR/SHUTTERSTOCK ©

★ BOOK AHEAD

Many museums and galleries have adopted a ticketing service with allocated entry times, so be sure to book ahead where required.

TRANSPARENCY & DIVERSIFICATION

A healthy debate about how to respectfully 'decolonise' these traditional cultural institutes has begun and seen some – such as the Museum of the Home (p137) – change their names. Look out for opportunities to offer your thoughts.

Best Free Spaces

- **Experience what life on the city's famous docks were like at the Museum of London Docklands.** (p137)
- **Enjoy an exhibition by a cutting-edge artist at the Whitechapel Gallery in hip East London.** (p137)
- **Go on a journey at the Natural History Museum that both kids and adults will love.** (p104)
- **See one of Da Vinci's actual notebooks along with many other amazing objects at The V&A.** (p104)

Above Victoria & Albert Museum (p104)

Peak Travel Season

Demand for accommodation peaks during summer. Book tours, flights and insurance in advance at lonelyplanet.com/bookings.

↘ Trooping the Colour

The Queen's official birthday is celebrated with much flag-waving, parades, pageantry and noisy flyovers on the second Saturday of June.

▶ trooping-the-colour.co.uk

← Open Garden Squares Weekend

Over a weekend in early June, 200-plus gardens, usually inaccessible to the public, open their gates.

↓ Wimbledon Lawn Tennis Championships

For two weeks in June and July, the South London village of Wimbledon becomes the central focus of the tennis world.

▶ Wimbledon

JUNE

Average daytime max: 17°C
Days of rainfall: 13

JULY

London in SUMMER

→ Pride London

The LGBTIQ+ community paints the town pink (and red and yellow and...) in this annual extravaganza.

▶ prideinlondon.org

↓ Great British Beer Festival

This booze fest cracks open casks of ale from across the world at Olympia London exhibition centre in the first week of August.

▶ gbbf.org.uk

← Wireless

One of London's top music festivals, with an emphasis on dance and R&B. Held in July at a large London park.

▶ wirelessfestival.co.uk

AUGUST

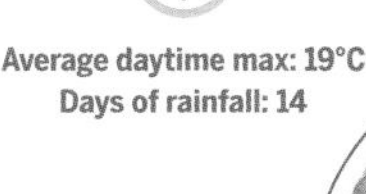
Average daytime max: 19°C
Days of rainfall: 14

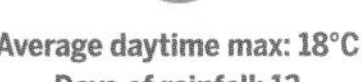
Average daytime max: 18°C
Days of rainfall: 13

← Notting Hill Carnival

Europe's biggest and most vibrant outdoor carnival celebrates Caribbean London over the August bank-holiday weekend.

▶ Notting Hill

Packing Notes

Summer hats, sunglasses and sunscreen for those occasional 'heatwaves' and a light packable rain jacket.

Check out the full calendar of events

→ The Mayor's Thames Festival

This cosmopolitan festival in September celebrating the River Thames culminates in an unmissable night procession.

▶ thamesfestivaltrust.org

↘ Open House London

For one weekend in mid-September over 800 heritage buildings, which are normally off-limits to public, open their doors.

▶ openhouselondon.org.uk

London Film Festival

The city's premier film event runs for two weeks in October, showing more than 100 British and international films before their cinema release.

▶ bfi.org.uk/lff

→ Affordable Art Fair

For four days in March and October, Battersea Park turns into a giant affordable art fair.

▶ Battersea, Wandsworth

▶ affordableartfair.com

SEPTEMBER

Average daytime max: 16°C
Days of rainfall: 15

OCTOBER

London in AUTUMN

→ Guy Fawkes Night

Fireworks light up the sky on 5 November, commemorating Guy Fawkes' failure to blow up Parliament in 1605.

↘ Lord Mayor's Show

A procession party as the new Lord Mayor of the City of London swears allegiance to the Crown.

▶ lordmayorsshow.london

↓ London Jazz Festival

Some of the world's greatest jazz musicians come to town for 10 days in November.

▶ efglondonjazzfestival.org.uk

NOVEMBER

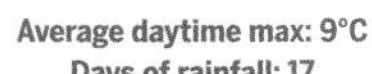

Average daytime max: 13°C
Days of rainfall: 15

Average daytime max: 9°C
Days of rainfall: 17

Wrap up and wander through London's tree-lined streets and parks to enjoy the stunning colours of the autumnal leaves.

Packing Notes

It's the season of layering - wear warm clothes that can be easily removed when the weather fluctuates or you go inside.

Christmas Holidays

Most people stay at home on Christmas Day, but come Boxing Day, the winter sales begin. Both are public holidays.

↘ Ice Skating

From mid-November to January, open-air ice rinks pop up across the city in exquisite locations.

← New Years

The countdown to Big Ben striking midnight is met with fireworks from the London Eye and celebrated by massive crowds.

→ Christmas Tree & Lights

Festival lights in central London get turned on and a huge Christmas tree is installed in Trafalgar Square.

DECEMBER

Average daytime max: 6°C
Days of rainfall: 17

JANUARY

London in WINTER

← London Art Fair

More than 130 major galleries participate in this contemporary art fair in January.

▶ londonartfair.co.uk

↓ Imagine Children's Festival

Twelve days of world-class children's music performances, literature, belly-aching comedy and parties every February at the Southbank Centre.

▶ Waterloo

→ Chinese New Year

In late January or early February, Chinatown fizzes, crackles and pops in this colourful Chinese street festival.

▶ Chinatown

Average daytime max: 6°C
Days of rainfall: 19

FEBRUARY

Average daytime max: 6°C
Days of rainfall: 16

← Pancake Races

Catch pancake races and silliness across town (Old Spitalfields Market, in particular) on Shrove Tuesday.

Packing Notes

Time for thick sweaters, scarves, gloves and winter coats, maybe extra tights or leggings too.

London is in full bloom, so head to the many gardens and large parks to see it in all its colourful glory.

↙ St Patrick's Day

Held the Sunday closest to 17 March, there's a colourful parade and lots of Guinness is consumed.

BAFTAs

The British Academy of Film & Television Arts rolls out the red carpet in mid-March for its annual cinema awards.

▶ bafta.org

→ Flare

This LGBTIQ+ film festival by the British Film Institute has film screenings, club nights, talks and events.

▶ bfi.org.uk/flare

MARCH

Average daytime max: 8°C
Days of rainfall: 16

APRIL

London in SPRING

← London Marathon

Some 40,000 runners go from Blackheath to the Mall in one of the world's biggest road races.

▸ tcslondonmarathon.com

↓ Boishakhi Mela

Running through Brick Lane and into neighbouring Weavers Fields, this explosion of colour, music and food celebrates the Bengali New Year in May.

▸ East End

↙ Chelsea Flower Show

The world's most renowned horticultural event attracts green-fingered and flower-mad gardeners.

▸ Chelsea

▸ rhs.org.uk

Average daytime max: 11°C
Days of rainfall: 16

MAY

Average daytime max: 14°C
Days of rainfall: 15

Oxbridge Boat Race

Crowds line the banks of the Thames to see the famous universities going oar-to-oar from Putney to Mortlake.

▸ theboatraces.org

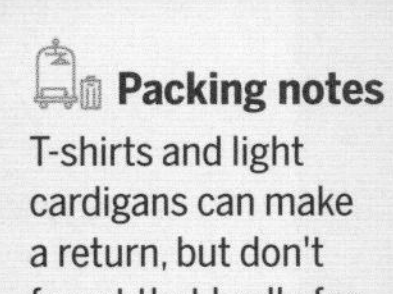

Packing notes

T-shirts and light cardigans can make a return, but don't forget that brolly for those April showers.

MY PERFECT DAY IN **LONDON**

By Hannah
@hannah_ajala

CYCLING, PARKS & STREET FOOD

It would be a spring or summer late afternoon. I would rent a nearby bicycle, ride around my favourite neighbourhoods and make pitstops for street food and iced coffee. Then I'd chill out at the greenest park I came across. It's the little things that make me appreciate and love my loud but mostly lovely London town. My outlook on life was shaped by the London culture I was born into and grew up in.

WHY I LOVE LONDON

I love London for making me feel closer to all the countries I've explored. I love London because it will always be home.

SUTTIRAT WIRIYANON/SHUTTERSTOCK ©

PAOLO PARADISO/SHUTTERSTOCK ©

Left Sandwich at Borough Market (p80) **Above** Cycling along the Regent's Canal in Hackney
Right Ginger cake at Borough Market

BREAKFAST IN THE CLOUDS. DINNER ON THE GROUND

By Demi
@girl_travels world

Wake up at Shangri-La The Shard, London Hotel then head for a swim in the 52nd-floor Sky Pool. I'd spend most of my morning here. For lunch I'd take a stroll down to Borough Market and wander around the stalls trying the different artisanal food vendors, then take in the sights along the South Bank until late afternoon. Walk past Tate Modern, the Oxo Tower and the pebbly Thames Beach. Keep heading towards the National Theatre and all the way to the London Eye – it's a magnificent walk!

BEST OF SOUTH BANK

Borough Market For coffee and freshly baked pastries.

The Market Porter Pub For a steak and ale pie with gravy and mash for lunch; inside Borough Market.

South Bank For a crisp walk and people-watching.

KIRILL LIVSHITSKIY/SHUTTERSTOCK ©

RIVERFRONT SIGHTS & ARCHITECTURAL GEMS

By Travis
@mister levius

Start at South Bank with an architecture tour of the National Theatre, one of London's brutalist landmarks. From London Eye Pier, take a scenic River Thames cruise and admire the city's bridges and landmarks. Hop off at Tower Pier and meander through the City of London for futuristic glass skyscrapers alongside Roman ruins and medieval-era churches. End the day with sunset drinks at Oblix – located inside The Shard, Western Europe's tallest building – where London's inimitable skyline is laid bare before you.

WHY I LOVE LONDON

I feel most alive here: the architecture and the charming parks, the creative scene, the remarkable diversity. London is not perfect – prices and moody weather being the main reality checks – but it's perfect for me.

By Tharik
@tharik_hussain
@_tharikhussain

ARTY, EDGY, ETHNIC QUARTERS

Start by taking in the latest exhibit at the Whitechapel Art Gallery before wandering through edgy Brick Lane. Stop and admire the stunning mural at the entrance and then grab a spicy light lunch at Graam Bangla. Snap the country's trendiest minaret when you visit the Lane's famous mosque, before spending the afternoon searching for a boutique gift or a vintage bargain in shops like Beyond Retro. And don't leave without devouring a delicious salt beef bagel from the Beigel Bake.

WHY I LOVE LONDON

London is less a city and more a collection of little worlds where you can taste or glimpse almost every corner of the globe.

MARC ZAKIAN/ALAMY STOCK PHOTO ©

BEST BARS

Sushi Samba (Heron Tower) A terrace bar with a view.

Bokan 37 (40 Marsh Wall) A rooftop bar with a laid-back vibe.

Dirty Martini (dirtymartini.uk.com) A stylish and dimly lit cocktail bar.

BARS, RESTAURANTS, PARKS, CULTURE

Head to East London, where you'll wander around the eclectic Brick Lane area to admire endless vivid murals painted by local artists. Then walk through the buzzy streets of Shoreditch to get to Boxpark for hearty meals paired with a drink. If the weather permits, spend your evening catching the sunset at Greenwich Park, where scenic views of London await. Otherwise, head to Sushi Samba on the 38th floor for wining and dining and a 360-degree view of London.

By Linda
@lyndakonde

Above Beyond Retro (p137) **Above right** Spitalfields Market **Right** Dishes at A Wong

By Qin
@qinxiesays

WILLY BARTON/SHUTTERSTOCK ©

MORNING TO NIGHT RESTAURANT- AND BAR-HOPPING

Fuel up with a decadent City Boy breakfast at Fox & Anchor, or opt for St John's cult-status bacon sandwich. For a deliciously eclectic street-food lunch, migrate east to Old Spitalfields Market where moreish shrimp burgers and silky hand-pulled noodles await. Now, amble west. Pick between coffee at HR Higgins' basement cafe or Selfridges' rooftop venue for sundowners. Dinner has to be in Chinatown, with Gerrard's Corner a firm favourite. Finish with a tipple at the Experimental Cocktail Club.

↓ BEST RESTAURANTS

Noble Rot (51 Lamb's Conduit St) Great food and excellent wines.

Bancone (39 William IV St) For serious pasta aficionados.

A Wong (70 Wilton Rd) Re-imagining Chinese food.

Brat (4 Redchurch St) Get the burnt cheesecake.

DAVID COTSWORTH/IMAGE SUPPLIED BY QIN XIE ©

7 Things to Know About LONDON

INSIDER TIPS TO HIT THE GROUND RUNNING

1 The Arts for Free

No other city in the world offers as much world-class culture for free as London. Here are just some of the internationally renowned institutes that charge nothing to enjoy their collections: The V&A, the National Portrait Gallery, the Tate Modern, the Tate Britain, Museum of London, Natural History Museum, Royal Academy of Arts, Science Museum and the British Museum.

▶ See more about free culture on p15

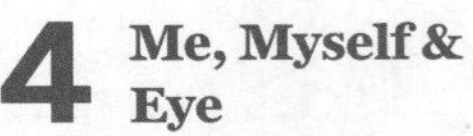

2 No Time for Tea

Once a proud nation of tea drinkers, the impact of coffee-loving immigrant communities from the Middle East, North Africa and the Mediterranean means you should no longer ask a Londoner if they want to go for a cup of tea – these days it's a skinny flat white or, if they're a real connoisseur, a cortado.

3 Rainbows

It rains a lot in London, so while this means you get to (briefly) see more rainbows than in most capital cities, don't leave home without an umbrella or a pack-away rain jacket.

▶ See more about the seasons on p16

4 Me, Myself & Eye

Londoners won't talk to you or make eye contact on public transport. If they do, they're tourists, drunk or both.

▶ See more about travel essentials on p217

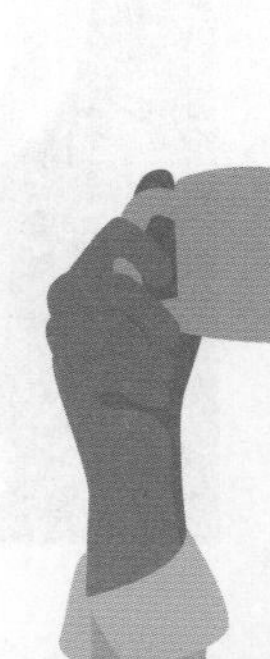

5 Day of Rest

Unusually for a modern metropolis, the tradition of Sunday being the 'day of rest' is still observed across London. Don't be surprised if a street heaving with people and businesses on a Saturday appears deserted the next day. The way around this is seek out the city's numerous Sunday markets.

6 London Lingo

'Ave a butchers - Have a look.

'Aving a bubble - Having a laugh.

Bloody... - An intensifier added toa word for effect ('bloody hell!', 'bloody marvellous!').

Hammering it down - It rains a lot and Londoners have loads of ways to describe rain. To 'hammer it down' means there's a deluge of rainfall.

Old Bill - Nope, he's not an elderly man named William; this is simply the police.

Fam - Short for 'family' and popular with young Londoners; it can be used to refer to anyone and everyone ('listen fam!').

A score - Not the football result but a £20 note, as in 'that's a score' when relaying the price of something.

Sarf or Noorf - Used to refer to London either side of the River Thames ('I'm from sarf London' or 'I live in noorf London').

Get lost! - Go away.

Have a good un - Have a good day

7 Multilingual London

Just because this is the capital of England does not mean everyone here speaks English – far from it. This was also once the capital of a vast Empire so expect to hear anything up to 300 languages (according to estimates) being spoken around London, from Swahili to German.

Read, Listen, Watch & Follow

READ

London Parks (Hunter Davies; 2021) The beauty, history and heritage of London's parks through the eyes of a Londoner.

London: The Biography (Peter Ackroyd; 2000) Still very much the authoritative text on the history of London.

London: Immigrant City (Nazneen Khan-Østrem; 2019) An immigrant's view of London written by someone who grew up in three different countries.

White Teeth (Zadie Smith; 2000) The multi-award-winning modern classic novel set in London and about multicultural Britain.

LISTEN

Gang Signs & Prayers (Stormzy; 2019) The first grime album to reach No 1 in the UK charts by the current king of the genre.

The Return of the Space Cowboy (Jamiroquai; 1994) Bestselling funk album of all time by the pioneering London band.

London Undone (London Undone) Podcast about the more unusual sites in and around London.

19 (Adele; 2008) The multi-award-winning debut album by the girl from Tottenham.

Londonist Out Loud (Londonist) Great podcast about London covering everything from iconic buildings to black cabs.

WATCH

Rocks (2020) A love letter to East London from its rooftops through the eyes of local teens.

Top Boy (2011) Gritty, crime drama series about life on inner London housing estates.

Withnail and I (1987) Two down-and-out actors escape '60s Camden Town for the British countryside.

Performance (1970) Mick Jagger stars in this ultimate London movie about rock stars and crooks.

Attack The Block (2011) Aliens invade Brixton; they just weren't ready for the mouthy youths living there.

ALLSTAR PICTURE LIBRARY LTD./ ALAMY STOCK PHOTO ©

MOVIESTORE COLLECTION LTD/ ALAMY STOCK PHOTO ©

FOLLOW

@StandardNews Breaking news and updates from the popular London daily on Twitter.

@TimeOutLondon The Time Out London Instagram account.

VISIT LONDON OFFICIAL VISITOR GUIDE (visitlondon.com) Information on special events, tours, accommodation, theatre and more.

Essential London (essentialldn.com) A blog filled with articles about London's best cultural and historical sites.

Transport for London (@TfL) Transport updates and a whole lot of fun on Twitter.

Sate your London dreaming with a virtual vacation at lonelyplanet.com/london#planning-a-trip

THE WEST END

ENTERTAINMENT | SHOPPING | HISTORY

Experience the West End online

CARNABY STREET
FOUBERT'S PLACE W1
MAC

THE WEST END
Trip Builder

TAKE YOUR PICK OF MUST-SEES AND HIDDEN GEMS

As a captivating hub known for its trendy and vibrant atmosphere, the West End is a district with myriad offerings. It is home to nine areas, each with its own distinctive character, housing many of London's most iconic sights, world-class shopping, the city'sentertainment quarter and a diverse dining scene.

Neighbourhood Notes

Best for Culture, history, nightlife, gastronomy and shopping.

Transport Central line, plus Victoria, Northern, Piccadilly, Bakerloo, Jubilee, Circle & District lines.

Getting around By Tube, bike and foot.

Tip The West End is always busy. Visit both in the day and the night to really get to know the area.

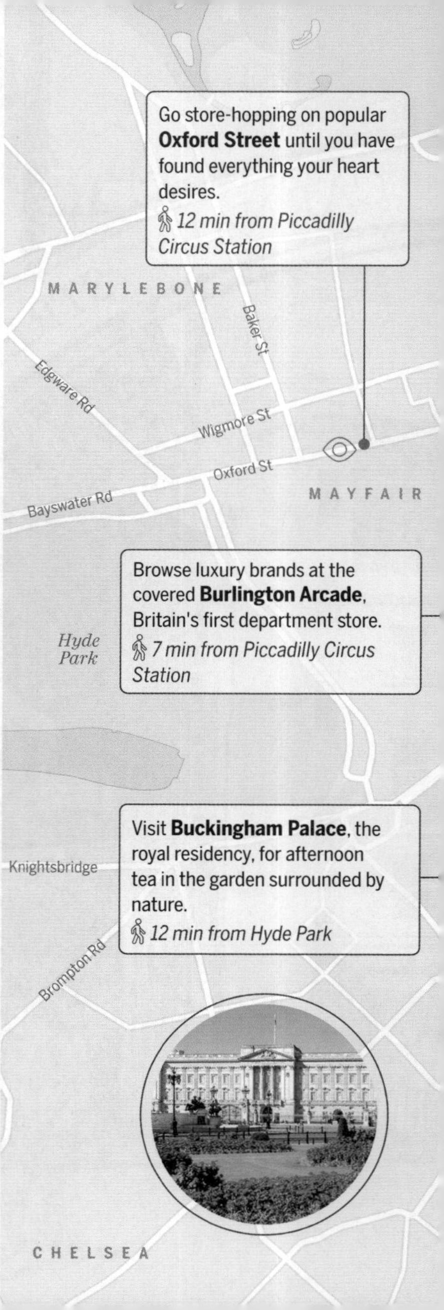

Go store-hopping on popular **Oxford Street** until you have found everything your heart desires.
12 min from Piccadilly Circus Station

Browse luxury brands at the covered **Burlington Arcade**, Britain's first department store.
7 min from Piccadilly Circus Station

Visit **Buckingham Palace**, the royal residency, for afternoon tea in the garden surrounded by nature.
12 min from Hyde Park

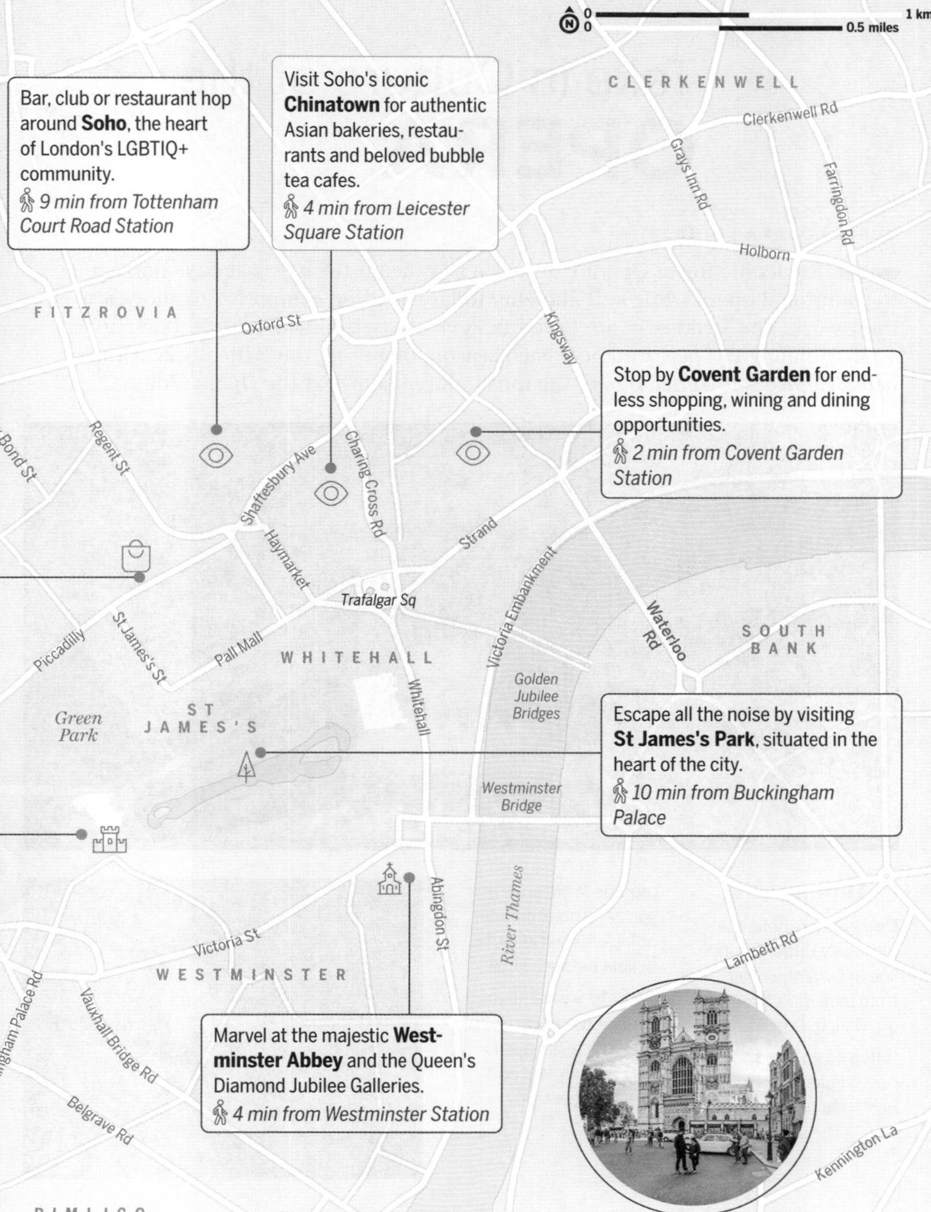

Bar, club or restaurant hop around **Soho**, the heart of London's LGBTIQ+ community.
9 min from Tottenham Court Road Station

Visit Soho's iconic **Chinatown** for authentic Asian bakeries, restaurants and beloved bubble tea cafes.
4 min from Leicester Square Station

Stop by **Covent Garden** for endless shopping, wining and dining opportunities.
2 min from Covent Garden Station

Escape all the noise by visiting **St James's Park**, situated in the heart of the city.
10 min from Buckingham Palace

Marvel at the majestic **Westminster Abbey** and the Queen's Diamond Jubilee Galleries.
4 min from Westminster Station

01 Take in Culture at the OPERA

MUSIC | OPERA | DINNER

The iconic Royal Opera House is a significant theatre that pays homage to traditional opera while still allowing today's leading composers to showcase their work. The striking white Baroque Revival–style edifice, built in 1858, hosts approximately 150 performances each season, including the critically acclaimed ballet *Romeo and Juliet*, one of the most adored shows at the Opera House.

YANG LIU/GETTY IMAGES ©

How to

Getting here Take the Piccadilly Underground line to Covent Garden; from here it's a two-minute walk to Bow St.

When to go The season runs September to July. Purchase tickets two months in advance if you are a non-member, or look for last-minute tickets before a show.

What to wear The dress code at the Royal Opera House is relaxed – as long as your feet and torso are covered.

ROBBIE JACK/GETTY IMAGES ©

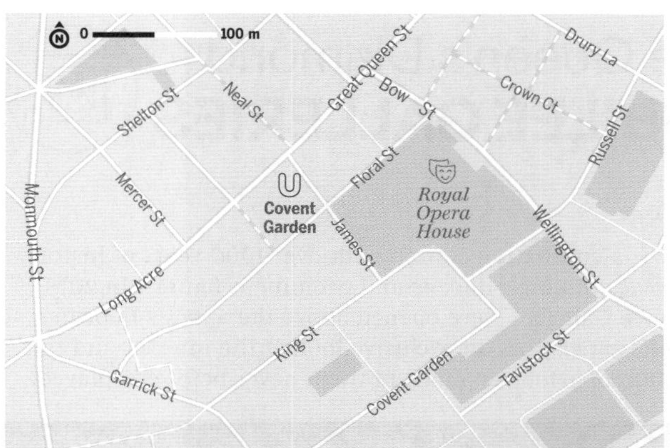

Left Royal Opera House **Below** John Tomlinson in a Royal Opera House production of *Faust*

Classical meets modern This celebrated performance venue in Covent Garden was a dance hall during WWII and became the Royal Opera House (ROH) that we know today when it opened its doors to the public in 1946. Since then it has been home to both the Royal Opera and the Royal Ballet. You can watch remarkable performances of operatic classics like *Macbeth*, *Tosca* and *The Marriage of Figaro* and ballets such as *Swan Lake* and *Giselle*, as well as exciting and unexpected contemporary productions. If you're unsure of what to see, consider the Royal Ballet's production of *Romeo and Juliet*, choreographed by Kenneth MacMillan; it has been a favoured showstopper since it first arrived at the ROH in 1965, amassing over 400 performances.

Opening to the street Significant renovations to the Royal Opera House were completed in 2018, which included opening the ground level to make it more inviting and attract a wider audience. As well as ballet and opera performances, the ROH offers the opportunity to join a dance class led by a member of the Royal Ballet, tour the ROH building, attend behind-the-scenes events and drop in for a lunchtime recital or performance (both free and ticketed events) featuring performances from the Royal Opera, the Royal Ballet, the orchestra and guest artists.

Drinking & Dining at the Opera

The Royal Opera House has eight restaurants and bars, each with a different ambience and price range. These venues are only open to ticket holders, except for the **Royal Opera House Café**, which is also open to the public during the day. The glass-vaulted dining area in **Paul Hamlyn Hall**, overlooking Covent Garden with an extraordinary U-shaped architectural design, is breathtaking. You can dine here without a reservation; try specialities like fish goujons or an appetising three-course meal for £17.50. Paul Hamlyn Hall is also home to the **Balconies Restaurant**, another stunning place to dine.

02 The Queen's Diamond JUBILEE GALLERIES

ROYALTY | GALLERY | HISTORY

Westminster Abbey is a coronation church with over 1000 years of history, as well as a royal resting place of kings, queens and prominent figures. In 2018 the Queen's Diamond Jubilee Galleries were opened above the abbey's floor in the medieval triforium, offering visitors an exclusive look at the interior and the abbey's fascinating collection of artefacts, many of them never before displayed.

LEON NEAL/GETTY IMAGES ©

How to

Getting here Take the Circle, District and Jubilee Underground lines to Westminster Station.

When to go Avoid the crowds by visiting early in the morning or late in the evening. Daily services at Westminster Abbey are open to the public.

The cost You can only purchase the Queen's Diamond Jubilee Galleries ticket (£5) in combination with admission to Westminster Abbey (£24).

JOHN STILLWELL/PA IMAGES/GETTY IMAGES ©

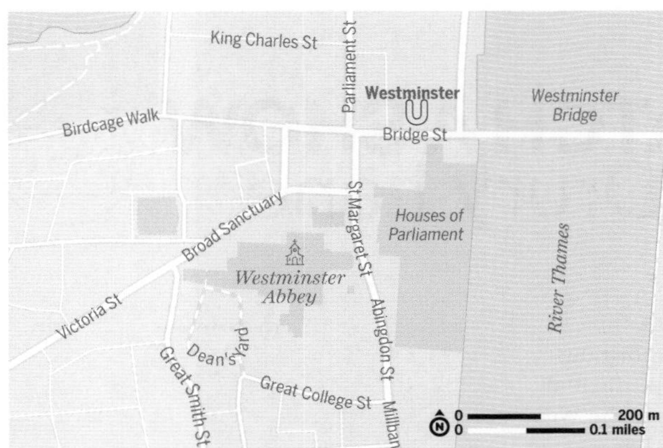

Open to the public The opening of the Queen's Diamond Jubilee Galleries in 2018 presented a surprising and new perspective of the iconic attraction. Located within the 13th-century triforium, 16m above the abbey's floor, this is the first time in the abbey's long history that this area, previously used for storage, has been open to the public. The unique attic space is accessed via the 30m-tall star-shaped Weston Tower (housing both stairs and lift), which opened along with galleries and is the first major addition to the abbey since 1745. As you ascend the stairs, admire views of the abbey's medieval Chapter House and the Palace of Westminster.

The collection The collection, which spans the abbey's 1000-year history, is broken into four key areas: Building the Abbey; Worship and Daily Life; the Abbey and the Monarchy; and the Abbey and National Memory. Among the 300 exhibits here, you will see 21 wonderfully preserved medieval funeral effigies, including the effigy head of Henry VII, Mary II's coronation chair, the royal marriage licence of Prince William and Kate Middleton and Henry V's battle gear, alongside art, sculptures and manuscripts from the abbey's library and archive collection. As you move around the neutral-coloured space under ancient oak beams, the bright stained-glass windows of the abbey create a beautifully serene atmosphere, with springs of light illuminating the wooden floor.

Left Funeral effigy of Catherine Sheffield and Robert Sheffield from 1735 **Below** The marriage license of Prince William and Kate Middleton

Westminster Abbey

Founded by Benedictine monks in 960 CE, Westminster Abbey is well known as a burial site for royalty and prominent figures (Sir Isaac Newton and 30 kings and queens among them) and for hosting royal weddings (16 in total), including the wedding of Prince William and Kate Middleton in 2011. 'People are naturally drawn to the tombs of the royals,' says Guy Fairbank, 'but there are also hidden delights to be seen.' Pass the Chapter House until you come to a thick oak door. Step inside and gaze over remnants of the original Norman abbey, with its stout, rounded columns, plain altar and medieval tiles.

Insights by Guy Fairbank, *London Blue Badge Guide at Urban Saunters, @guyfairbank*

03 CATCH A SHOW at Drury Lane

THEATRE | MUSICAL | SHOWS

After nearly 400 years, the Theatre Royal Drury Lane continues to tell a story through the spectacular shows it stages in the heart of the West End. The historic landmark has earned its accolade with the original building dating back to 1663, making it the oldest theatre in use in London. The auditorium remains a momentous place for modern and classic performances.

How to

Getting here Take the Piccadilly Underground line to Covent Garden; from here it's a four-minute walk on the main streets to Theatre Royal Drury Lane.

When to go The theatre is open every day, but it is best to purchase tickets early.

Good to know One of the theatre's entrances has step-free access; wheelchair-friendly spaces are present on all floors, excluding the balcony.

Extraordinary performances Celebrated composer Andrew Lloyd Webber, the mastermind behind world-renowned productions such as *Phantom of the Opera* and *Cats*, purchased the Theatre Royal Drury Lane in 2004 and it is today managed by his company LW Theatres. A significant restoration project took place between 2019 and 2021, bringing the theatre into the modern day, with improvements made to the auditorium and building accessibility and the addition of several sleek drinking and dining venues, while

Right Production of *42nd Street* at Theatre Royal Drury Lane
Below Exterior of Theatre Royal Drury Lane

GAVIN RODGERS/ALAMY LIVE NEWS ©

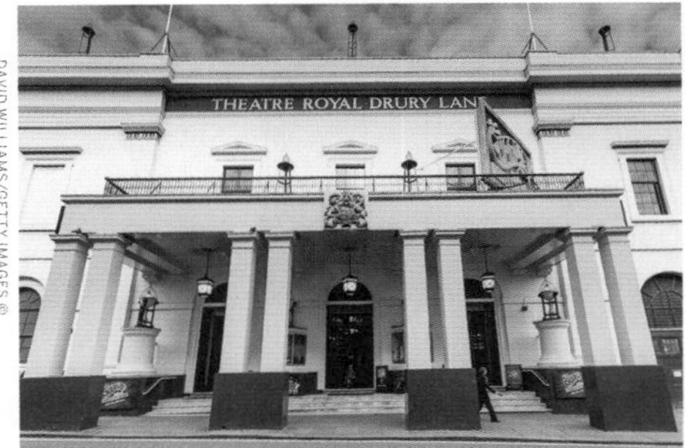

DAVID WILLIAMS/GETTY IMAGES ©

A Fascinating History

Originally founded in 1663, the Theatre Royal Drury Lane is the oldest theatre site in London. The building has gone through various changes and restorations over the years; today's structure dates back to 1812 and is the fourth theatre to be built on this site.

reviving many of the theatre's elegant original features. The grand stage, which has seen countless classic musical productions including *My Fair Lady* and *42nd Street*, is today impressive as ever and ready to usher in a new era with immersive shows such as *Frozen the Musical*.

An enchanting restaurant Next door to the theatre is **The Garden**, an intimate venue tucked away from the street. Part of LW Theatres, the contemporary cafe and bar is a meeting point for those looking to combine their love for culture, entertainment and gastronomy. Spend an hour or two at the leafy venue, sipping a cocktail or a speciality coffee, or sampling cheese served on the theatre's old stage boards or desserts created by renowned London baker Lily Vanilli. Both theatre goers and the general public are welcome.

04 BUCKINGHAM Palace for a Day

ROYALTY | AFTERNOON TEA | PALACE

Home to Queen Elizabeth II, Buckingham Palace – a former townhouse built in 1703 – has attained iconic status worldwide and attracts millions of visitors each year. It is one of the few working royal palaces remaining in the world today. Despite its exclusivity, visitors can tour the palace in the summer months and enjoy an afternoon tea in the private garden.

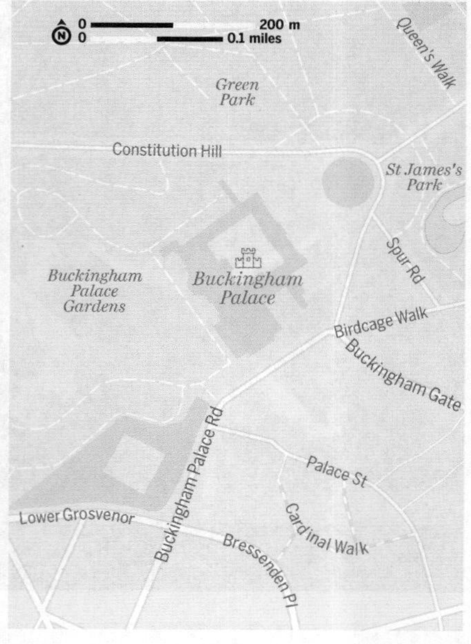

How to

Getting here Take the Victoria or Piccadilly Underground line to Victoria, Green Park or Hyde Park. Avoid driving as parking is limited and expensive.

When to go Buckingham Palace can be visited by the public between July and September, when the Queen is not in residence. The Changing of the Guard ceremony takes place throughout the year.

The cost Prices for hot beverages from the garden cafe, including tea, start at £3. Pair your drink with a dessert like a carrot cake, or opt for a wrap or sandwich.

A royal experience Walking through the vividly coloured State Rooms on a guided tour allows visitors a glimpse into an illustrious world. There are more than 775 rooms at Buckingham Palace, 19 of which are State Rooms. These opulent rooms were designed for receiving guests and official and ceremonial occasions and are filled with an extensive collection of sculptures, furniture and art

Right Buckingham Palace's ballroom **Below** Buckingham Palace Gardens

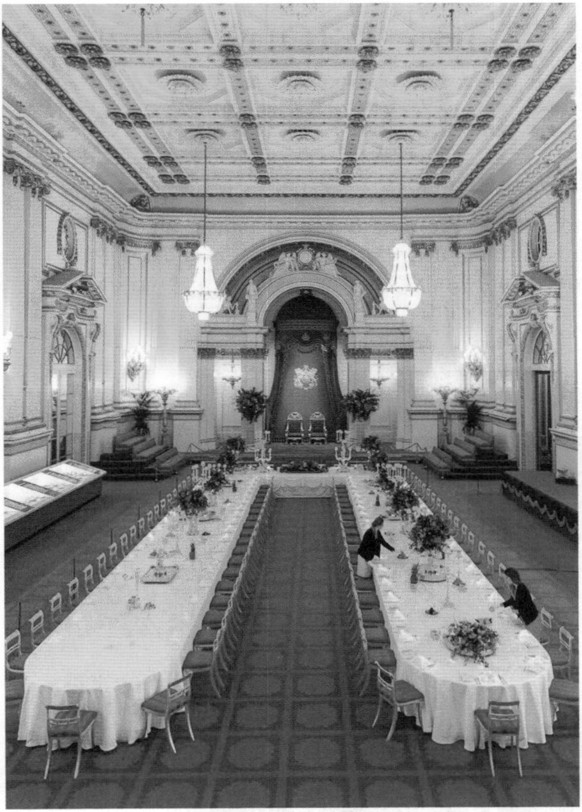

PA IMAGES/ALAMY STOCK PHOTO ©

GARY BLAKE/ALAMY STOCK PHOTO ©

The Palace Flags

When the Royal Standard flies atop Buckingham Palace, it signifies that the Queen is in London. But when the Union Flag is present, it means she's out.

■ **Tip by Justin Roxburgh,** *Blue Badge Tourist Guide, @just_in_london_tours*

from the Royal Collection. On the tour you will see the ballroom, throne room, white drawing room and music room, among others.

Tea in the garden Enjoying afternoon tea is a quintessential British custom and cultural norm. After the State Rooms guided tour, head to Buckingham Palace Garden and find a seat on the well-maintained grass, preferably with a view that overlooks the 19th-century lake, for a picnic with afternoon tea. Nibble on a selection of sandwiches, cakes and scones as you take in the surprisingly tranquil ambience in the centre of London (this is London's biggest private backyard, after all). Afterwards, explore the royal grounds – the 16-hectare garden was built to impress – and the never-ending corners at your own pace before exiting one of Britain's most popular attractions.

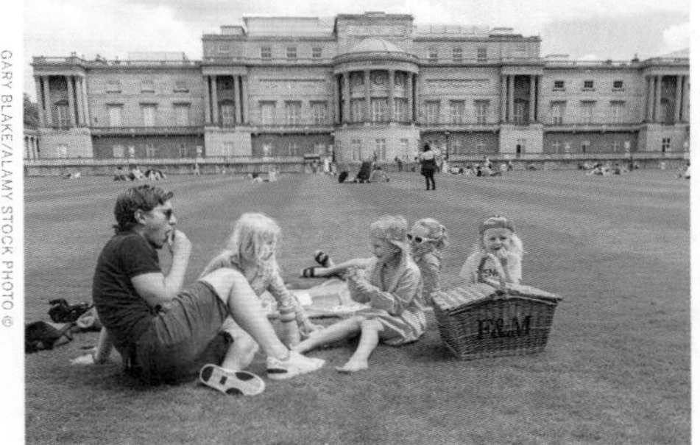

05 Walk the Historic WEST END

HISTORIC | WALKING | MONUMENTS

One of the best ways to uncover the West End is by foot or bike. With a surplus of famous attractions and historical monuments, it is chock-full of offerings. Soak up the city's deep and complex history and learn about how each sight became significant and a representation of Britain.

WILLY BARTON/SHUTTERSTOCK ©

How to

Getting there Catch the Bakerloo and Northern lines to Charing Cross Station to get to Trafalgar Square; from here it's a two-minute walk to the plaza.

When to go The area tends to be busy, particularly in the summer and on the weekend. Take the main roads to spot all the sights.

Tip Make sure you wear comfortable shoes. While the walk is straightforward and short, you might end up strolling for longer than expected.

With thanks to Shabby Flanders, CEO of Urban Saunters in London, @urbansaunters

Ancient London

Immerse yourself in over 1000 years of history as you stroll around the West End area, learning about the city's political history and the prominent figures who have shaped the nation. Stop by cultural sights such as the 1940s **Regency Cafe**, which embodies London's 'caff culture' and serves a traditional English fry-up.

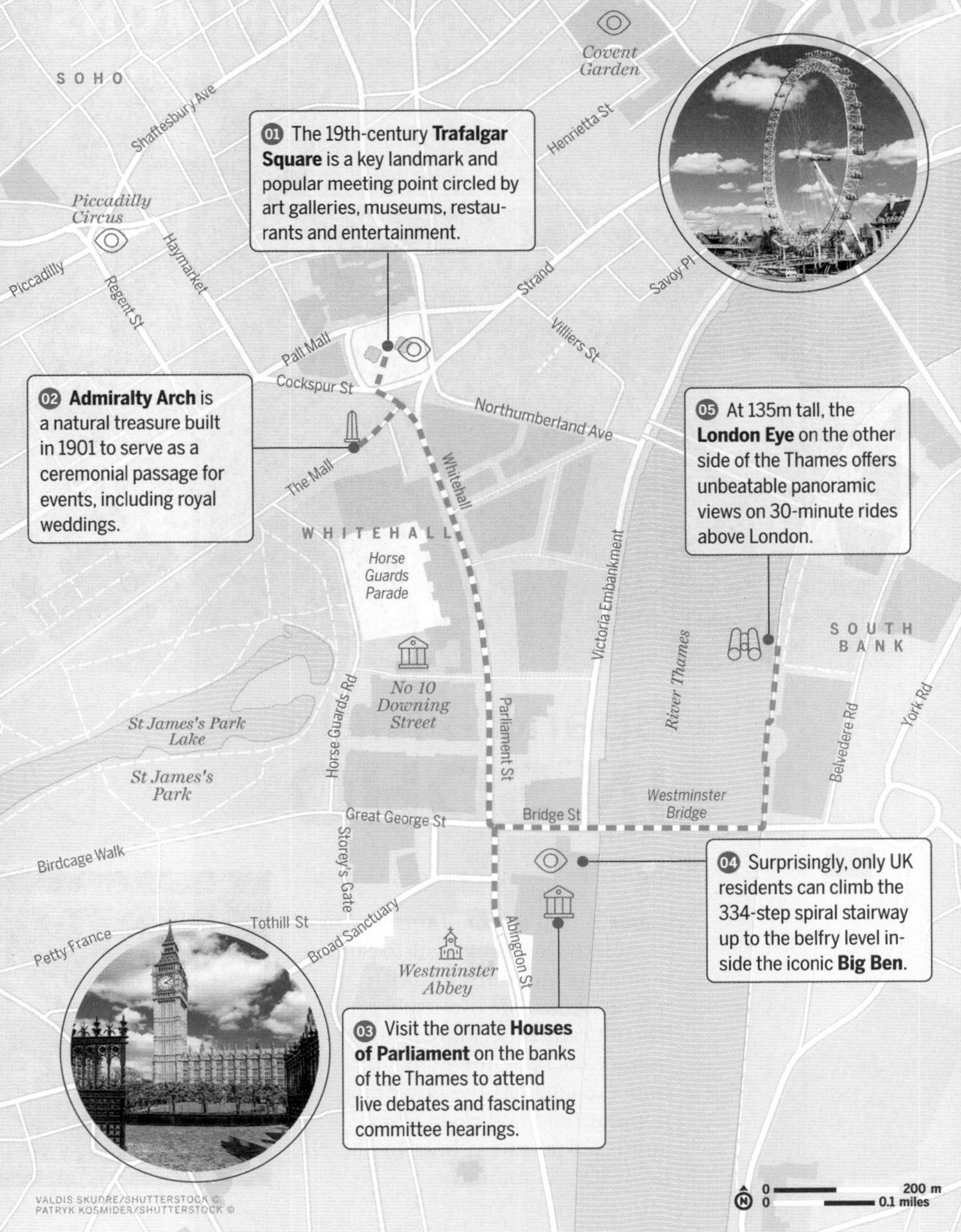
SOHO
Covent Garden
Shaftesbury Ave
Henrietta St
Piccadilly Circus
Piccadilly
Regent St
Haymarket
Strand
Savoy Pl
Villiers St
Pall Mall
Cockspur St
Northumberland Ave
The Mall
Whitehall
WHITEHALL
Horse Guards Parade
No 10 Downing Street
Horse Guards Rd
Parliament St
Victoria Embankment
River Thames
SOUTH BANK
Belvedere Rd
York Rd
St James's Park Lake
St James's Park
Great George St
Bridge St
Westminster Bridge
Birdcage Walk
Storey's Gate
Tothill St
Petty France
Broad Sanctuary
Abingdon St
Westminster Abbey
01 The 19th-century **Trafalgar Square** is a key landmark and popular meeting point circled by art galleries, museums, restaurants and entertainment.
02 **Admiralty Arch** is a natural treasure built in 1901 to serve as a ceremonial passage for events, including royal weddings.
03 Visit the ornate **Houses of Parliament** on the banks of the Thames to attend live debates and fascinating committee hearings.
04 Surprisingly, only UK residents can climb the 334-step spiral stairway up to the belfry level inside the iconic **Big Ben**.
05 At 135m tall, the **London Eye** on the other side of the Thames offers unbeatable panoramic views on 30-minute rides above London.
0 200 m
0 0.1 miles
N

06 Spend a Night IN SOHO

NIGHTLIFE | RESTAURANTS | LGBTIQ+

A trip to London isn't complete without a visit to Soho, a small neighbourhood with a larger-than-life atmosphere. The vibrant area, known for its boisterous bohemian vibe, is home to some of the city's most popular bars and restaurants and is a prominent hub for the LGBTIQ+ community.

FOTOMATON/ALAMY STOCK PHOTO ©

How to

Getting here Take the Victoria Underground line to Oxford Circus, from where you can walk to Soho. Alternatively, take the Central or Northern Underground line to Tottenham Court Road and walk from there.

When to go While the area is always busy, weekends tend to get packed with energetic party people and tourists roaming around.

The cost Drinks are generally more expensive in central London. But some of the LGBTIQ+ bars offer cheaper drinks.

CHRISTO MITKOV CHRISTOV/SHUTTERSTOCK ©

Bars and clubs What Soho lacks in size, it makes up for it with its wide range of entertainment. Nearly every narrow street in this dynamic area is home to a range of bars, nightclubs and pubs that quickly get filled with people from all walks of life. Britain's pub culture has evolved through the years and is considered a key part of a community, hence why pubs like the **Dog & Duck** are often crowded. Immerse yourself in the pub culture by socialising with locals – chances are they are regulars. Head over to **Zebrano** for a dance, or visit **Salsa Soho** to listen to salsa, bachata, merengue and reggaeton. If you're into cocktails, enter **the Vault**, a warm cocktail bar disguised as a bookstore. Some bars, such as **Simmons Bar**, have

ALENA VEASEY/SHUTTERSTOCK ©

A Celebrated Venue

In the middle of Old Compton St is **She Soho** – London's first and only lesbian venue. The small, crowded space is a safe spot for queer women, in a basement-style setting. DJs are always present and ready to bring the excitement up at this lively modern bar and nightclub.

Above left Simmons Bar **Above** The Dog & Duck **Left** Neon signage in Soho well-appreciated happy hours, offering a selection of drinks, including mojitos, for as little as £10.

Essential dining Experiencing a culinary craving in Soho is not necessarily a bad thing – the area's dining scene reflects London's diverse culture. The diminutive size of **10 Greek Street**, a neighbourhood favourite, provides an opportunity to dine in an intimate setting in an otherwise lively area. If you are craving Mexican food, your go-to place is **Temper**, a barbecue and steakhouse with an impressive drinks menu. For Japanese, head to **Shack-Fuyu Soho** to try its famous pudding – it's meant to be the best in London! Those looking for high-end dining will not be disappointed at the upscale **Bob Bob Ricard**. Here a luxury Russian and English menu offers oysters

A Colourful World

The Yard Bar Not a milk-shake in sight, but boys you will find in this roomy courtyard and loft bar. An abundance of flowers and wooden furnishings make this a relaxing place to mingle.

Comptons of Soho This Victorian-style pub has knocked around since the 1890s, evoking Soho's covert queer past. Now with some modern renovations, it's a must for a pint with a side of history.

G-A-Y Bar It's campy, it's 'basic', but cynics always change their tune after a few happy-hour specials at this iconic night out starter. Grab a wristband outside for free entry to G-A-Y Late or Heaven to keep the party going.

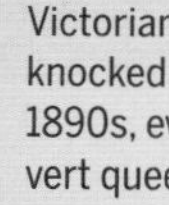

Recommended by Andrew Headspeath, *editor & member of the LGBTIQ+ community, @thescottipino*

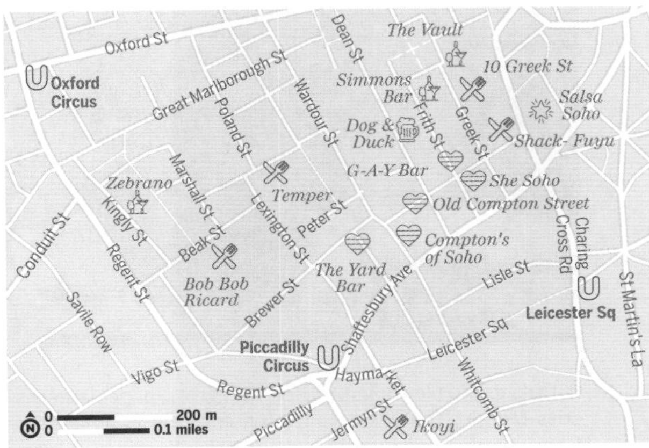

Left Interior of Bob Bob Ricard
Below Old Compton Street, Soho

and caviar paired with champagne. Experience the flavours of Nigeria at **Ikoyi**, a Michelin-star restaurant that blends West African tastes with British micro-seasonality.

London's LGBTIQ+ heart Bright neon-coloured signs and pride flags are just a few of the common sights around **Old Compton Street**, famous for being an important LGBTIQ+ centre. Despite being a short road, it's home to London's main gay bars and clubs, attracting large crowds throughout the night every weekend. With so many venues to visit, including **G-A-Y**, London's longest-running gay nightclub, you can easily bar-hop throughout the night. Just be sure to arrive at your first destination before midnight; some venues start refusing entrance around that time as they might have reached maximum capacity.

By Angela Hui
Angela is a food and drink writer at Time Out London. She is a double-award winning freelance writer and editor covering lifestyle, food and travel.
@angelahuii

London's Evolving Chinatown Food Scene

MAKING WAY FOR CONTEMPORARY DINING CONCEPTS

The number of Cantonese restaurants in Soho's Chinatown is dwindling, making way for more specialist, regional Chinese and pan-Asian businesses that appeal to a younger demographic. But as chains move in, have the traditional family-run businesses that are the area's lifeblood had their day?

Left Golden Phoenix Chinese restaurant **Right** Laksa medan **Far right** Ube bilong ice cream at Mamasons Dirty Ice Cream

PICTURE CAPITAL/ALAMY STOCK PHOTO ©

With its grand tile-roofed, red-pillared gates, paper lanterns criss-crossing the streets and intriguing aromas emanating from bakeries, restaurants and butchers, it's impossible to miss London's Chinatown. The streets between Leicester Square and Piccadilly Circus have been a hub for Chinese businesses in London since the 1960s. But Chinatown hasn't always had a W1 postcode. London's original Chinatown started life in Limehouse, East London, catering to Chinese sailors in the Georgian docklands. After the bombing of the area during WWII, many Chinese immigrants who lived near the docks were forced to resettle across town where they opened up shop in the then-seedy area of Soho.

Today, in the face of rising rents, shifts in immigration patterns, customers' changing tastes and a global pandemic, London's Chinatown is going through a constant metamorphosis. What was once a predominantly Cantonese neighbourhood of restaurants and lunch spots has diversified to create a new wave of street food, takeaway and dessert shops that are more cost-effective. But many of these establishments don't offer the slower sit-down experience that brings families and friends together to a table to converse and bond, which was one of the many things that made Chinatown so special.

Welcome to Snacktown

For a long time, restaurants in London's Chinatown offered Western diners a taste of the East – albeit a somewhat diluted version. Old-school banquet hall restaurants and dim sum parlours such as Golden Phoenix, Joy King Lau and Golden Dragon, which served staples like sweet and sour pork and aromatic crispy duck, were what diners came to

ARIYANI TEDJO/SHUTTERSTOCK ©

NATHANIEL NOIR/ALAMY STOCK PHOTO ©

know and expect in the area. Today the diversity and breadth of China and its cuisine, as well as its Southeast Asian neighbours, is finally being reflected on menus. Within an acre area it's now possible to feast on Malaysian curry laksa at C&R Cafe, Food House's *rou jia mo* flatbreads from Xi'an, Filipino *ube bilog* from Mamasons, as well as a simple Cantonese egg fried rice at Cafe TPT, one of the last remaining Hong Kong dai pai dongs. While traditional restaurants do remain, they coexist with contemporary concepts – Instagram-friendly waffles from Hong Kong, fluffy Japanese soufflé and Taiwanese gold-leaf black-sugar bubble tea – that appeal more to younger affluent diners.

> London's original Chinatown started life in Limehouse, East London, catering to Chinese sailors in the Georgian docklands.

Looking to the Future

As Chinatown restaurants fight to get customers through the door, the area is having something of an identity crisis, slowly transforming into a replica of what can be seen in many of Mainland China's urban centres: a soulless pan-Asian Disneyland of chains, brands and snacks that offer a bit of everything from everywhere and appeal to all. Looking into the future, it might not be about the survival of the fittest or even reviving old restaurants, but more about reminding Londoners and visitors to the city why Chinatown has always been worth visiting: the discovery of new flavours and cuisines, coming together with family and friends over a meal, and a shared connection to the identity of Britain itself.

Chinatown's Changing Face

Even before the global Covid-19 pandemic hit in 2020, many Chinatown businesses were already under pressure due to sky-high commercial rents. Traditional, family-run businesses that rely on cash flow to survive or can't compete with innovative newcomers to the area are hanging on by a thread or have been edged out by big-money international players. Some businesses like the iconic Cantonese roast meat caff Hung's have closed for good, while others have relocated outside of Zone 1. 'Mini Chinatowns' can now be found in King's Cross, Angel, Holborn, Aldgate, Lambeth and Victoria – meaning the same diners who once travelled specifically to Soho to eat Chinese food can now find it on their doorstep.

Listings

BEST OF THE REST

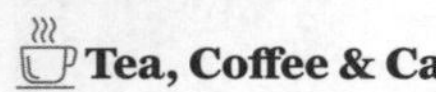

Tea, Coffee & Cake

Söderberg £££

A two-storey Swedish bakery with a minimalist Swedish aesthetic. Stop by for freshly baked cinnamon buns, open sandwiches, waffles, pastries or the famous Swedish meatballs.

Chez Antoinette £

A cheerful French restaurant on the ground floor of the Covent Garden Market Building with an amazing menu, including sweet tartines, cheeseboards and a rich cured ham salad.

Biju Bubble Tea Room Soho

This fun Taiwanese cafe serves authentic bubble tea to its many dedicated fans. Try the Black Cream Tea and Hong Kong Milk Tea, both signature beverages.

Cocktails & Beers

Aqua Nueva

A stylish top-floor contemporary restaurant specialising in Spanish cuisine with an equally impressive terrace bar overlooking central London. Walk-ins are welcome, but best to arrive early for guaranteed entry.

The Rooftop at The Trafalgar St James

You can find cheaper drinks elsewhere but nothing beats the view from the Rooftop. Gaze upon picture-perfect views of London's famous skyline, preferably at sunset, while sipping on a drink.

Opium

An intimate cocktail bar in Chinatown that transports you to 1920s Shanghai. Perfectly hidden behind a bright jaded door, there are several dimly lit seating areas across the two floors.

The Harp, Covent Garden

An award-winning pub in Trafalgar Square that is famous for its welcoming atmosphere, great service and a large selection of beers. Suitable for avid beer lovers. Situated near the National Gallery

Shochu Lounge

A contemporary rustic-chic basement bar celebrating Japanese culture in the centre of Fitzrovia. Cherry blossom trees illuminate the sophisticated space, creating a laid-back atmosphere. There's also a shisha lounge.

Green Spaces

Regent's Park

One of the biggest parks in London, Regent's Park is a beautiful space if you want to escape the city and lounge in the park.

St James's Park

St James's Park is a charming 23-hectare park and an ideal place to find stunning photography locations near St James's Park Lake or if you're looking for a bit of tranquillity.

St James's Park

Victoria Tower Gardens

A small green space near some of London's historic sites, including Houses of Parliament, Big Ben and Westminster Abbey. Stop by to enjoy the surroundings on a warm summer day.

Retail Therapy

Burlington Arcade

Opened in 1819, this historic covered shopping arcade is hailed as the first department store in Britain. It's home to ultra-luxurious brands; you can expect to find exclusive fashion pieces.

Oxford Street

The world's biggest high street with over 300 stores dotted from Tottenham Court Road to Marble Arch Station. You can find just about anything, from fashion to electronics.

Liberty

A high-end department store set in a Tudor Revival building near Carnaby St. Expect to find luxury goods from some of the world's biggest brands across six floors.

Carnaby Street

Historic Carnaby St is a London hot spot. It's home to many shops, including independent clothing stores and popular chain stores, as well as Kingly Court, a three-storey food court with world cuisines.

International Dining

Sketch, Soho £££

This quirky gastro-brasserie is known for its fun decor and enchanted atmosphere. Rooms are fuelled by art, with the main room transforming into a vibrant cocktail lounge in the evening.

Gaucho £££

This Argentinian steakhouse is often praised for serving the best steak in London. The critically acclaimed chain has restaurants around town, but the townhouse Piccadilly branch is the flagship venue.

WILLY BARTON/SHUTTERSTOCK ©

Oxford Circus

Akoko £££

A culinary experience that showcases the best of West African cuisine via Nigeria in the heart of London. The charming restaurant serves mouth-watering dishes in a classy venue in Fitzrovia.

Blacklock ££

A lively steakhouse serving juicy steaks and burgers in a basement-style former brothel in the heart of Soho.

Brasserie Zédel ££

Experience a piece of France at Zédel, an elegant brasserie that pays homage to 1930s Paris and is known for its good-value set menu of traditional French cuisine.

Imperial China ££

One of the largest Cantonese restaurants in Chinatown, Imperial China is set over two floors and has been serving traditional Chinese dishes and dim sum since 1993. There are also karaoke-ready rooms for groups.

Scan to find more things to do in the West End online

CITY OF LONDON

HISTORY | ARCHITECTURE | GARDENS

BUTLERS WHARF

CITY OF LONDON
Trip Builder

TAKE YOUR PICK OF MUST-SEES AND HIDDEN GEMS

The City of London's key attraction is its fascinating history and unusual architecture. Here glass skyscrapers offer a futuristic backdrop to centuries-old ruins. Delve a little deeper and you'll find hidden gardens, gorgeous churches and a wealth of public art in this very walkable neighbourhood, with some great pubs to boot.

Neighbourhood Notes

Best for Architecture and history.

Transport Central, District, Circle and Northern lines (also Metropolitan, Waterloo & City, Hammersmith & City, DLR, Thames Clippers)

Getting around It's always faster on foot.

Tip Plan a weekend visit if you want to avoid the crowds but check bars and restaurants are open before you go.

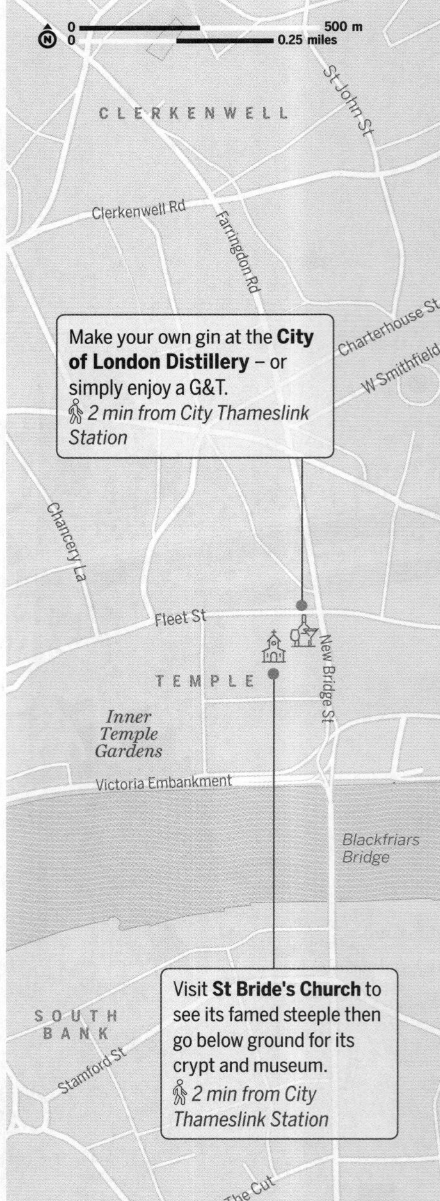

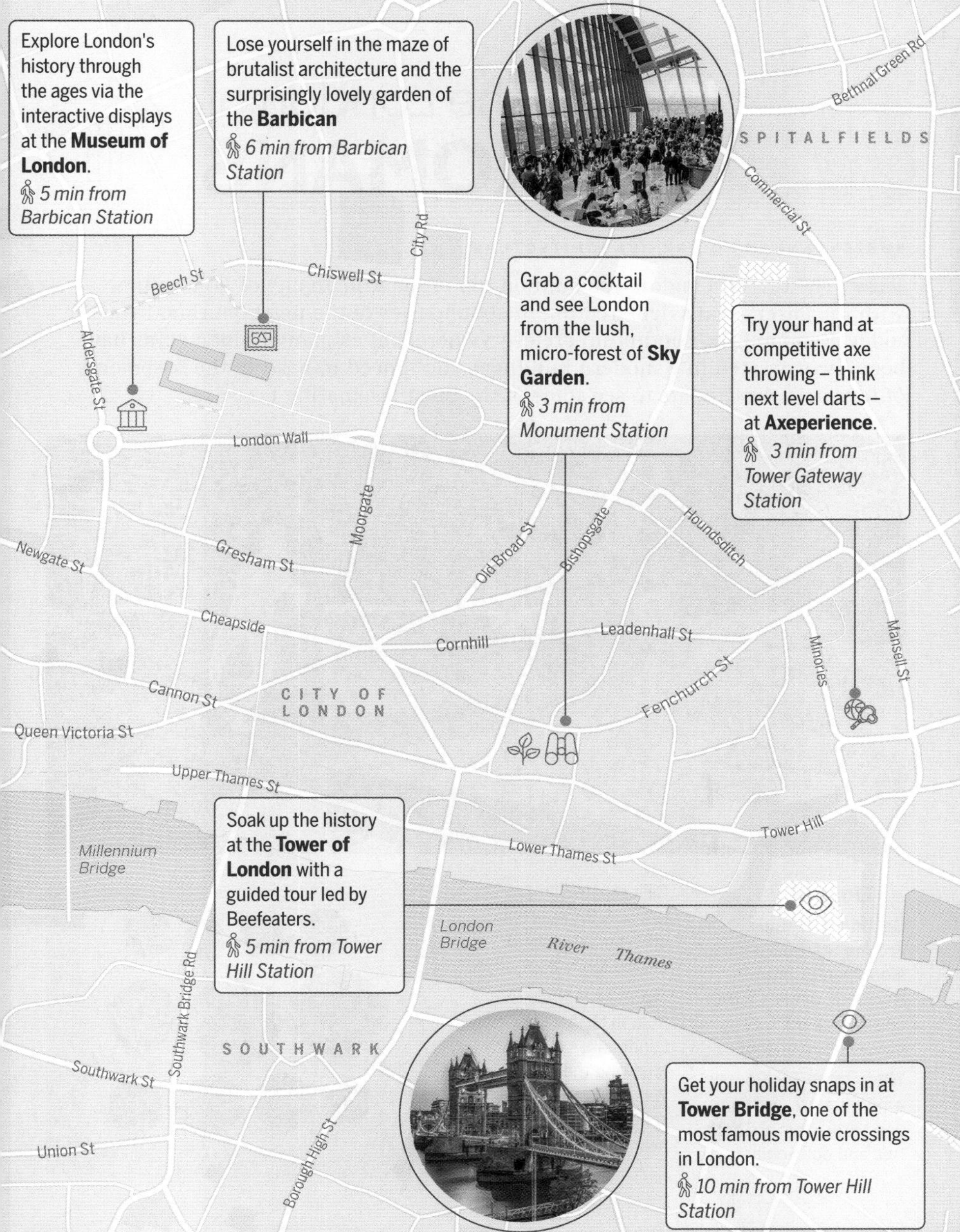

Explore London's history through the ages via the interactive displays at the **Museum of London**.
5 min from Barbican Station
Lose yourself in the maze of brutalist architecture and the surprisingly lovely garden of the **Barbican**
6 min from Barbican Station
Grab a cocktail and see London from the lush, micro-forest of **Sky Garden**.
3 min from Monument Station
Try your hand at competitive axe throwing – think next level darts – at **Axeperience**.
3 min from Tower Gateway Station
Soak up the history at the **Tower of London** with a guided tour led by Beefeaters.
5 min from Tower Hill Station
Get your holiday snaps in at **Tower Bridge**, one of the most famous movie crossings in London.
10 min from Tower Hill Station
Bethnal Green Rd
SPITALFIELDS
Commercial St
City Rd
Chiswell St
Beech St
Aldersgate St
London Wall
Moorgate
Houndsditch
Bishopsgate
Old Broad St
Newgate St
Gresham St
Cheapside
Cornhill
Leadenhall St
Minories
Mansell St
Fenchurch St
Cannon St
CITY OF LONDON
Queen Victoria St
Upper Thames St
Lower Thames St
Tower Hill
Millennium Bridge
London Bridge
River Thames
Southwark Bridge Rd
SOUTHWARK
Southwark St
Union St
Borough High St

07 Explore the London of THE ROMANS

SUBTERRANEAN | QUIRKY | ARCHITECTURE

The City of London was built on top of the Roman city of Londinium, with the latter's walls demarcating the boundaries of the neighbourhood you see today. Remnants of Londinium are everywhere, but as many Roman ruins have been incorporated into modern buildings, you'll need to head to the basements of towering skyscrapers to see some of the most fascinating treasures.

DAVID WILLIAMS/AFP VIA GETTY IMAGES ©

How to

Getting here and around Start from Bank/ Monument (Central, Northern, Circle, District and Waterloo & City lines) and go on foot.

When to go The Roman Amphitheatre and London Mithraeum are both free and open daily. Billingsgate Roman House & Baths is only open on Saturday for guided tours; book ahead.

Tip You can trace the Roman city of Londinium's outline by following the London Wall Walk, a 21-stop self-guided tour starting near Tower Hill Station.

DANIEL LEAL-OLIVAS/AFP/GETTY IMAGES ©

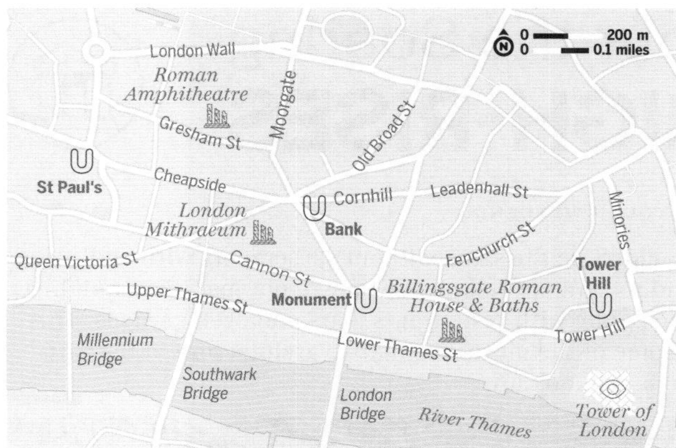

Underneath the ample art collection at the Guildhall Art Gallery is the **Roman Amphitheatre**. Originally built around 70 CE, the structure was made entirely from timber. It was enlarged in the 2nd century CE, and some of the timber was replaced with Kentish ragstone. The portions that remain – the entrance tunnel, east gate and arena walls – are all from the later version; a CGI projection shows you what the amphitheatre would have looked like.

The **London Mithraeum** is the reconstructed remains of a temple dedicated to the Iranian god Mithras, founded around the 3rd century CE and rediscovered in 1954. Considered by Romans to be a cult in its heyday, the temple admitted only men. In the collection of artefacts displayed by the entrance are two wax tablets; one details a financial transaction – apt given the space sits underneath the offices of Bloomberg – while the other is one of the earliest records mentioning Londinium. The display also features an immersive sound-and-light show every 20 minutes that re-imagines the temple in use.

Sitting in the basement of an office building, with an unceremonious entrance in the back, is **Billingsgate Roman House & Baths**. Originally built as a Roman villa around 150 CE, the bathhouse wasn't added until around 100 years later. Today it's one of the best-preserved Roman baths in the UK. See it on a guided tour.

Left Guildhall Art Gallery
Below Roman coins at the London Mithraeum

Roman Wall

The section of the Roman Wall by Tower Hill Station is the oldest in London. It's built in the Mediterranean style that's seen throughout the Roman Empire, from Rome to Istanbul. The design is distinctive. It features four or five layers of stone, followed by tiles, and then more stone and tiles. This layering gives the wall some flex so that it can withstand earthquakes. The same design is seen all over the Roman world, even in locations with zero or few earthquakes like the UK. The building material is local, though – it's Kentish ragstone harvested from the Medway Valley.

Recommended by Dr Simon Elliott, *archaeologist, historian and broadcaster, Twitter @SimonElliott20*

08 Tour the Soaring HIGH-RISES

ARCHITECTURE | WALKING TOUR | WEEKEND

London's skyline wouldn't be the same without skyscrapers with endearing names like the Gherkin and the Walkie Talkie. But they're not just office buildings – some are also open to the public with restaurants, bars and even gardens. This short walk links together some of the most imaginative architecture in the City where you can do more than just look up.

ARCHITECTS: CHAMBERLIN, POWELL AND BON. JO CHAMBERS/SHUTTERSTOCK ©

How to

Getting there From Bank/Monument (Central, Northern, Circle, District and Waterloo & City lines), or Aldgate (Circle and Metropolitan lines) if doing the tour in reverse.

When to go Weekends, especially mornings, are quietest, while Thursday evenings are busiest.

Tip The Walkie Talkie and the Gherkin both have a restaurant and bar at the top with great views. Book ahead and bring ID for the Gherkin. You can also visit Sky Garden at the Walkie Talkie for free.

Barbican Highlights

Barbican Water Gardens Surrounded by the Barbican's brutalist architecture with sunken alcoves and seating.

St Giles Cripplegate A medieval church that survived the Great Fire of London in 1666.

Barbican Highwalk A raised pedway that skirts the estate.

Tips by Richard Vines, *journalist and Barbican resident, @richardvines*

01 Designed by Rafael Viñoly, the concave glass exterior of the **Walkie Talkie** (20 Fenchurch St) famously melted a car by reflecting sunlight onto it. It's since been fitted with special shades.

02 Richard Rogers designed the **Lloyd's building** (1 Lime St) to be 'inside out' – the interior is open plan while pipes and elevators are on the outside, just like Paris's Centre Pompidou.

03 The **Scalpel** (52-54 Lime St) has a tapered top because architectural firm Kohn Pedersen Fox had to comply with rules designed to protect views of St Paul's Cathedral.

04 The **Cheesegrater** (122 Leadenhall St), officially the Leadenhall Building and designed by Rogers Stirk Harbour + Partners, was also shaped to protect views of St Paul's.

05 Foster + Partners' the **Gherkin** (30 St Mary Axe), known officially by its address, is the bullet-like skyscraper dominating the London skyline. The restaurant and bar in its dome are open to the public.

By Chris Rogers
Chris is a London-based author and historian of architecture and visual culture.
chrismrogers.net

London's Hidden Skyscrapers

THE FIRST GENERATION, OVERSHADOWED YET STILL IMPRESSIVE

Building tall for users other than church or state only began in the 1930s, and it took two more decades for true towers to appear. Overcoming legal barriers, uncertain geology and architectural conservatism, these pioneers remain distinctive and intriguing today.

Left Shell Office **Middle** London Hilton **Right** Hyde Park Barracks residential tower

The first, reaching a height previously attained only by St Paul's, was the 27-floor, 107m tower of the Shell Centre on the South Bank. Opened in 1962 and designed by Howard Robertson as the centrepiece of a corporate campus, it was the tallest office block in Britain. Controversial for this reason – in a goodwill gesture, Shell left the lights on in selected rooms for several nights to create a giant Christmas tree for London – and the employees' pool, cinema and shops below it, the neoclassical aesthetic also distressed some critics. The public viewing gallery, open-air sculptures and those staff amenities all proved forward-looking, however, and its Portland stone architecture has aged well.

Just weeks later, the taller (118m) Vickers Tower was completed on the opposite bank for the noted British engineering conglomerate Vickers; fittingly, its form was far more radical. A waisted or pinched plan generated two convex and two concave elevations, which were sheathed in glass curtain walling and detailed with projecting stainless steel mullions to emphasise their sheer verticality. Pat Keely's Tube poster that year showing an ethereal modernist tower on the Thames is clearly inspired by Ronald Ward & Partners' elegant building which, now as the Millbank Tower, remains one of the best of its era.

The London Hilton opened on Park Lane in 1963. It was only the chain's second hotel outside the United States and combined Mayfair prestige with American glamour. A transatlantic collaboration between Lewis Solomon Kaye & Partners and William B Tabler Architects yielded a 123m, Y-shaped tower with balconies toward Hyde Park and in the wing junctions, gold and black anodised aluminium windows and fast Otis lifts. Rooms had iced

WILLY BARTON/SHUTTERSTOCK ©

CERI BREEZE/ALAMY STOCK PHOTO ©

water on tap and key-operated hatches for the shoe cleaning service, while the Roof Restaurant's contemporary interior by Hugh Casson contrasted with the faux-Polynesian Trader Vic's in the podium.

Around the corner, Basil Spence struggled throughout the 1960s to fit new stables, messes, a parade ground and accommodation into the long, thin site of the Household Cavalry's Hyde Park Barracks. For the married other ranks' quarters he employed a tower, as a pragmatic response and architectural counterpoint. Completed in 1970, this extruded a square plan to a height of 94m with four flats per floor and squash courts and terraces at the summit. Its crown of concrete fins is seen by some as a guardsman's helmet, by others as a chess piece – the king to the Hilton's queen.

> Shell left the lights on in selected rooms for several nights to create a giant Christmas tree for London.

Even more protracted was the birth of the National Westminster Tower in the Square Mile. First planned two decades earlier by one of the bank's predecessors as a shorter, more conventional pair, the single 183m skyscraper that finally opened in 1981 was by R Seifert & Partners and packed with technology. Three polygonal 'leaves' were cantilevered from a reinforced concrete core, as is dramatically clear at street level, and double-deck lifts with sky lobby interchanges saved space. Bronzed glazing between stainless steel mullions was cleaned by a window-washing robot. It remained Britain's tallest building until a new generation emerged in a new quarter of London: Canary Wharf.

Forward in the Fifties

After Royal objections to the 14-storey Queen Anne's Mansions overlooking Buckingham Palace, the occupiable height of future buildings in the capital was limited to 80ft (24.4m) by an Act of 1894 that was only repealed in 1956. The clay familiar to any London gardener was thought incapable of supporting anything much taller until civil engineer Alec Skempton, an expert in soil mechanics, showed in a 1959 academic paper that friction would grip bored concrete piles firmly enough. And although glass towers in the International Style were too radical for most British clients and architects, New York's Lever House of 1952 proved influential.

09 Relax in Hidden GARDENS

UNEXPECTED | SUMMER | NATURE

With so many skyscrapers tightly packed together, it's hard to imagine the City of London as a green space. But it has a clutch of gardens and courtyards hidden in unexpected places, where office workers come for a lunchtime screen break and tourists can see a different side of the neighbourhood – the only thing is, you've got to know where to look.

ARCHITECT: RAFAEL VIÑOLY DRIMAFILM/SHUTTERSTOCK ©

How to

Getting here Bank/Monument (Central, Northern, Circle, District and Waterloo & City lines) or Fenchurch Street Railway Station (National Rail).

When to go Year-round, although summer is best for some gardens. Weekdays are always quieter, as long as you avoid the lunchtime rush.

Tip Dozens of gardens, courtyards and green spaces are hidden down medieval alleys and between high-rises. Many are unmarked, but most have seating – bring a small picnic and enjoy.

JONATHAN HOSEANA/SHUTTERSTOCK ©

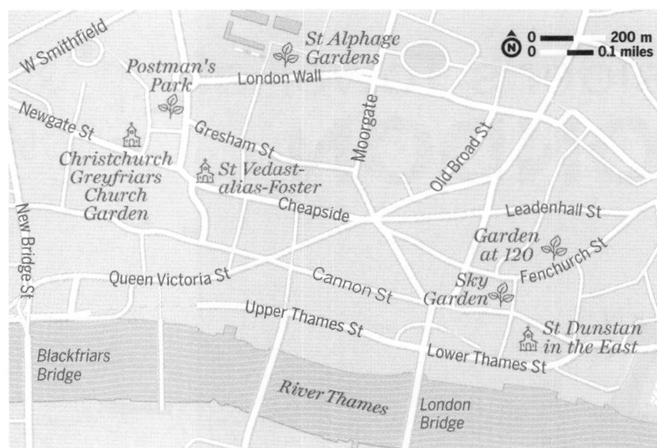

Left Sky Garden at the Walkie Talkie building **Bottom left** St Dunstan-in-the-East

Crowning the top three floors (Levels 35 to 37) of the Walkie Talkie building is **Sky Garden**. The interior resembles a giant greenhouse, with exotic plants creating a rainforest-style garden on staggered terraces, while an outdoor viewing platform offers unrivalled views south. There are two restaurants and three bars inside (so don't pack a picnic for this one). It's free to visit, but you have to book; tickets are released weekly.

Nearby is **The Garden at 120**, a rooftop garden occupying the 15th floor of the Fen Court building. As well as a water feature, there are fruit trees and wisteria providing shade. While not as high as the Walkie Talkie, the glass barriers here mean you get 360-degree views of London. Those afraid of heights might want to stay away from the edge. No need to book – it's first come, first served.

For somewhere firmly grounded, **St Dunstan-in-the-East** is gorgeous all year. The 12th-century church was damaged in the Great Fire of London in 1666, then mostly destroyed during the Blitz of 1941. Today nature has taken over its Gothic arches, making it look hauntingly beautiful.

Head to **Christchurch Greyfriars Church Garden** to see a surprising flourish of roses in the summer, planted in flower beds that mark out the original church's pews.

More Green Spaces

Walk through a set of inconspicuous church doors to explore the courtyard garden of **St Vedast-alias-Foster**. It's fairly small, with a single tree at its centre, but it's that extra barrier that makes it feel even more intimate.

Postman's Park is particularly beautiful in summer when all the flowers are in full bloom. It's also one of the biggest gardens and features a memorial for local heroes.

In winter, go to **St Alphage Gardens**. Similar to St Dunstan-in-the-East, when all the foliage has died away, you still have the ruins of the St Alphage Church as well as part of the Roman wall to see.

Tips by Katie Wignall, *Blue Badge Tourist Guide, Instagram @look_uplondon*

10 Insider's Tower of LONDON

FAMILY | HISTORY | FUN

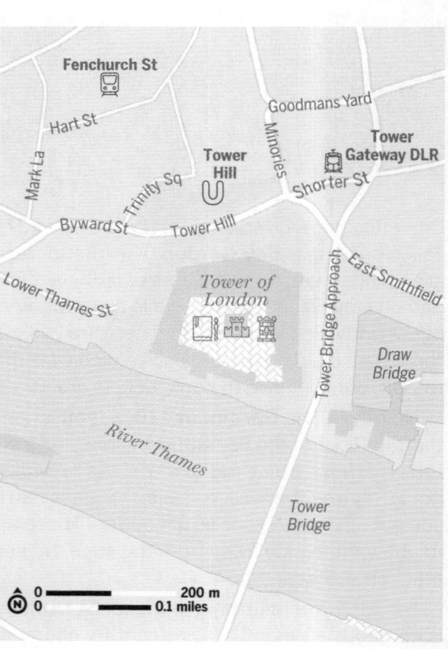

With history stretching back almost a millennia, the Tower of London is an imposing palace and fortress that guards the eastern entrance to the City of London. This family-friendly attraction – and a favourite with tourists – is a place to discover myths and legends, learn about the kings and queens of the past and see the dazzling Crown Jewels.

How to

Getting here Tower Hill (Circle, District, DLR, Thames Clippers)

When to go Go early in the morning and dedicate a whole day; avoid school holidays if you can.

How much From £28.90/14.40 per adult/child

Tip Special events such as the Ceremony of the Constable's Dues, the gun salutes and twilight tours take place a handful of times a year.

Take a tour Begin your visit with a free hour-long highlights tour led by a Yeoman Warder. These ceremonial guardians, also known as Beefeaters, were historically personal bodyguards to the monarch. Even today, they must be ex-armed forces to get hired. The warders live on the grounds with their families so you won't find a better guide. Alternatively, book a private guided tour to hear more of the tower's secrets. Designed for groups, these can be quite expensive but you'll see areas normally closed to the public, including the prison cell where St Thomas More was held before his execution in 1535.

Jewels and ravens The Crown Jewels are an essential

Right A Yeoman Warder
Below The British Crown Jewels

CHRISDORNEY/SHUTTERSTOCK ©

JOSEPH M. ARSENEAU/SHUTTERSTOCK ©

Ceremony of the Keys

During this ceremonial event, which has taken place every night for some 700 years, a Yeoman Warder locks and secures the outer and inner gates of the Tower under the escort of soldiers from its military garrison. Since 1826, it has begun at exactly 9.53pm. Tickets must be pre-booked.

Tip by Pete McGowran, *Chief Yeoman Warder, @TowerOfLondon*

stop – head there first thing to avoid queues – but for some the real gems are the ravens that live on-site and roam the grounds during the day. Legend has it that if the six resident ravens leave the tower, it and the kingdom will both fall. This hasn't been tested yet, but there's always a spare raven just in case.

Hidden surprises Key attractions aside, there are some small surprises, too. As you pass through Byward Tower on the way in, look left for a glass brick. Inside, there's a fake human hand that was installed as a joke. Also look out for the lamppost by the New Armouries Café – it's repurposed from a cannon. There's even a pub in the grounds that's only open to Beefeaters and their guests.

11 Imbibe on a Historic PUB CRAWL

PUBS | WALKING TOUR | HISTORY

The wooden beams and faded walls of London's oldest pubs have played witness to centuries of history. Some date back to the 1600s while others have been faithfully rebuilt in the style of their predecessors. This itinerary is a chance for you to dive into the stories behind their quirky interior over a cool and refreshing pint.

CHRIS LAWRENCE TRAVEL/SHUTTERSTOCK ©

How to

Getting there On foot from Holborn (Central line), or Bank/Monument (Central, Northern, Circle, District and Waterloo & City lines) if doing the itinerary in reverse.

When to go Thursday afternoons are very busy and there's usually a lunchtime rush, which adds to the atmosphere. Most of the pubs are closed on Sunday.

Tip Some of the pubs were rebuilt in the last 100 years and they combine architectural elements from different times in history.

London Gin Distillery

The gin craze famously depicted by English painter William Hogarth gripped London in the early 18th century. The multiple Gin Acts that followed then closed all the distilleries. In 2012 the **City of London Distillery** became the first new distillery in the area for almost 200 years. Book ahead to taste – and make – your own gin here.

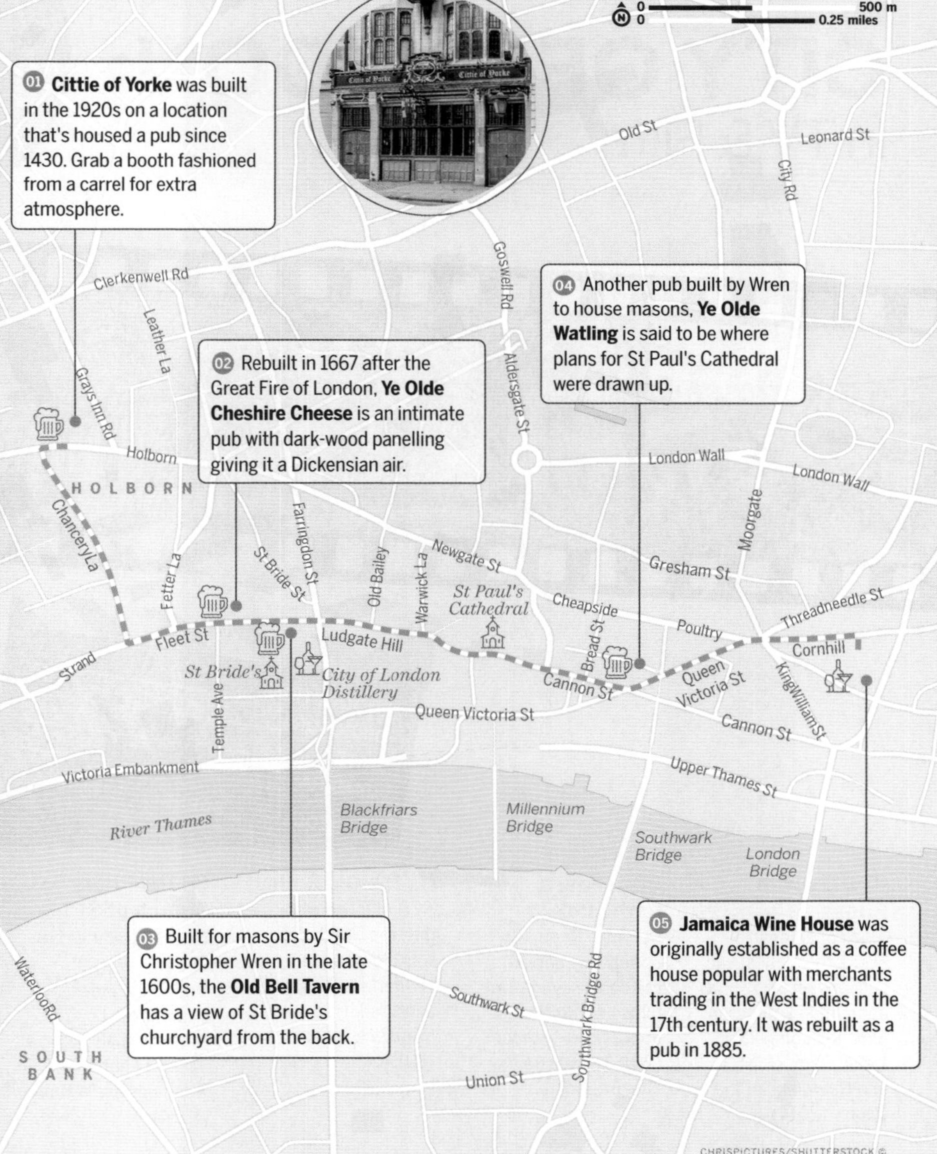
01 **Cittie of Yorke** was built in the 1920s on a location that's housed a pub since 1430. Grab a booth fashioned from a carrel for extra atmosphere.
02 Rebuilt in 1667 after the Great Fire of London, **Ye Olde Cheshire Cheese** is an intimate pub with dark-wood panelling giving it a Dickensian air.
03 Built for masons by Sir Christopher Wren in the late 1600s, the **Old Bell Tavern** has a view of St Bride's churchyard from the back.
04 Another pub built by Wren to house masons, **Ye Olde Watling** is said to be where plans for St Paul's Cathedral were drawn up.
05 **Jamaica Wine House** was originally established as a coffee house popular with merchants trading in the West Indies in the 17th century. It was rebuilt as a pub in 1885.
Cittie of Yorke
0 500 m
0 0.25 miles
Old St
Leonard St
City Rd
Goswell Rd
Clerkenwell Rd
Leather La
Grays Inn Rd
Aldersgate St
Holborn
HOLBORN
London Wall
London Wall
Moorgate
Chancery La
Farringdon St
Newgate St
Gresham St
St Bride St
Old Bailey
Warwick La
Fetter La
St Paul's Cathedral
Cheapside
Threadneedle St
Poultry
Bread St
Cornhill
Fleet St
Ludgate Hill
Strand
St Bride's
City of London Distillery
Cannon St
Queen Victoria St
King William St
Temple Ave
Queen Victoria St
Cannon St
Victoria Embankment
Upper Thames St
Blackfriars Bridge
Millennium Bridge
River Thames
Southwark Bridge
London Bridge
Waterloo Rd
Southwark St
Southwark Bridge Rd
SOUTH BANK
Union St

CITY OF LONDON
in TV & Film

01 Millenium Bridge
Since opening in 2000, this pedestrian suspension bridge has appeared in numerous films including *28 Weeks Later* (2007) and *Guardians of the Galaxy* (2014).

02 St Paul's Cathedral
St Paul's frequently appears as part of London's skyline, but films like *Mission: Impossible – Fallout* (2018) reveal its stunning interior.

03 The Old Bailey
A criminal court by day, the Old Bailey was blown up in *V for Vendetta* (2005) and captured by terrorists in *Justice League* (2017).

04 The Priory Church of St Bartholomew the Great
One of the oldest churches in London, St Barts is also St Julian's church in *Four Weddings and a Funeral* (1994).

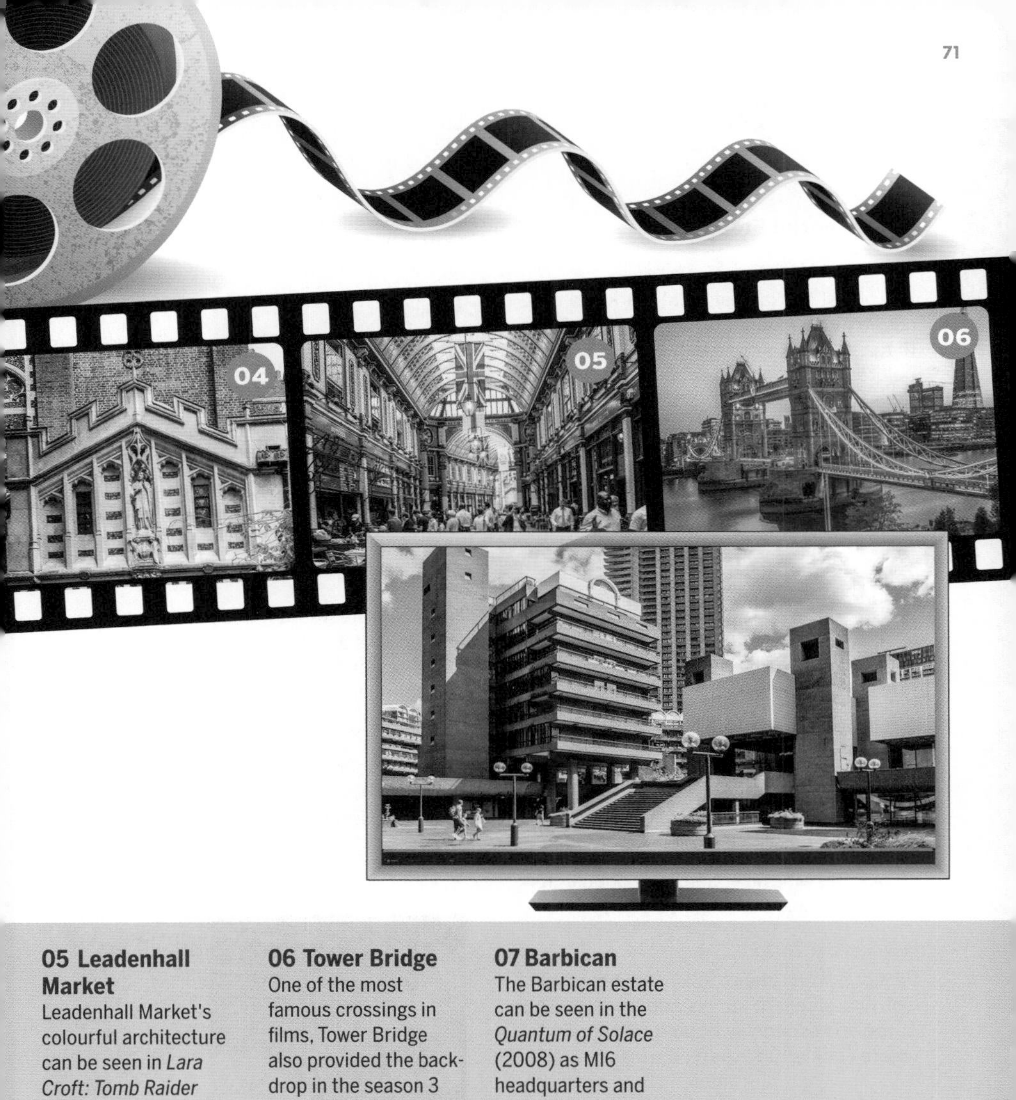

05 Leadenhall Market

Leadenhall Market's colourful architecture can be seen in *Lara Croft: Tomb Raider* (2001) and *Harry Potter and the Philosopher's Stone* (2001).

06 Tower Bridge

One of the most famous crossings in films, Tower Bridge also provided the backdrop in the season 3 finale of the TV series *Killing Eve*.

07 Barbican

The Barbican estate can be seen in the *Quantum of Solace* (2008) as MI6 headquarters and in Netflix's *The One* (2021).

Listings

BEST OF THE REST

Essential Stops

Smithfield Market

The oldest and largest meat market in the country with interesting architecture dating to the 1860s. It's open to the public – go before 7am to see it in action.

41 Cloth Fair

This unassuming property, built between 1597 and 1614, is the only one that survived the Great Fire of London in 1666, making it the City's oldest house.

The Royal Exchange

Luxury shopping and dining in a grand building dating back to 1844. The first Royal Exchange on this site was opened by Queen Elizabeth I in 1566.

Steaks & Views

Goodman £££

New York–style steakhouse with moody interiors, including wood panelling and leather banquettes. Expensive but good-quality steaks and wine selection. Very popular for business lunches.

Hawksmoor Guildhall ££

Part of a small chain, this place nevertheless has excellent steaks and burgers. This outpost is especially popular for breakfast where cocktails are served with your fry-up.

Duck & Waffle ££

Named after its signature dish, this 24-hour restaurant has sweeping views of London from the 40th floor. Great for weekend brunch but popular for sunrise breakfasts, too.

Madison £££

An upscale restaurant with up-close views of St Paul's Cathedral. Book the outdoor terrace bar for drinks only. There are also live-music and DJ nights.

Yauatcha £££

Intricate and opulent Cantonese-inspired dim sum from the Hakkasan group, plus a patisserie shop, great views of Broadgate Circle and a small rooftop terrace.

Koya £

Japanese udon noodles in the heart of Bloomberg Arcade with covered outdoor seating. Popular with City workers.

City Social £££

Fine-dining restaurant and bar from Michelin-starred chef Jason Atherton. Located on the 24th floor of Tower 42, with close-up views of the Gherkin.

Jin Bo Law Skybar £

The 14th-floor bar at Dorsett City Hotel faces the City of London. The outdoor terrace gets very busy during the summer months.

West Smithfield Meat Market

Churches with Secrets

All Hallows by the Tower

Founded in 675 CE, this is the oldest church in the City of London. A section of Roman pavement dating back to the 2nd century is hidden in its crypt.

St Bride's Church

Famed for its wedding-cake spire, this Sir Christopher Wren–designed church near Fleet St has a museum in the crypt.

St Stephen Walbrook

While not much to look at from the outside, inside you'll see the magnificent Wren-designed dome that's said to be the precursor to St Paul's dome.

A Dose of Culture

Barbican Centre

Multipurpose venue at the heart of the Barbican estate that includes a cinema, theatre and art gallery. There are always free exhibits but book well ahead for performances.

St Mary-le-Bow

A Wren-designed church (since rebuilt by architect Laurence King) that hosts regular lunchtime organ recitals as well as public lectures and discussion panels on a range of subjects.

Bank of England Museum

Interactive and family-friendly museum filled with interesting exhibits where you can learn about the history of the bank and its place in today's economy.

Museum of London

Learn about the history of London at this family-friendly museum. It's also the best place to see Roman artefacts.

KIT LEONG/SHUTTERSTOCK ©

Interior of All Hallows by the Tower

Get Competitive

Baranis

Intimate subterranean bar with an indoor pétanque court (boules are supplied). Sip herb-infused cocktails as you play.

Swingers

Enormous indoor crazy golf venue with two bespoke courses, food stalls and bars. Best enjoyed in a small group.

Axeperience

Axe throwing – think darts but with 600g axes instead. Instructors are on hand for safety and technique. Popular for date night.

Create Your Own Walks

Sculpture in the City

A 'sculpture park' that uses spaces in the Square Mile for its installations. The theme and location of the public art changes every year.

City Trees

There are around 70 species of trees in the dense urban environment of the City. Use Tree Talk *(treetalk.co.uk)* to plot your own walk.

SOUTH BANK

VIBRANT | FOODIE | FAMILY FUN

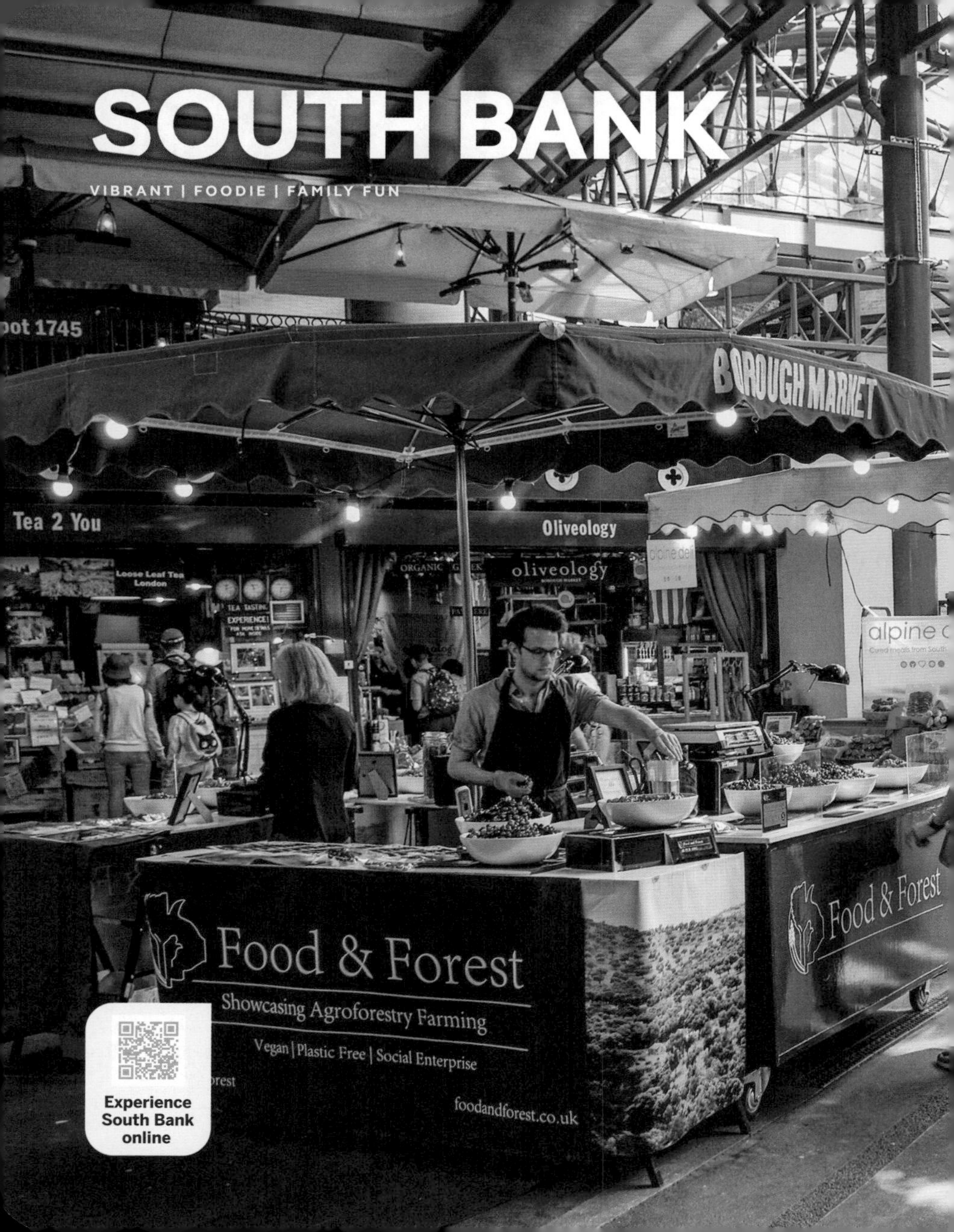

Experience South Bank online

alpine deli
Cured meats from South Tyrol, Italy

SOUTH BANK
Trip Builder

TAKE YOUR PICK OF MUST-SEES AND HIDDEN GEMS

The South Bank is known for its eclectic art spaces and theatres that rival the West End, but it is also the go-to neighbourhood for food markets. There's lots to do for free and the huge number of family-friendly attractions make it perfect for a rainy day.

Neighbourhood Notes

Best for Food and culture.

Transport Northern, Jubilee, National Rail (also Waterloo & City, Bakerloo, Thames Clippers).

Getting around Best on foot but take the underground if hopping from Waterloo to London Bridge.

Tip Look out for festivals and special events. In the summer there's free theatre and live music, and in winter there's a Christmas market.

SOUTH BANK BUILD YOUR TRIP

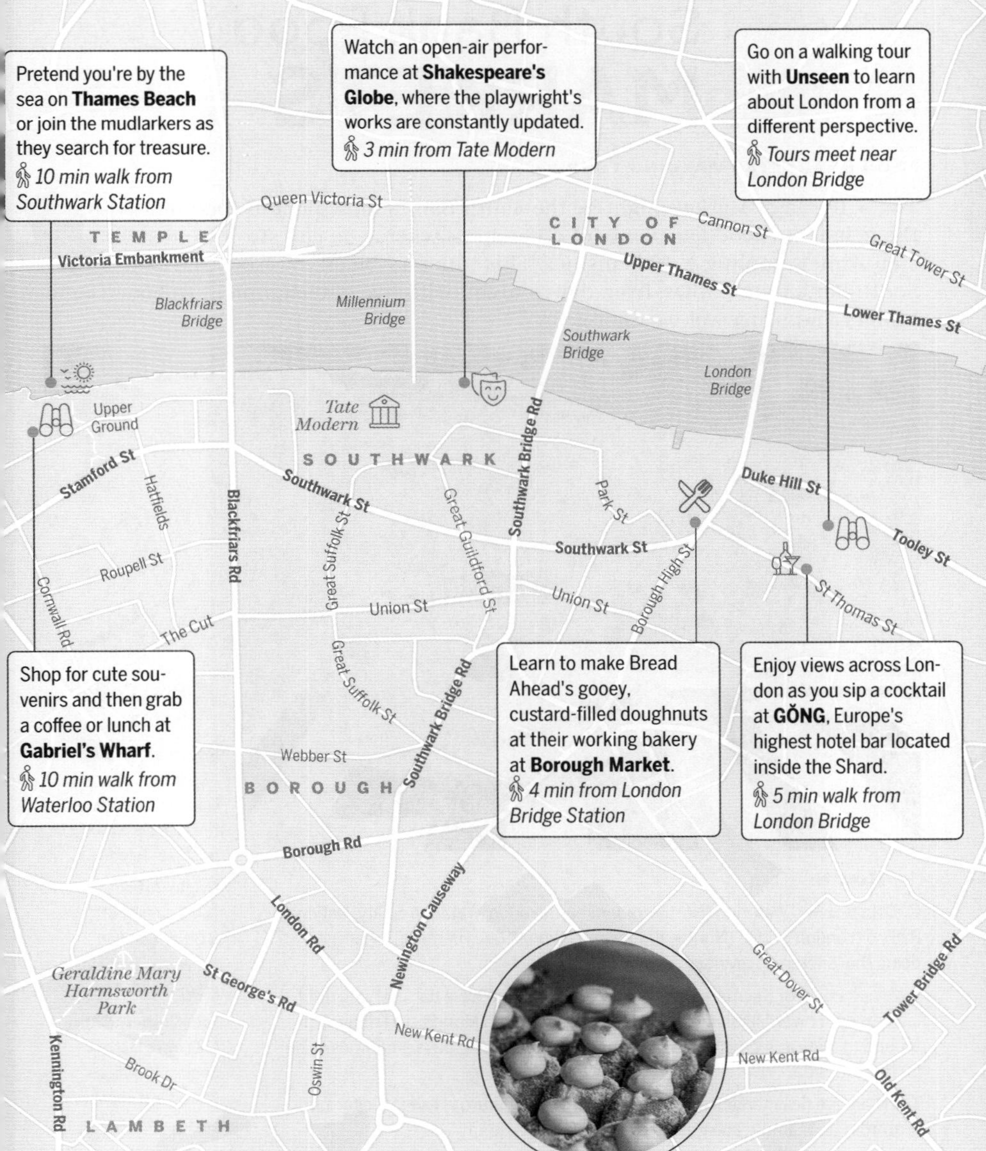

Pretend you're by the sea on **Thames Beach** or join the mudlarkers as they search for treasure.
10 min walk from Southwark Station
Watch an open-air performance at **Shakespeare's Globe**, where the playwright's works are constantly updated.
3 min from Tate Modern
Go on a walking tour with **Unseen** to learn about London from a different perspective.
Tours meet near London Bridge
Shop for cute souvenirs and then grab a coffee or lunch at **Gabriel's Wharf**.
10 min walk from Waterloo Station
Learn to make Bread Ahead's gooey, custard-filled doughnuts at their working bakery at **Borough Market**.
4 min from London Bridge Station
Enjoy views across London as you sip a cocktail at **GŎNG**, Europe's highest hotel bar located inside the Shard.
5 min walk from London Bridge
Queen Victoria St
TEMPLE
Victoria Embankment
CITY OF LONDON
Cannon St
Great Tower St
Upper Thames St
Lower Thames St
Blackfriars Bridge
Millennium Bridge
Southwark Bridge
London Bridge
Upper Ground
Tate Modern
SOUTHWARK
Stamford St
Hatfields
Blackfriars Rd
Southwark St
Great Suffolk St
Great Guildford St
Southwark Bridge Rd
Park St
Duke Hill St
Tooley St
Borough High St
St Thomas St
Roupell St
Cornwall Rd
The Cut
Union St
Webber St
BOROUGH
Borough Rd
London Rd
Newington Causeway
Geraldine Mary Harmsworth Park
St George's Rd
New Kent Rd
Great Dover St
Tower Bridge Rd
Old Kent Rd
Kennington Rd
Brook Dr
Oswin St
LAMBETH

12 South Bank Food MARKETS

FOOD | MARKETS | WALKING TOUR

Borough Market might be the South Bank's most famous food market but the neighbourhood has plenty of other spots where you can stroll from stall to stall while sampling world cuisines. This itinerary takes you from one side of the South Bank to the other, from day to night, with live entertainment to boot. Come hungry and bring wet weather gear.

LOOP IMAGES LTD/ALAMY STOCK PHOTO ©

How to

Getting around Waterloo (Northern, Jubilee, Bakerloo, Waterloo & City, National Rail), or London Bridge (Northern, Jubilee, National Rail, Thames Clippers) if doing the itinerary in reverse.

When to go All of the markets are open on Friday and have bars serving until late, except Lower Marsh Market, which closes at 3pm Monday to Friday. Start around midday and check individual markets for opening days and times to be on the safe side.

Tip There are flea markets at Lower Marsh Market (Saturday) and Vinegar Yard (Saturday and Sunday) on weekends.

Best Coffee Spots

Roasting Plant Coffee (4 Borough High St) Upscale cafe where the beans are always freshly roasted.

Origin Coffee (84 Scoresby St) B Corp–certified coffee shop with Instagram-friendly decor.

Four Corners Cafe (12 Lower Marsh) Speciality coffees served in a kitsch space.

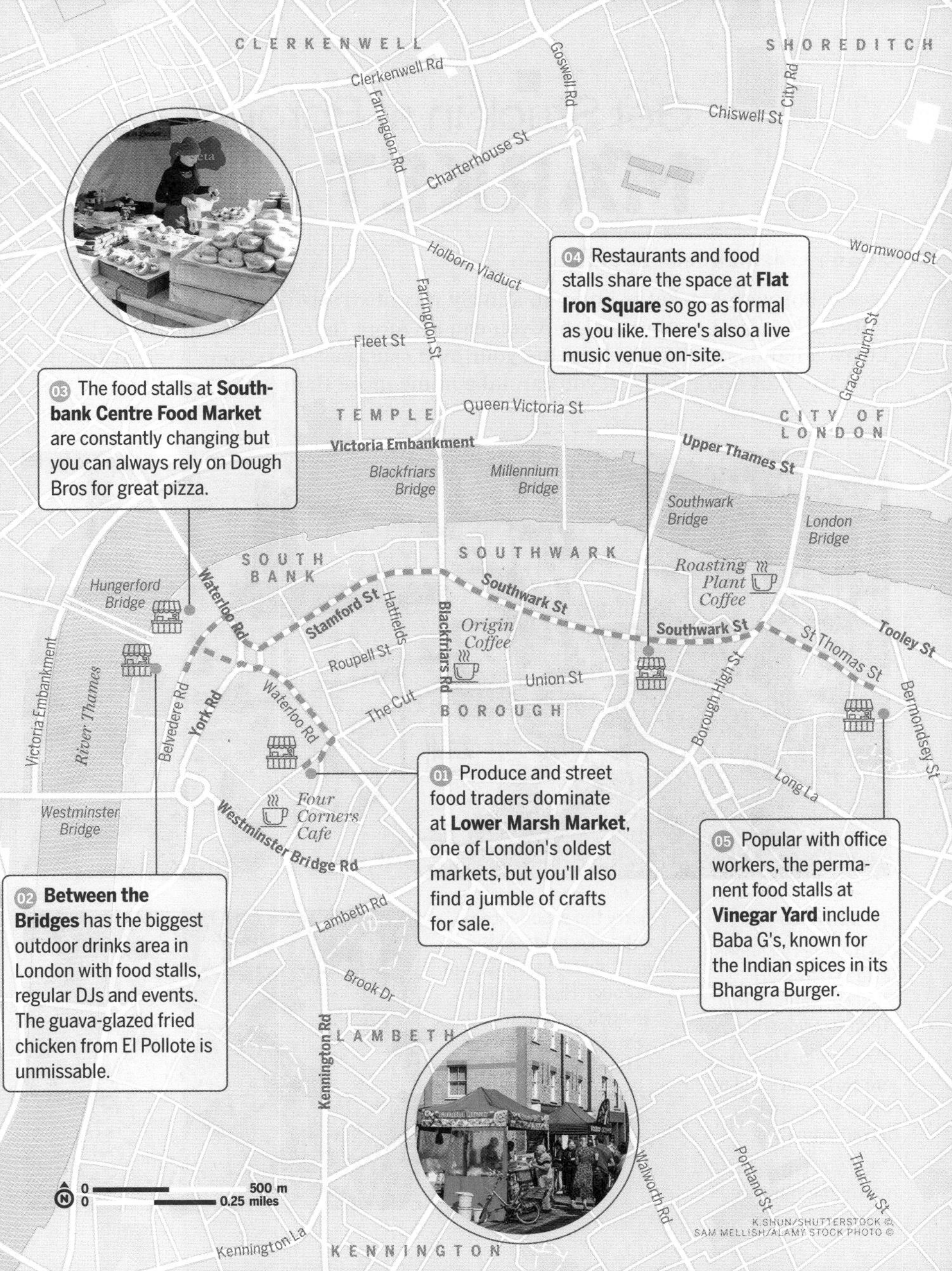

01 Produce and street food traders dominate at **Lower Marsh Market**, one of London's oldest markets, but you'll also find a jumble of crafts for sale.
02 **Between the Bridges** has the biggest outdoor drinks area in London with food stalls, regular DJs and events. The guava-glazed fried chicken from El Pollote is unmissable.
03 The food stalls at **Southbank Centre Food Market** are constantly changing but you can always rely on Dough Bros for great pizza.
04 Restaurants and food stalls share the space at **Flat Iron Square** so go as formal as you like. There's also a live music venue on-site.
05 Popular with office workers, the permanent food stalls at **Vinegar Yard** include Baba G's, known for the Indian spices in its Bhangra Burger.
CLERKENWELL
SHOREDITCH
Clerkenwell Rd
Goswell Rd
City Rd
Chiswell St
Farringdon Rd
Charterhouse St
Holborn Viaduct
Wormwood St
Farringdon St
Fleet St
Gracechurch St
TEMPLE
Queen Victoria St
CITY OF LONDON
Victoria Embankment
Upper Thames St
Blackfriars Bridge
Millennium Bridge
Southwark Bridge
London Bridge
SOUTH BANK
SOUTHWARK
Roasting Plant Coffee
Hungerford Bridge
Waterloo Rd
Stamford St
Hatfields
Blackfriars Rd
Southwark St
Origin Coffee
Tooley St
St Thomas St
Roupell St
Union St
Victoria Embankment
River Thames
Belvedere Rd
York Rd
The Cut
BOROUGH
Borough High St
Bermondsey St
Long La
Four Corners Cafe
Westminster Bridge
Westminster Bridge Rd
Lambeth Rd
Brook Dr
LAMBETH
Kennington Rd
Walworth Rd
Portland St
Thurlow St
0 500 m
0 0.25 miles
Kennington La
KENNINGTON

13 Get Stuck in at Borough MARKET

FOOD | EXPERIENCES | SHOPPING

Borough Market is home to a lively mix of street-food stalls, produce traders, bars and restaurants, but you can do more than just eat and drink here. Learn a hands-on skill like making your own sausages or try your hand at frying up a batch of doughnuts so you can take home more than just memories.

51NORTH/ALAMY STOCK PHOTO ©

How to

Getting here London Bridge (Northern, Jubilee, National Rail, Thames Clippers)

When to go Most traders are closed on Sunday. Experiences require advance booking.

Tip If you buy food from one of the stalls, don't hurry the experience by eating kerbside. At the junction of Bedale St and Borough High St there's an enclosed space with seating. Otherwise walk to Bankside where you can perch by the Thames with unrestricted views of the London skyline.

CRISTINA.A/SHUTTERSTOCK ©

Skip the doughnut queue outside **Bread Ahead** and go straight into the adjacent bakery where you can learn how to make these tasty treats yourself. In just two hours, you'll leave with a small bundle of 'custard grenades' – a doughnut overfilled with creamy custard – that you've made yourself. If desserts aren't your thing, they also have half-, full- and multi-day courses specialising in different breads and pastries. Courses often sell out a month in advance.

If you don't mind getting a bit messy, make your way to **the Ginger Pig**. The upscale butcher's shop runs a popular sausage-making course at its Borough Market branch. You'll learn the basics of sausage-making – from getting the lean meat to fat ratio just right, to adding the perfect combination of flavour – before getting hands on with a mincer and sausage stuffer to make your own links.

Bedales of Borough Market combines a wine shop, bar and bistro in one. Book ahead (ideally at least 36 hours in advance) for a self-guided wine tasting with a Prosecco and three table wines, all accompanied by fresh sourdough and olives. A tasting booklet is provided. It's the perfect excuse to try before you buy.

Left Spice Mountain **Bottom left** Window display at Bread Ahead

Shop Borough Market

Spice Mountain *(spice-mountain.co.uk)* Fabulous tubs of spices and spice blends for you to experiment with at home.

Oliveology *(oliveology.co.uk)* Sachets of wonderful dried Greek herbs.

From Field & Flower *(fromfieldandflower.co.uk)* An extensive selection of delicious honeys with varying intensities of flavour.

Food & Forest *(foodandforest.co.uk)* Sustainably produced raw, roasted or sweet nuts.

Borough Kitchen Cook Shop *(boroughkitchen.com)* If luggage space allows, pick up *The Borough Market Cookbook* by Ed Smith, or Mark Ridaway's *Borough Market: Edible Histories*.

Recommended by Angela Clutton, *freelance food writer and host of the Borough Market Cookbook Club, @angela_clutton*

14 Discover Vibrant STREET ART

GRAFFITI | OUTDOORS | EXPLORING

Having established galleries like the Tate Modern on the South Bank means its street art is often overlooked. But if you know where to go, there are artworks to rival those found in Shoreditch. The works here are more spread out so you'll need to get your explorer's hat on and keep your eyes peeled for everything from captivating graffiti to diminutive mosaics.

BAILEY-COOPER PHOTOGRAPHY/ALAMY STOCK PHOTO ©

How to

Getting here Waterloo (Northern, Jubilee, Bakerloo, Waterloo & City, National Rail), or London Bridge (Northern, Jubilee, National Rail, Thames Clipper) in reverse.

Before you go Visit *streetartbio.com* to find out more about the artists and their work.

Tip Works by celebrated artists such as Banksy have appeared on the South Bank in the past, but the nature of these pieces mean they don't stay for long as some are removed and others are painted over. So even if you've already been, it's still worth coming back.

CHAMELEONSEYE/SHUTTERSTOCK ©

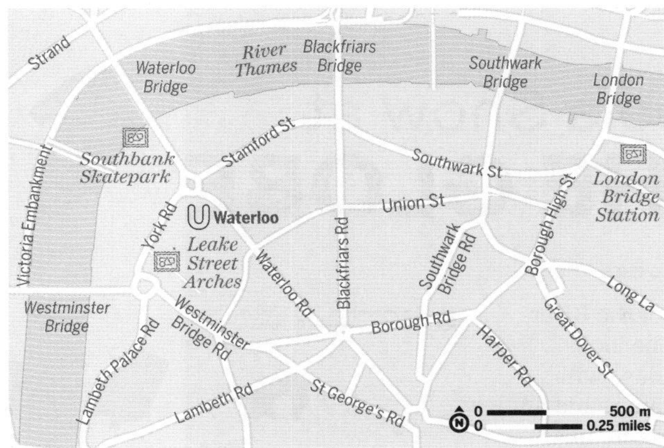

Leake Street Arches is the South Bank's best-known street-art hub. The disused railway arches had been largely abandoned before Banksy hosted the first Cans Festival here in 2008 and gave it a new lease of life. Since then, it's become a multi-venue space with theatres, live music and restaurants – all accessed via the brightly spray-painted tunnel entrance. You'll always see art in progress and there are occasionally events where you can have a go yourself.

Sitting directly beneath the Southbank Centre is the **Southbank Skatepark**, a public space that's frequently regarded as the home of British skateboarding. Having been used by skaters for over 40 years, it was refurbished and extended in 2019 following a public campaign to save it from redevelopment. Now it features the largest collection of tags and throw-ups on the South Bank.

As you walk along the river from Waterloo to London Bridge, you'll see some street art clustered around each of the bridges. Look out for colourful murals on feature walls and small mosaics higher up. The biggest collection can be found around the arches at **London Bridge Station**. Unlike Leake Street Arches and Southbank Skatepark, the artworks here are much more spread out so this section is where you can really lose yourself.

Left Leake Street Arches **Bottom left** Southbank Skatepark.

Illuminated River

Connecting east London to the west is **Illuminated River** *(illuminatedriver.london)*, a major public art project. The idea is to fit 15 bridges – from Tower Bridge in the east to Albert Bridge in the west – with coloured LED lights that illuminate the structures at night. The lighting design was created by American light artist Leo Villareal, with each bridge given a unique sequence to enhance its features. Nine bridges have already been completed and you can see them in action after dark – just take a walk along the River Thames at night.

If you want to learn more, there is also a programme of events around the bridges, including special river cruises, guided walking tours and magical guided night kayaking trips.

15 See a Show at THE GLOBE

THEATRE | SUMMER | OUTDOORS

Sitting on the bank of the River Thames, Shakespeare's Globe looks every part the Tudor playhouse with its thatched roof, timber frames and an open yard that's standing-room only and exposed to the elements. When you're in the yard, the experience mirrors that of the average Elizabethan, while the shows are thoroughly modern, making this experience truly unique.

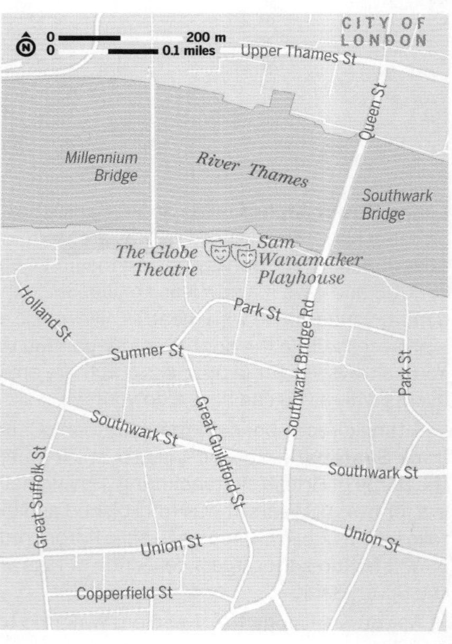

How to

Getting here Bankside (Thames Clippers) or a short walk from London Bridge (Northern, Jubilee).

When to go Evening performances at The Globe are more atmospheric but matinees are less busy.

How much From £5.

How long Upwards of 1½ hours. Not all performances have intervals.

Tip Prepare for all weather, even if seated. You can't use umbrellas in the yard so pack a raincoat.

Shakespeare's Globe is actually two venues in one: the **Globe Theatre** (outdoors, summer only) and **Sam Wanamaker Playhouse** (indoors, year round). While both are worth experiencing, the Globe feels more authentic to Shakespeare and is much more affordable, making it great for a first visit.

The shows performed at the Globe are exclusively Shakespeare's works, albeit reinterpreted for a modern audience, so expect plenty of singing, dancing and special effects, all accompanied by a live band. Almost all performances are family-friendly,

Top right Performance of *The Tempest* by the Lions Part performers **Right** Exterior of the Globe Theatre

PADMAYOGINI/SHUTTERSTOCK ©

The Third Globe

The Globe Theatre that you see today was completed in 1997 and features many Elizabethan design elements, including a real thatched roof. The original theatre was located nearby, a street back from the river. When it burned down in 1613, a second was built in its place, but it was closed by order of Parliament in 1642 when the English Civil War began.

although the evening shows can run late into the night, which might not be suitable for young children. Select performances have British Sign Language interpreters or audio description; these are indicated when you book your tickets.

The yard is the cheapest place to be but it's also the most fun. You're right in the middle of the action as the actors tend to interact more with the audience here, and will even run through the crowd as part of the show. You can also walk around to get a different perspective or even a better view – just as Elizabethans would have done in their time. Those who get tired easily might want to find a spot at the back of the yard where leaning against the banister is de rigueur.

RON ELLIS/SHUTTERSTOCK ©

16 Best Free Views of LONDON

LANDSCAPES | ARCHITECTURE | FREE

The City of London might be packed with skyscrapers but the best views of the skyline are found south of the river. There are multiple vantage points along the riverfront - some elevated and some right at the water's edge - where you can get the perfect shot. And you don't have to pay for the privilege either.

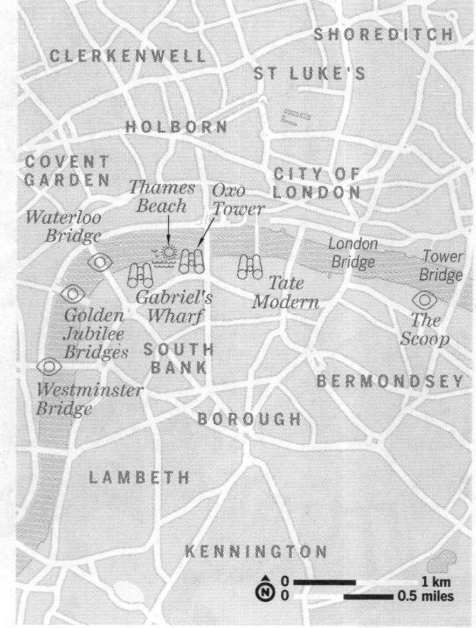

How to

Getting here Waterloo (Northern, Jubilee, Bakerloo, Waterloo & City, National Rail) or London Bridge (Northern, Jubilee, National Rail, Thames Clipper).

When to go Great year round but best at dawn, sunset or after dark.

Top tip Instead of a river cruise, take one of the Thames Clippers. Services run from Putney to Woolwich but the most interesting stretch is in the Central Zone. The RB2 serves South Bank stops.

For virtually unobstructed views of the city, cross a bridge. **Westminster Bridge** offers the view of the Houses of Parliament that you frequently see in films. Of the two pedestrian-only **Golden Jubilee Bridges**, the upstream one has slightly better views, especially of the London Eye as you walk from north to south. For the perfect panoramic downriver, go to **Waterloo Bridge** and cross just over half way.

For views from up high, there's a little-known public viewing platform on Level 8 of the **Oxo Tower**, by the restaurant. From here, look

Top right Big Ben **Right** City skyline seen from Tate Modern's Blavatnik Building

River View

The South Bank is all about interacting with the water and it's better when you're lower down. The **Thames Beach** is right at the water level and you can go mudlarking on the river bank.

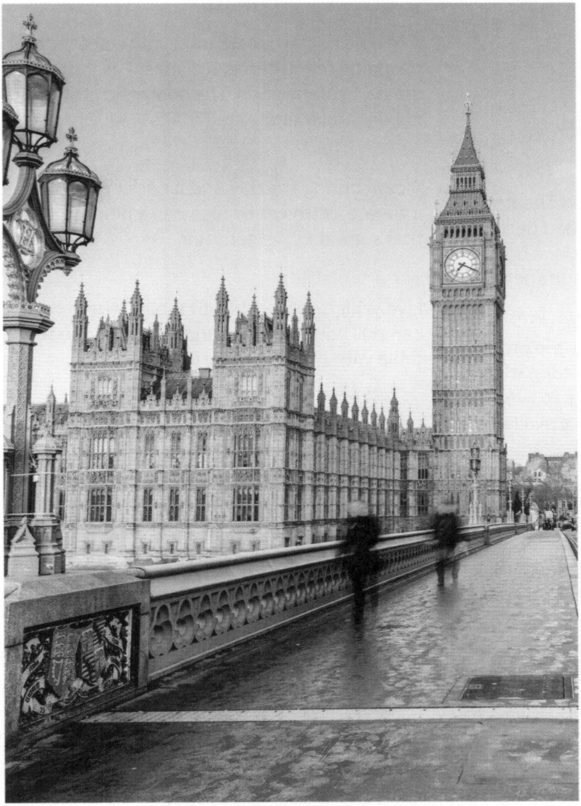

Tip by Alex Lifschutz, *Founding Director of Lifschutz Davidson Sandilands architects @lds_architects*

left for Somerset House and right for St Paul's Cathedral and the City of London. Further along the river you have the viewing platform on Level 10 of **Tate Modern's Blavatnik Building**. St Paul's is pretty much straight ahead when you face north while the City is further east. Be prepared to wait a while for the elevators, though, as it can get crowded.

You can walk along the river all the way from Westminster Bridge to London Bridge and there are multiple viewpoints along the way. The observation point by **Gabriel's Wharf** offers virtually the same view as Oxo Tower from the ground, but even better is the view from the stretch by **the Scoop** near Tower Bridge. Look west to see the City skyline in all its glory.

Listings

BEST OF THE REST

More than a Show

National Theatre

The Olivier, Lyttelton and Dorfman Theatres are all venues at this publicly funded performing arts centre. Free shows take place outside the venue frequently during the summer.

The Old Vic

A large-capacity (1000 seats) not-for-profit theatre with over 200 years of history, where you can see everything from plays to live music. Discounted preview tickets are available for new shows.

The Young Vic

Originally an Old Vic offshoot, the Young Vic is well known for its boundary-pushing programming with shows from younger playwrights and plays inspired by world events.

The Vaults

Housed inside disused railway arches, this multi-space venue is known for hosting alternative performances and immersive experiences, including dinner theatre. It's accessed via Leake Street Arches.

Space to Refuel

Casa do Frango £

Airy Portuguese restaurant specialising in freshly grilled piri-piri chicken and small plates to share. The space gets quite busy and loud, even during the week.

Trivet £££

Fine-dining restaurant serving creative British food with a hefty price tag. The co-founders are both alumni of the three-Michelin-starred Fat Duck.

Arabica £

A Middle Eastern restaurant with a seasonal changing menu of meze dishes. The flatbreads are particularly good. The energetic atmosphere and friendly staff make it a joy to visit.

Scootercaffe £

A cafe during the day and a bar at night, this intimate, retro venue also has a hidden garden that's great in the summer.

The Thirsty Bear £

Lively, high-tech pub with tables where you can pull your own pint and order food to the table with the help of an iPad.

GŎNG ££

Located on the 52nd floor of the Shard, this is the highest hotel bar in Europe. There's a minimum spend but it's cheaper than the viewing gallery lower down.

Art Yard Bar & Kitchen ££

Bankside Hotel's hospitality offering features a huge collection of art and excellent cocktails inspired by the local area.

Family-Friendly Attractions

London Eye

The world's largest cantilevered observation wheel with 32 glass pods. A single rotation

National Theatre

takes 30 minutes and there's enough space in the pods for a small group.

SEA LIFE Centre London Aquarium

Spanning the ground floor of County Hall, the layout of this aquarium creates hidden corners that make exploring its shark walk and underwater tunnel feel like an adventure.

The London Dungeon

A walk-through experience with a mixture of rides and live actors that retell important points in history. A hit with teens but not suitable for young kids.

Electric Gamebox

Interactive and immersive gaming experience in an enclosed room. Touch-sensitive walls, sensors and cameras are used to track your progress. Each session lasts 30 or 60 minutes.

Golden Hinde

A full-sized replica of the vessel that Sir Francis Drake used to circumnavigate the world. On board this seaworthy ship, you'll learn about the history of the original expedition.

Clink Prison Museum

Built on the grounds of the original Clink Prison, this gruesome museum tells the stories of the colourful inmates. There are also displays of torture devices.

Tours with Purpose

Unseen London Bridge

Unseen gives a voice and income to those who have been homeless, and this walking tour offers insight into another side of London with a dose of history.

PPTARA/SHUTTERSTOCK ©

London Eye

Balkan Tastes & Culture

A collaboration between tour operator Intrepid and social enterprise Women in Travel, which supports underprivileged women, this walking tour reveals the South Bank's many Balkan connections.

Shop for Souvenirs

Gabriel's Wharf

A cluster of cute boutiques selling clothing and accessories, many of which are handmade. You can also pick up works and prints by local artists.

Oxo Tower Wharf

Split across different floors of the building are studios and shops home to makers and designers. Most sell handmade jewellery but you can also find ceramics and furniture.

Southbank Centre Book Market

A secondhand book market under Waterloo Bridge, with everything from comics to classic novels in paperback and hardback. Antiques are occasionally sold here, too.

Scan to find more things to do in South Bank online

KENSINGTON & HYDE PARK

PARKS | MUSEUMS | SHOPPING

Experience Kensington & Hyde Park online

KENSINGTON & HYDE PARK
Trip Builder

TAKE YOUR PICK OF MUST-SEES AND HIDDEN GEMS

The term 'world-famous' is often attached to sites within this culturally (and financially) rich section of town: The V&A. Hyde Park. Harrods. Kensington Palace. There are few areas more classic and quintessentially British than here; plan a visit to witness the multifaceted capital's opulent, polished side.

Neighbourhood Notes

Best for Culture, parks, luxury shopping and dining.

Transport Piccadilly, Circle, District and Victoria lines (and National Rail trains to Victoria Station).

Getting around It's a highly walkable area, otherwise buses and Underground trains are readily available.

Budget tip Neighbourhood shopping and dining can be pricey, but museums remain free.

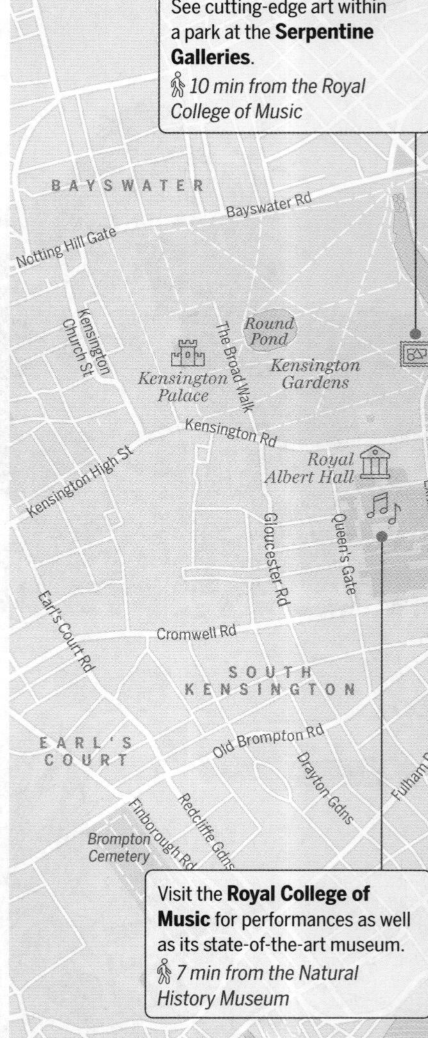

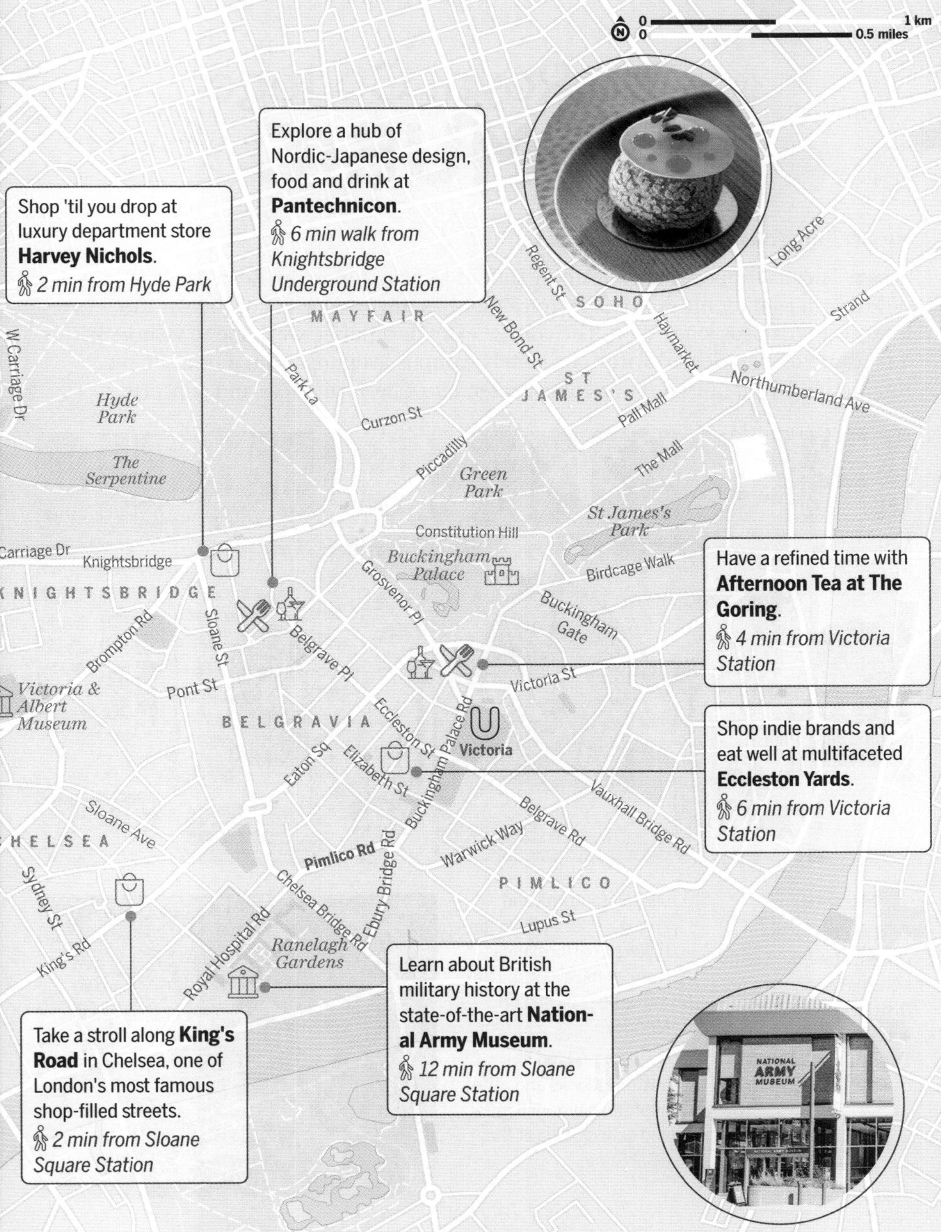
0 1 km
0 0.5 miles
Shop 'til you drop at luxury department store **Harvey Nichols**.
2 min from Hyde Park
Explore a hub of Nordic-Japanese design, food and drink at **Pantechnicon**.
6 min walk from Knightsbridge Underground Station
Have a refined time with **Afternoon Tea at The Goring**.
4 min from Victoria Station
Shop indie brands and eat well at multifaceted **Eccleston Yards**.
6 min from Victoria Station
Learn about British military history at the state-of-the-art **National Army Museum**.
12 min from Sloane Square Station
Take a stroll along **King's Road** in Chelsea, one of London's most famous shop-filled streets.
2 min from Sloane Square Station
MAYFAIR
SOHO
ST JAMES'S
KNIGHTSBRIDGE
BELGRAVIA
CHELSEA
PIMLICO
Hyde Park
The Serpentine
Green Park
St James's Park
Buckingham Palace
Victoria & Albert Museum
Ranelagh Gardens
Victoria
W Carriage Dr
Carriage Dr
Knightsbridge
Park La
Curzon St
Piccadilly
Regent St
New Bond St
Haymarket
Long Acre
Strand
Northumberland Ave
Pall Mall
The Mall
Constitution Hill
Birdcage Walk
Buckingham Gate
Grosvenor Pl
Belgrave Pl
Sloane St
Brompton Rd
Pont St
Victoria St
Eccleston St
Buckingham Palace Rd
Elizabeth St
Eaton Sq
Sloane Ave
Pimlico Rd
Ebury Bridge Rd
Chelsea Bridge Rd
Warwick Way
Belgrave Rd
Vauxhall Bridge Rd
Lupus St
Sydney St
King's Rd
Royal Hospital Rd
NATIONAL ARMY MUSEUM

17 The Royal College OF MUSIC

MUSIC | HISTORY | PERFORMING ARTS

Located opposite Royal Albert Hall in Kensington is the Royal College of Music, a leading music conservatoire that has nurtured some of the world's brightest virtuosos since 1883. The college extends a public welcome to visitors with a plethora of experiences within its stately campus grounds, from a brand-new, interactive music museum to a robust calendar of performances and concerts.

ROBERTO LA ROSA/SHUTTERSTOCK ©

How to

Getting there The closest station – South Kensington on the Circle, District and Piccadilly line – is a half-mile away. The 360 bus brings you closest to its doorstep.

When to go During the typical college semester season (autumn and spring); check online for ticketed performances (rcm.ac.uk/events). The museum is closed on Monday.

Buyer's tip Find mugs, buttons, books and other affordable branded gifts and collectables at the RCM Shop.

HEATHCLIFF O'MALLEY - WPA POOL/ GETTY IMAGES ©

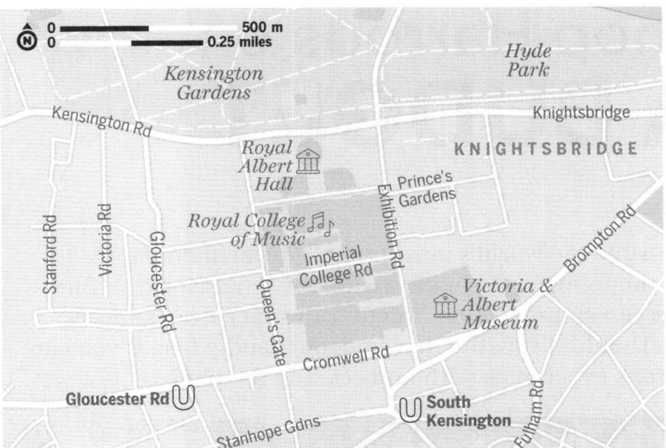

The sound of history The new, state-of-the-art **Royal College of Music Museum** is the crown jewel of the institution's ongoing multimillion-dollar facelift. From 2021, visitors can explore an interactive space housing thousands of items – from the earliest known string keyboard instrument, the clavicytherium, to portraits of leading 18th-century musicians. Audio guides will take you through five centuries of music history under an attractive atrium venue. Go on a Friday to catch one of the weekly in-museum **chamber performances**, or try your hand at crafting your own sound inside its family-friendly **Weston Discovery Centre**.

Catch a show Where can you find the next classical music superstar? Chances are, they could be a student performing or composing at any given recital or concert on this campus – and you can see them in action for free or for as little as £5. The semester season is rife with open-to-the-public shows in refreshed performance spaces, including the **Britten Theatre**, a grand opera house where costumed students belt notes to the tune of an 80-person orchestra. Catch a masterclass by a world-renowned violinist in a concert hall; sway to jazz from a student ensemble in one of the theatres; or enjoy a chamber music session inside the new 150-seat performance hall.

Bottom left The Royal College of Music **Below** Students performing at the college

Museum Must-Sees

The **oldest guitar** in the world, made in Lisbon by Belchior Dias in 1581.

Famous portraits of celebrated Italian baroque singer Farinelli and Austrian composer Joseph Haydn.

A beautifully **painted harpsichord** made in Venice by Alessandro Trasuntino in 1531.

A collection of **early viols** made in London from the end of the 16th century.

Autographed manuscripts from the RCM Library collection, including works by Edward Elgar, Frédéric Chopin and Wolfgang Mozart.

Recommended by Gabriele Rossi Rognoni, *Curator of the Royal College of Music Museum, @RossiRognoni*

18 Shop Harrods on A BUDGET

SHOPPING | DINING | FASHION

Harrods is quite possibly the world's most famous department store, a grand temple of high-end shopping based in ultra-affluent Knightsbridge. But not every Harrods shopper can splurge £1 million on ruby-encrusted slippers, or buy a yacht on a whim. Thankfully, with a few budget-friendly hacks, you can have a quintessential Harrods experience without breaking the bank.

STEVE VIDLER/ALAMY STOCK PHOTO ©

How to

Getting there A stone's throw from the Underground's Knightsbridge Station entrance; otherwise, use Knightsbridge area-bound buses.

When to go Harrods is open seven days a week. Mornings are best to sidestep the daily afternoon and early evening rush; winter holiday season is a popular but enchanting time to visit.

Just browsing Everyone's a window shopper – no matter the budget – from 11.30am to noon on Sunday, as that is Harrods' dedicated 'browsing only' period.

PEN_85/SHUTTERSTOCK ©

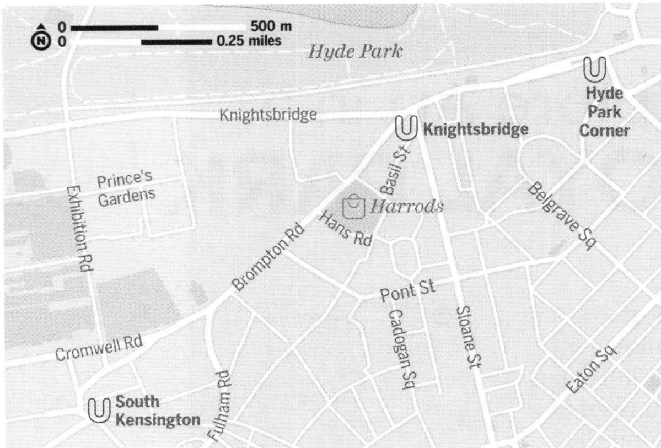

Left Chocolate Hall
Bottom left Harrods Tea Room

Wallet-friendly eats Though Harrods is known for its varied (and often outrageously expensive) collectables and luxury fashion stock, its edible offerings remain the most popular and more cost-friendly aspect of the visitor shopping experience. The famous, ornate Food Halls recently completed their four-year renovation in 2021; the latest from the taste emporium is **Chocolate Hall**, with an in-house chocolatier, where you can grab Harrods' signature Gold Bar for £10. (It's a better deal than, say, £350 for limited-edition Ecuadorian chocolate bars also sold on-site.) Buy affordable fresh breads and pastries at the **Roastery & Bake Hall**, or grab takeaway fare from Fresh Market Hall's **The Deli** and make a picnic of it at nearby Hyde Park.

Souvenirs and sales With over 300 departments selling mostly luxury items, bargain-hunting at Harrods can feel intimidating and downright unfeasible. The general shopping rule of thumb is to bypass the fashion, home goods and jewellery departments and focus on souvenirs. Harrods-branded souvenirs, especially, tend to be more cost-friendly than other brands on display. But don't overlook sale season for clothing and accessories that might have been out of reach: you can save up to 50% during the summer and winter holiday seasons if you stay on top of announcements (and arrive in-person as early as possible).

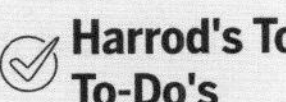

Harrod's Top To-Do's

See the **store's exterior by day** and drool over London's caramelised Vatican of Shopping.

Feast your eyes with a stroll through the **Food Halls**, decked with original Royal Doulton tiling.

Find the perfect scent at **Salon de Parfum**, London's preeminent perfume shop, with fragrances found nowhere else in the world, presided over by fabled Professeur de Parfum Roja Dove.

Savour a champagne afternoon tea at the **Harrods Tea Room** for prime people-watching in elegant surroundings.

Don't miss the building's exterior at night, a shimmering fairy tale of **12,000 lightbulbs on display**.

Tips by Frank Burgess, *a Blue Badge Tour Guide with Premium Tours, @FrankTourGuide*

19 Explore Art in a ROYAL PARK

NATURE | ART | CULTURE

Kensington Gardens, bordering Hyde Park to the west, is known for its affiliation with Kensington Palace, an iconic, functioning royal residence since the 17th century. Beyond the palace and expansive park grounds, however, the garden is also a hub of the arts, with two esteemed contemporary galleries and a patchwork of abstract and lifelike statues to discover.

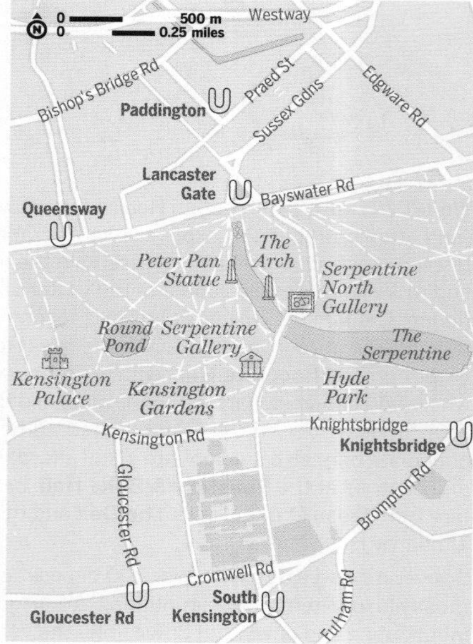

How to

Getting there Use the Underground – Central line's Lancaster Gate or Queensway; District line's Bayswater; and Circle and District line's High Street Kensington – or a plethora of buses.

When to go The summer season (June to August) has the most extensive art events calendar.

Green thumb Next to Serpentine North Gallery is the Allotment, a small community garden where you can relax or learn urban gardening tips.

Serpentine Galleries No leading London contemporary art gallery can claim residence within a Royal Park other than this mighty pair – the **Serpentine Gallery** and the striking **Serpentine North Gallery** designed by Iraqi-British architect Zaha Hadid (1950–2016) – split by the eponymous lake. Since 1970, art luminaries such as Damien Hirst, Jeff Koons and Ai Weiwei have showcased their talent through several exhibits and events throughout the year. From the interactive Bridge Commission Audio Walks to the lively Park Nights and an acclaimed

Top right The Magazine restaurant at the Serpentine Galleries
Right *Peter Pan* statue

ARCHITECT: ZAHA HADID
RON ELLIS/SHUTTERSTOCK ©

ANTON_IVANOV/SHUTTERSTOCK ©

Don't Miss the Arch

Head west of Serpentine North Gallery, towards Long Water, for a glimpse of Henry Moore's *The Arch* (1980), a 6m-tall travertine sculpture gifted to Serpentine Gallery after Moore's 80th birthday exhibition.

art bookshop, a visit between the two galleries is a plum choice for art aficionados. The summer months see the Serpentine Gallery (the elder of the two) hosting the **Pavilion**, a rotating commission of global architectural talent on the gallery's lawn.

Talking tales The world has witnessed JM Barrie's Peter Pan come to life in books, plays and films over the last 120 years, and the character remains Kensington Gardens' most famous resident (in statue form). However, the century-old bronze sculpture on Long Water's west end can now be seen and heard with an interactive audio feature accessed with the scan of a smartphone. Run in partnership with **Talking Statues London** (talkingstatueslondon.co.uk), the sculpture of the mischievous pipe-playing fictional boy is given a voice through British actor Danny Roche, and the humorous monologues make for a fun family pit stop.

20 Go Indie on KING'S ROAD

SHOPPING | FOOD & DRINK | LUXURY

An initial walk along Chelsea's famous, nearly 2-mile strip of pricey high-street brands and UK dining chains might discourage someone seeking one-off places, but a closer look reveals a handful of independent spots worth exploring along this princely corridor.

MAGDANATKA/SHUTTERSTOCK ©

How to

Getting there Sloane Square Station (on the Underground's District & Circle line) places you at the top of King's Road. Buses along the road can shuttle you to specific areas.

Rock and frocks Shop one of the pioneers of British punk fashion at World's End, the original boutique of designer icon Vivienne Westwood.

Nights out Though the evening hours see most fashion shops and galleries closed, it is the best time to soak in the road's buzzy dining and cocktail bar scene.

Blooming Season

King's Road is one of the best locations to witness **Chelsea in Bloom** *(chelseain-bloom.co.uk)*, an annual, neighbourhood-wide spectacle of storefront floral arrangements. Held in May and lasting a week, the free art show competition sees several King's Road shops and cafes outdoing one another with elaborate, vivid botanical displays.

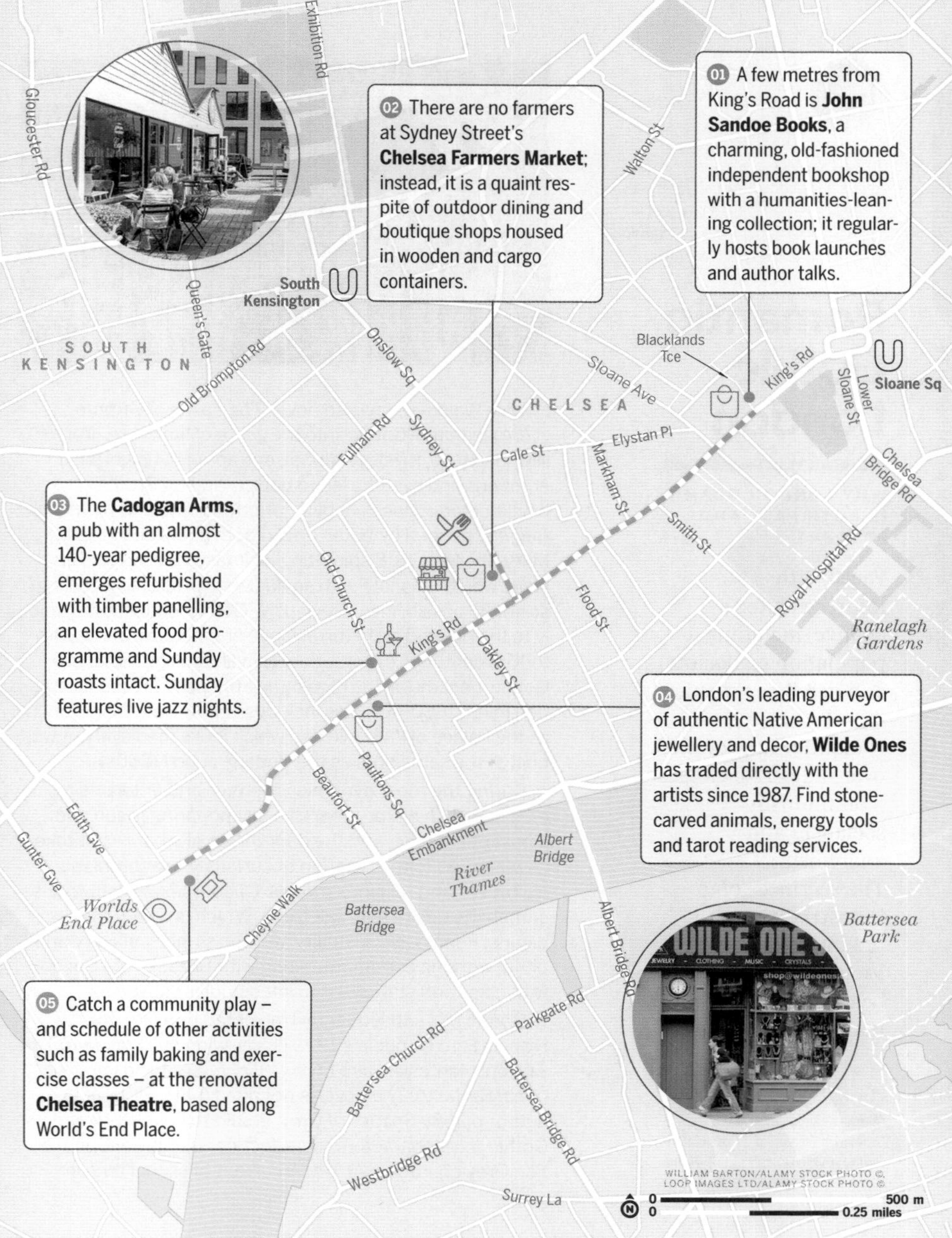

01 A few metres from King's Road is **John Sandoe Books**, a charming, old-fashioned independent bookshop with a humanities-leaning collection; it regularly hosts book launches and author talks.
02 There are no farmers at Sydney Street's **Chelsea Farmers Market**; instead, it is a quaint respite of outdoor dining and boutique shops housed in wooden and cargo containers.
03 The **Cadogan Arms**, a pub with an almost 140-year pedigree, emerges refurbished with timber panelling, an elevated food programme and Sunday roasts intact. Sunday features live jazz nights.
04 London's leading purveyor of authentic Native American jewellery and decor, **Wilde Ones** has traded directly with the artists since 1987. Find stone-carved animals, energy tools and tarot reading services.
05 Catch a community play – and schedule of other activities such as family baking and exercise classes – at the renovated **Chelsea Theatre**, based along World's End Place.
Exhibition Rd
Gloucester Rd
Walton St
South Kensington
SOUTH KENSINGTON
Queen's Gate
Old Brompton Rd
Onslow Sq
Blacklands Tce
Sloane Ave
King's Rd
Sloane Sq
Sloane St
Lower
CHELSEA
Fulham Rd
Sydney St
Cale St
Elystan Pl
Markham St
Chelsea Bridge Rd
Smith St
Royal Hospital Rd
Old Church St
Flood St
King's Rd
Oakley St
Ranelagh Gardens
Paultons Sq
Beaufort St
Edith Gve
Gunter Gve
Chelsea Embankment
Albert Bridge
River Thames
Worlds End Place
Cheyne Walk
Battersea Bridge
Albert Bridge Rd
Battersea Park
WILDE ONES
Parkgate Rd
Battersea Church Rd
Battersea Bridge Rd
Westbridge Rd
Surrey La
0 500 m
0 0.25 miles

By Julia Robson
Julia is a fashion journalist. Here she explores how London is a city that is a time traveller's paradise well-suited to vampires and lovers of vintage.

Romantic Gothic London

WHY LONDON GOTHIC IS BOTH PAST AND PRESENT

Faced with unprecedented change, including a population explosion and deadly epidemics like cholera, romanticism prevailed over radical ideologies (communism, socialism and anarchism). The sacrifices of industrialisation taught 19th-century Victorians to revere beauty and whatever makes your heart race.

Left Palace of Westminster facade **Middle** Keanu Reeves and Gary Oldman in Francis Ford Coppola's *Bram Stoker's Dracula* (1992) **Right** Highgate Cemetery

Horace Walpole's stylised novel, *The Castle of Otranto* (1764) initiated 'Gothic' into the genre of literature. Tropes like suspense, mystery, gloom, entrapment, heightened emotions and hysteria led to bodice-ripping Brontë blockbusters: *Jane Eyre* by Charlotte Brontë and *Wuthering Heights,* penned by sister, Emily (both published in 1847). Mary Shelley's 1818 spine-tingling masterpiece, *Frankenstein,* would resonate with an audience processing chilling scientific possibilities. Previously, 'Gothic' had referred solely to the pointed arch/turret/spire architecture of the 13th to 16th centuries. 'The Gothic Revival', or High Victorian Gothic, became all the rage during the peak of industrialisation (circa 1860-90). This includes London landmarks such as the Palace of Westminster, which looks medieval but was built at the same time as the Underground (1860s).

During the most dynamic, inventive and enterprising eras in British history, fear of a disappearing green and pleasant England, and the dark threat of what might take its place, led to the creation of curiously anachronistic narratives and religious morals. Of course, with new rules comes the desire to break them. Which is where the fun begins. Repressive sexuality, women's rights, slavery and pitiful working conditions, along with Britain's obsession with class and status, led to spectacular subversion.

Gothic has subsequently translated into film, from Francis Ford Coppola's 1992 Oscar-winning *Dracula* to Tim Burton's fantasies, film (*The Twilight Saga*) and gaming (*Final Fantasy*). The novel is not dead (yet). EL James, author of *Fifty Shades of Grey,* is said to have studied Gothic male characters to perfect her diabolical Christian Grey character. An undercurrent of sexual tension

PHOTO 12/ALAMY STOCK PHOTO ©

JUST ANOTHER PHOTOGRAPHER/SHUTTERSTOCK ©

reflects then-fashionable theories of Freud and Jung's 'Jekyll & Hyde' human behaviours. Victorians were called the 'Last Romantics'. As we enter the fourth industrial revolution and its blurred boundaries of physical and virtual worlds, we can imagine them smiling at us from beyond the grave.

With fog, Jack the Ripper, carriage wheels on cobbles and danger lurking, London is the perfect Gothic setting, as John Landis' comic horror, *American Werewolf in London* (1981), can testify. So much of the gritty capital feels like a time warp because Victorian buildings form much of the housing stock. You can imagine Sherlock Holmes sleuthing at 221b Baker St or Van Helsing heading off to ghostly Highgate Cemetery to drive a stake through the heart of the vampire Lucy Westenra (as told in Bram Stoker's *Dracula,* 1897). You can visit a painting of Pre-Raphaelite poster girl, Elizabeth Siddal, Dante Gabriel Rossetti's flame-haired wife, at the Guildhall Art Gallery then hop on bus to Highgate Cemetery where she is buried.

> With fog, Jack the Ripper, carriage wheels on cobbles and danger lurking, London is the perfect Gothic setting...

'I love old things. I need things that have lived,' declared fashion designer and Biba founder Barbara Hulanicki, who reinvented Victoriana with her Biba boutique (1964-76). Fashion historian Tony Glenville believes the British royal family are key also. Queen Victoria triggered the cult of black. The off-shoulder, 'Revenge dress' designed by Christina Stambolian worn by Diana, Princess of Wales (1994), vies for the most iconic Gothic outfit ever, rivalled only by her silk taffeta Royal wedding dress (1981), with its leg o' mutton sleeves, 7.6m train and 140m tulle veil.

Jack the Ripper & Gothic Fashion Horror

In his definitive book, *The Victorians* (2003), AN Wilson writes of the 'pornographic fascination of the Jack the Ripper murders'. Alexander McQueen's Central Saint Martins 1992 graduate collection, entitled 'Jack the Ripper Stalks His Victims' saw the son of a London cabbie explode onto the international fashion stage. In it he used locks of hair sewn into garments, a reference to 19th-century prostitutes who would sell their hair. 'I find beauty in the grotesque' he once said. McQueen's darkly Gothic aesthetic took inspiration from Victorian mental asylums, circus freaks, music halls, crinolines and corsets.

Listings

BEST OF THE REST

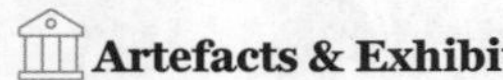

Artefacts & Exhibits

Victoria & Albert Museum

Affectionately known as the V&A, this essential site along the famed Exhibition Road is the world's largest decorative arts museum, with more than two million objects spread over seven floors.

National Army Museum

Learn about the trials, feats and global impact of the British Army in this profound collection of galleries based alongside the Royal Hospital Chelsea. There are child-friendly sections, too.

Natural History Museum

One of London's premier family attractions. Gawk at a blue whale skeleton suspended from the ceiling, confront lifelike dinosaurs and see millions of insects in this wildly intriguing museum on Exhibition Road.

Science Museum

Feed your sense of wonder with the family at this museum on Exhibition Road. Beyond the impressive science artefacts collection are flight simulators, live experiment shows and an IMAX theatre.

Great Meals

Dinner by Heston Blumenthal £££

The culinary flagship of Mandarin Oriental Hyde Park, next to Knightsbridge Station, is one of the world's foremost fine-dining temples. Book well ahead for Blumenthal's Michelin-starred, history-obsessed food experience.

Claude Bosi at Bibendum £££

An enormous stained-glass Bibendum, aka 'Michelin Man', overlooks this airy Chelsea dining room – formerly the tyre company's headquarters – where chef Bosi creates exquisite haute French fare.

Regency Café £

This 'greasy spoon' institution between Pimlico and Westminster has been a no-frills favourite since the 1940s. It's one of the best places for an English breakfast.

Phat Phuc Noodle Bar £

However amusing this pan-Asian restaurant's name might be (it translates as 'Happy Buddha' in Vietnamese), this cheap gem tucked off King's Road offers delicious pho and more for under £10.

Market Hall Victoria £

Head inside this trendy food hall for a plethora of tasty, wallet-friendly stalls, then take to the spacious terrace for bang-on views of Victoria Station across the street.

Pantechnicon ££

There are five minimalist-chic floors to explore at this so-called 'village' of Nordic-Japanese cuisine and culture in Belgravia, including a rooftop bar, Japanese bottle shop and a fusion restaurant.

Blue whale skeleton at the Natural History Museum

Rabbit £££

Savour bucolic farm-to-fork eating in the heart of Chelsea's King's Road. It's a culinary showcase of West Sussex county, from where sustainably raised livestock and several wines on the menu are sourced.

Tea Time

Afternoon Tea at The Goring £££

A classic among classics, in a hotel beloved by the Royal Family. Choose the Bollinger Afternoon Tea – with strawberries and cream and rosé – for an extra dollop of fancy.

The Kensington's London Landmarks Afternoon Tea £££

Taste the British capital in a unique hotel tea offering with sweet treats depicting the likes of Big Ben (a lemon curd tart) and the Red Telephone Box (a rhubarb mousse).

Prêt-à-Portea at The Berkeley £££

The ultimate afternoon tea for the high-fashion set, appropriately located in a five-star Knightsbridge hotel. Mini-cakes are moulded into stilettos, brand handbags and dresses in seasonal 'collections'.

Spa Breaks

The Lanesborough Club & Spa

London's most exclusive and lavishly appointed hotel wellness club, based in Hyde Park Corner. Though covertly advertised, day passes and non-member spa packages are available for bookings.

Ushvani

Behind a heavy wooden door near Chelsea's Sloane Square is a sumptuous Malaysian-themed day retreat. Though open to all, the steam room and plunge pool facilities are for women only.

CKTRAVELS.COM/SHUTTERSTOCK ©

Eccleston Yards

Ilapothecary Spa

Sound baths and customised body treatments are the norm for the eponymous brand's flagship on Kensington High Street, set in a homely wood-clad space.

Style File

Harvey Nichols

Oft overlooked for Harrods a mere block away in Knightsbridge, this department store is the less touristy option for luxury fashion, beauty and gifts, plus restaurants on the 5th floor.

Worn

Shop luxe for (a little) less at a high-end secondhand clothing store on Chelsea's Elystan St, carrying labels from Hermès to Victoria Beckham.

Eccleston Yards

Since its 2018 opening, this open-air destination has brought much-needed liveliness to the quietly elegant Belgravia neighbourhood. Find boutique fashion stores, local restaurants and yoga studios centered on a mural-lined courtyard.

Scan to find more things to do in Kensington & Hyde Park online

Experience Clerkenwell, Shoreditch & Spitalfields online

CLERKENWELL, SHOREDITCH & SPITALFIELDS

HISTORY | FOOD | MUSIC

CLERKENWELL, SHOREDITCH & SPITALFIELDS
Trip Builder

TAKE YOUR PICK OF MUST-SEES AND HIDDEN GEMS

Rooted in history but with a bunch of modern live-music venues, pioneering bars, independent retailers and a thriving food culture, this end of London refuses to play it small. Some suggest that the neighbourhood has lost its edge, but it continues to pull in the big crowds.

Neighbourhood Notes

Best for Live music, food and bars. There's a mix of restaurants, cafes, trucks, markets and stalls serving food from around the world.

Transport Get here on the Northern, District and Hammersmith & City lines on the Tube.

Getting around Best explored on foot or bike; easier to get around the one-way systems.

Tip This area is great for a night out. Londoners rarely party in the big city, opting for smaller, quirkier venues such as those found in this neighbourhood.

CLERKENWELL, SHOREDITCH & SPITALFIELDS BUILD YOUR TRIP

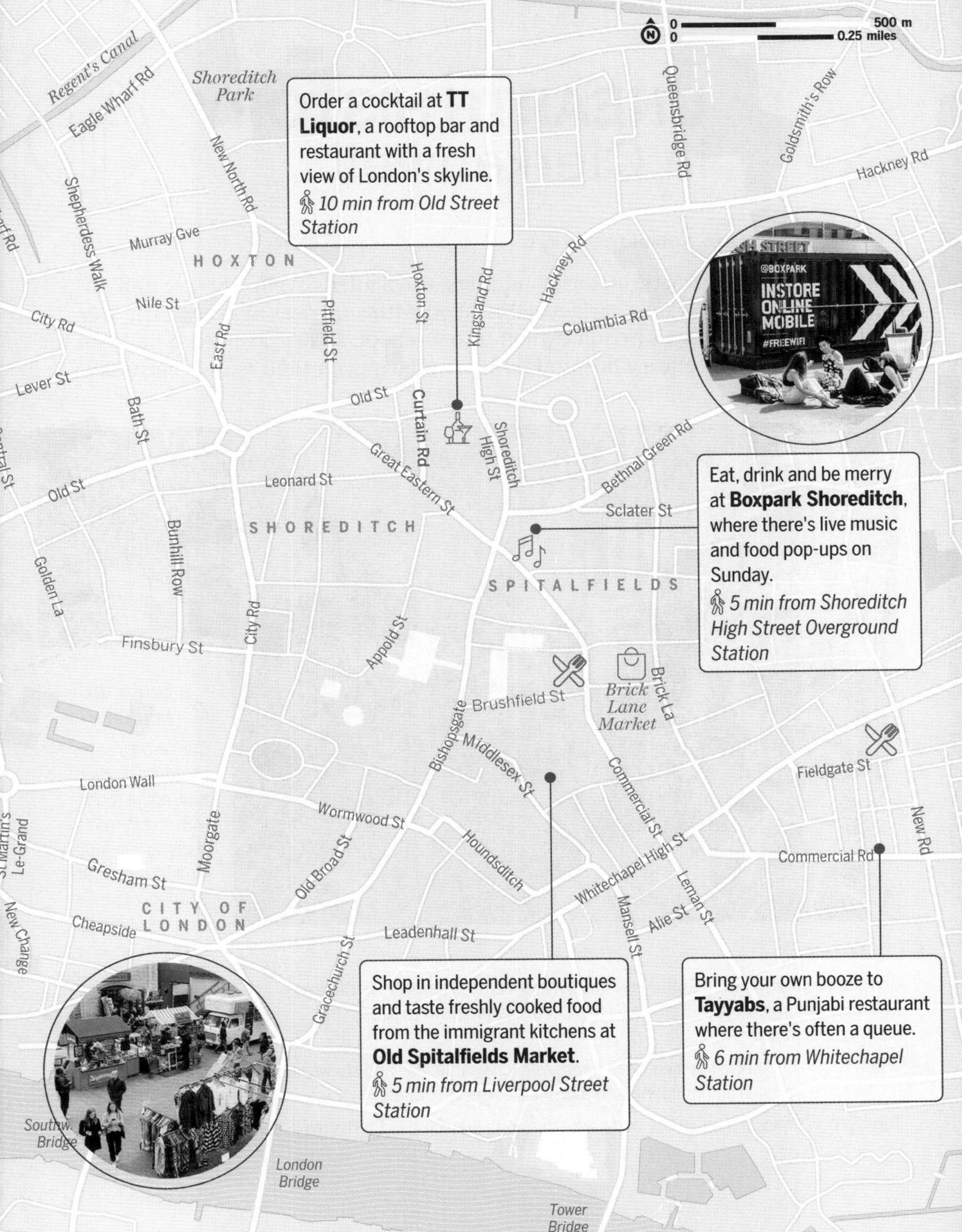
0 500 m
0 0.25 miles
N
Order a cocktail at **TT Liquor**, a rooftop bar and restaurant with a fresh view of London's skyline.
10 min from Old Street Station
Eat, drink and be merry at **Boxpark Shoreditch**, where there's live music and food pop-ups on Sunday.
5 min from Shoreditch High Street Overground Station
Shop in independent boutiques and taste freshly cooked food from the immigrant kitchens at **Old Spitalfields Market**.
5 min from Liverpool Street Station
Bring your own booze to **Tayyabs**, a Punjabi restaurant where there's often a queue.
6 min from Whitechapel Station
@BOXPARK
INSTORE
ONLINE
MOBILE
#FREEWIFI
Regent's Canal
Eagle Wharf Rd
Shoreditch Park
New North Rd
Shepherdess Walk
Murray Gve
HOXTON
Nile St
City Rd
East Rd
Pitfield St
Hoxton St
Kingsland Rd
Hackney Rd
Queensbridge Rd
Goldsmith's Row
Columbia Rd
Lever St
Bath St
Old St
Curtain Rd
Shoreditch High St
Great Eastern St
Bethnal Green Rd
Sclater St
Leonard St
Central St
SHOREDITCH
SPITALFIELDS
Bunhill Row
Golden La
Finsbury St
Appold St
Brick La
Brick Lane Market
Brushfield St
Bishopsgate
Middlesex St
Commercial St
Fieldgate St
New Rd
Commercial Rd
London Wall
Wormwood St
Houndsditch
Whitechapel High St
Leman St
Mansell St
Alie St
Moorgate
Old Broad St
Gresham St
St Martin's Le-Grand
New Change
Cheapside
CITY OF LONDON
Leadenhall St
Gracechurch St
Southwark Bridge
London Bridge
Tower Bridge

21 UNEARTH HISTORY in Clerkenwell

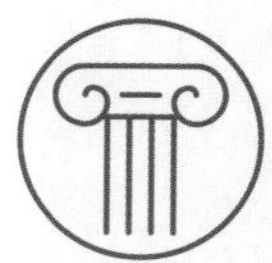

FOODIE | HISTORIC | UNDISCOVERED

With leafy streets, historic buildings, the Sadler's Wells Theatre and an underrated food market, Clerkenwell is filled with surprises at every turn. Here you will find a women's prison turned into a school, an art-deco town hall and the remains of a 12th-century hospital built for pilgrims on their way to Jerusalem.

JOE DUNCKLEY/SHUTTERSTOCK ©

Exmouth Market

Clerkenwell's Exmouth Market is all about food, with street-food stalls selling Indian, Mediterranean and a variety of other cuisines lining the street on weekdays. But you'd better get here before 1pm – the food sells out quickly. The market, which takes its name from the very street it's on, comes alive in the evening as restaurants start their dinner service.

How to

Getting here Angel Tube Station on the Northern Line is nearest for Clerkenwell, plus Farringdon Tube Station on the Circle, Hammersmith & City and Metropolitan lines.

When to go Clerkenwell Design Week happens each year in May and showcases UK and international independent architectural and design brands.

Top tip Don't miss a meal at the wonderful Sessions Arts Club in Clerkenwell.

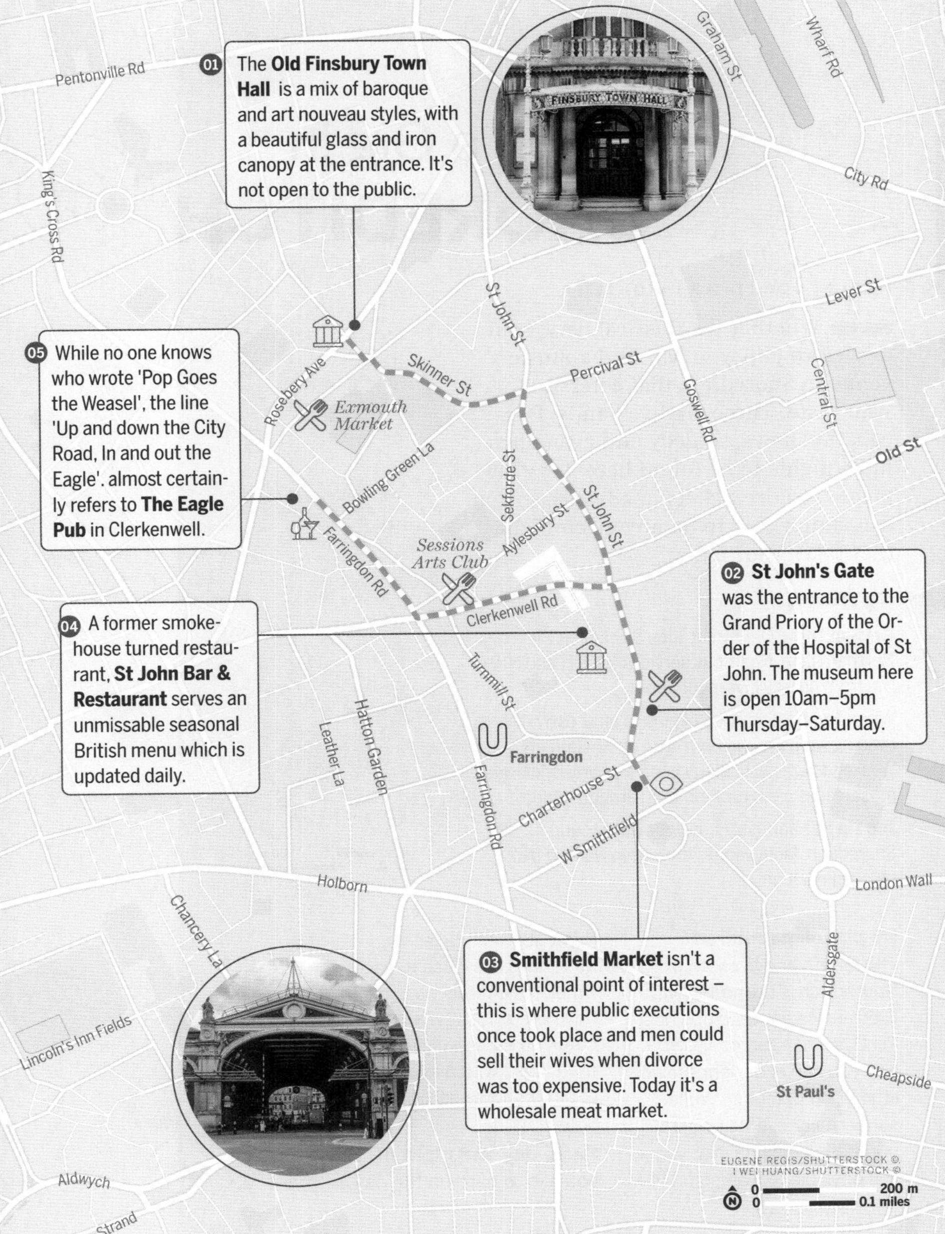

EUGENE REGIS/SHUTTERSTOCK ©, I WEI HUANG/SHUTTERSTOCK ©

22 Catch a Gig in SHOREDITCH

MUSIC | COCKTAILS | NIGHTLIFE

Whether it's classical, jazz, soul or electro pop, you will find a music venue in Shoreditch that caters to your taste. There are live bands, DJs, cabaret shows, comedy and even open-mike nights to be found here. Very few places require tickets in advance so you can simply join in on any given night that takes your fancy.

How to

Getting there Old Street Tube Station on the Northern Line. Night bus services 23, N11 and N133 run from nearby Liverpool Street.

When to go Shoreditch begins to buzz early evening from around 6pm even on weeknights. Weekends are particularly good for early drinks and most places open for food from around midday.

Top tip Bar-and-club-hop your way around Shoreditch. Most venues are within walking distance of each other.

No planning required
The length and breadth of Shoreditch is brimming with live-music venues, clubs hosting DJs and cabaret shows – and you can experience it with little or no planning. While some major events require purchasing tickets in advance, it is possible to walk-in on the night at most places. And, as venues are close to each other, it's entirely possible to have pre-drinks on a rooftop, catch an early live gig and then finish with a late-night cabaret show – all on the same night.

Party day and night If you like to party in the day,

Top right Jack Broadbent performing at the Blues Kitchen **Right** Concert at Boxpark Shoreditch

OLLIE MILLINGTON/REDFERNS/GETTY IMAGES ©

Late-Night Jazz

In the Truman Brewery, **Ninety One Living Room** is an acclaimed late-night jazz club with live music. Stop by on a weeknight for £5 happy-hour cocktails between 5pm and 7pm. Check the schedule for special events such as the London Jazz Festival.

Boxpark Shoreditch runs day and evening events, from quiz nights to DJs. RCRD Shop hosts a party here (Sundaze) from 3pm to 8pm Sunday with a live band showcasing new talent, from R&B to neo soul. The vibe is spot on and there are also food stalls, clothes and gift shops. The **Blues Kitchen** has a consistently great evening line-up of live blues and soul music – most gigs are free so just walk-in.

Drag it out Colours is a multi-art bar and club that has a brilliantly inclusive schedule of live gigs and events, such as drag disco, cabaret and live music from new and big-name artists (buy tickets in advance). Go Wednesday or Thursday for £5 cocktails all night long.

SHAKEYJON/ALAMY STOCK PHOTO ©

23 TASTE CULTURE in Spitalfields

HISTORY | FOOD | DIVERSITY

It's hard to imagine that Spitalfields was once the home of 'the worst street in London' – Dorset St – where Jewish, Irish and Huguenot immigrants lived in squalid conditions and Jack the Ripper murdered three of his victims. Today immigrant communities continue to make this neighbourhood their home and the thriving restaurant scene here has them to thank.

How to

Getting here Aldgate East and Whitechapel Stations on the District and Hammersmith & City lines.

Getting around The area is cycle friendly but best explored on foot. Buses are frequent and connect to Central London and beyond. Cabs are also plentiful and an efficient way to get around.

Top tip Old Spitalfield Market is great for artisan food and souvenirs all made by small, independent businesses.

Spitalfields is the perfect place to try a bit of everything, with restaurants, food trucks and street-food stalls plating up cuisine from all over. For a taste of Jamaica, head to **Cafe Caribbean**, which serves homemade regional dishes from St Catherine, as well as classic dishes such as ackee and salt fish and rice and peas. **Tayyabs** has been serving the community reasonably priced Punjabi curries, naans and grills at the same location since 1972. It gets very busy here in the eve-

Top right Lamb chops at Tayyabs restaurant **Right** Merkamo Ethiopian food stall

MARC ZAKIAN 2/ALAMY STOCK PHOTO ©

Brick Lane

Brick Lane is unmissable for its renowned independent curry houses, vintage clothing stores, art galleries and live-music venues. Sundays are particularly great here for mixing with Londoners browsing for vintage or having a beer alfresco when the weather is mild. The neighbourhood attracts a creative crowd that is incredibly inclusive.

nings and weekends so be prepared to wait for a table or a takeaway. Bring your own wine and spirits.

Vegans will love **Merkamo Ethiopian** (Old Spitalfields Market), which serves a variety of award-winning flavours and traditional dishes with a twist. The menu is divided up into low-carb high-protein, half and half, green plates. **Nilly's Turkish Kitchen** (Old Spitalfields Market) serves traditional Turkish wraps as they'd be sold and eaten on the streets of Istanbul. Wraps are filled with seasoned meat and fish, but it's the meat-free *gözleme* option with cheese and potato that is a crowd favourite.

JULIO ETCHART/ALAMY STOCK PHOTO ©

Shoreditch STREET ART

02

01

03

01 Octopus Eating an Ice Lolly

Painted outside the Petticoat Lane Market on Toynbee St by London-based Polish artist Woskerski who specialises in surrealism.

02 Silent Sea

Inspired by the harsh realities of orca captivity, Jim Vision created this piece on Jerome St as part of his Colourful Women series.

03 Black Lives Matter

Another mural by artist Jim Vision, this political statement following the Black Lives Matter movement, is located on Whitby St.

04 Political Sanitiser

This political statement on Brick Lane is from an unknown artist.

05

06

07

05 Wu Tang Clan

Dave Bonzai is the creator of this liquid chrome sign for the hip-hop group Wu Tang Clan. The mural can be found on Corbet Pl.

06 Audrey Hepburn Holding Tulips

Painted above Brick Lane Brasserie, this is the signature style of London-based French artist Zabou and is inspired by a photo by Yousuf Karsh.

07 The Pink Bear

The trademark of artist Luap who works in paint, print and photography can be seen under a bridge on Bateman's Row.

Listings

BEST OF THE REST

Delightful Dining

Sessions Arts Club £££

An unmissable dining experience in Clerkenwell. It's a decadent dream of a space with stripped-back walls and velvet curtains where whimsical dishes such as clams, Reisling and lovage are served.

Som Saa Thai Restaurant £

Regional dishes from Northern Thailand such as *kua kling plaa* (stir-fried mackerel with lemongrass) have made Som Saa a favourite in Shoreditch.

Smoking Goat £

Inspired by late-night canteens in Bangkok, Smoking Goat in Shoreditch has an entirely traceable menu of British and Thai products and suppliers. Try dishes like red sambal mackerel grilled in banana leaf.

Christina's Shoreditch £

An all-day cafe great for both coffee and cocktails. Order an espresso, chai latte or Japanese moriuchi koucha black tea accompanied by a sweet treat from the Chestnut Bakery.

Leroy ££

This Shoreditch restaurant headed by two sommeliers and with a focus on mindfully simple dining was awarded a Michelin star in 2019 – the year after it opened. A two-course lunch starts from only £24 per person.

Map Maison £

A premium cocktail bar on Kingsland Rd in Haggerston with great mixologists and a curated Japanese cocktail menu. You can also enjoy all-day tapas, brunch or a ridiculously good afternoon tea here.

Rapsa ££

This incredible Filipino fusion restaurant in Hoxton offers a fantastic bottomless weekend brunch. It lasts for 100 minutes and includes Prosecco, lychee daiquiri and a variety of drinks along with a brunch dish.

F Cooke £

Experience a traditional East End pie, mash and gravy at this Hoxton cafe. It's one of the few places left which still serve old classic dishes such as jellied eels.

E Pellicci £

Few places reflect authentic British cafe culture as much as Pellicci's in Bethnal Green. Grab yourself a classic English breakfast or an Italian favourite such as lasagna.

High-End Restaurants

Moro £££

A busy restaurant in Clerkenwell serving a seasonal menu of North African and Spanish dishes. Get lucky and try the seared pigeon breast with garlic puree and sun-dried peppers.

F Cooke

St John Bar & Restaurant £££

Around the corner from Smithfield Market, this restaurant serves wonderfully British dishes such as mutton and barley broth and grouse. The building was a former smoke-house, and apart from a coat of white paint, it has changed very little.

Bourne & Hollingsworth Buildings £££

Dishes are created from seasonal British produce such as smoked halibut and seared venison at this part restaurant and part greenhouse in Clerkenwell.

Galvin La Chapelle £££

The Galvin brothers have put together a special dining experience in a wonderful neoclassical building in Spitalfields, where they serve up traditional French fare with a modern twist.

Brat £££

You'll feel like you're sitting in the kitchen in this full-on Michelin-starred food fest serving traditional Basque country cooking in the heart of Shoreditch; the signature dish is a turbot cooked on an iron grill.

Beer & Food

The Exmouth Arms

You can't miss this green-tiled Victorian pub which gave the market here its name. Find old-fashioned chip butties on the same menu as kimchi arancini and wash it all down with a pale ale from the tap.

Coin Laundry

This spacious bar and kitchen serves seasonal food with craft and draught beer. A great place to enjoy a traditional British Sunday roast.

ALEX SEGRE/ALAMY STOCK PHOTO ©

E Pellicci

The Angelic

A fabulously spacious pub for a great British menu and Sunday roast with good beer. There's an upstairs lounge, plus outdoor seating for milder weather.

TT Liquor

The humble liquor store entrance to TT Liquor gives nothing away of the spectacular view of London from its rooftop bar. Enjoy an 'nduja pizza with a craft beer or watermelon martini.

London Shuffle Club

A great evening of either lane shuffle or table shuffle can be had at the London Shuffle Club. Enjoy a pizza and beer with friends as you battle it out in a classic game of shuffle.

Vintage Finds

Rokit

Rokit has been a vintage clothing store in London since the 1980s. Rummage around for extra-special designer finds, denim and military wear at this iconic store.

Scan to find more things to do in Clerkenwell, Shoreditch & Spitalfields online

EAST LONDON

CULTURE | MARKETS | DRINKING

Experience East London online

EAST LONDON
Trip Builder

TAKE YOUR PICK OF MUST-SEES AND HIDDEN GEMS

Be it the docks or Whitechapel at the edge of the City of London, this was always 'migrant London' – now it's just uber-cool London, where those decades of cultural concocting has birthed deliciously exotic foodie markets in Brick Lane, edgy drinking spots near Hackney Wick and the most fascinating history and heritage.

Neighbourhood Notes

Best for Indo-Asian culture, busy markets and cutting-edge microbreweries.

How long Give yourself four days.

Getting around Use the Tube, buses and TfL bikes.

Tip If you're on a budget look for the cheap local markets, like the one on Whitechapel Rd, where everything costs a lot less.

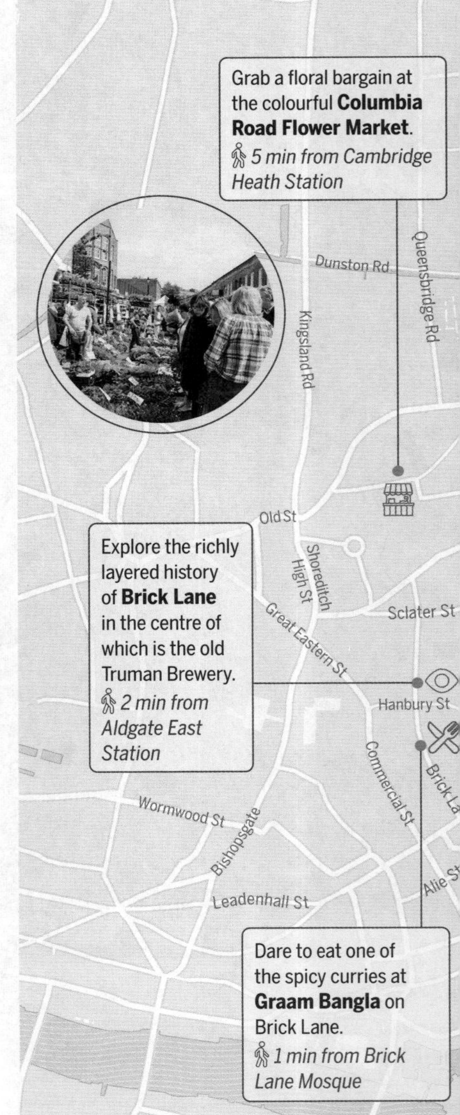

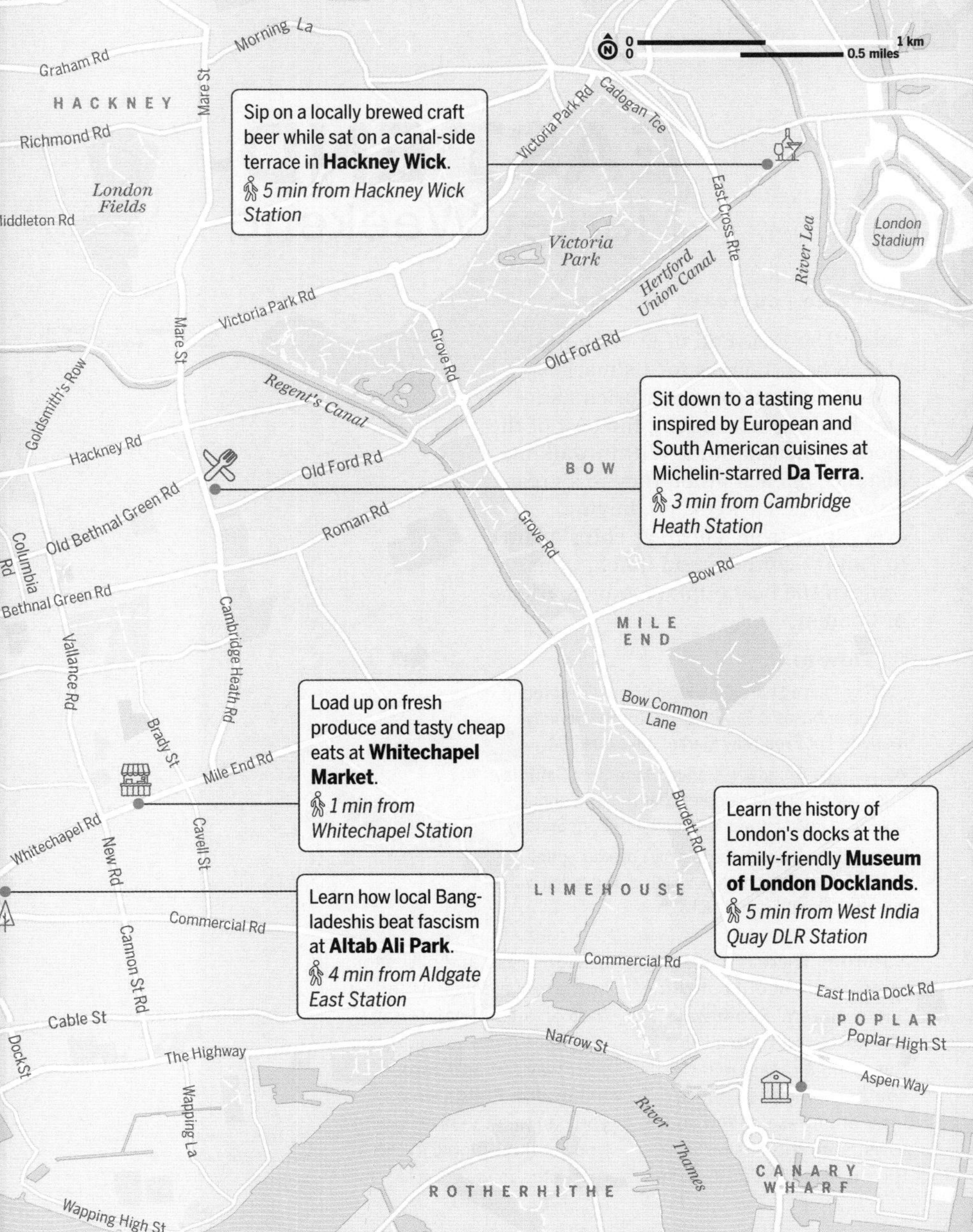

Sip on a locally brewed craft beer while sat on a canal-side terrace in **Hackney Wick**.
5 min from Hackney Wick Station
Sit down to a tasting menu inspired by European and South American cuisines at Michelin-starred **Da Terra**.
3 min from Cambridge Heath Station
Load up on fresh produce and tasty cheap eats at **Whitechapel Market**.
1 min from Whitechapel Station
Learn how local Bangladeshis beat fascism at **Altab Ali Park**.
4 min from Aldgate East Station
Learn the history of London's docks at the family-friendly **Museum of London Docklands**.
5 min from West India Quay DLR Station
0 1 km
0 0.5 miles
HACKNEY
London Fields
Victoria Park
London Stadium
BOW
MILE END
LIMEHOUSE
POPLAR
CANARY WHARF
ROTHERHITHE
River Lea
River Thames
Regent's Canal
Hertford Union Canal
Morning La
Graham Rd
Richmond Rd
Middleton Rd
Mare St
Victoria Park Rd
Cadogan Tce
East Cross Rte
Goldsmith's Row
Hackney Rd
Old Ford Rd
Grove Rd
Old Bethnal Green Rd
Roman Rd
Columbia Rd
Bethnal Green Rd
Bow Rd
Vallance Rd
Cambridge Heath Rd
Bow Common Lane
Brady St
Mile End Rd
Whitechapel Rd
New Rd
Cavell St
Burdett Rd
Commercial Rd
Cannon St Rd
East India Dock Rd
Cable St
Narrow St
Poplar High St
Dock St
The Highway
Aspen Way
Wapping La
Wapping High St

24 EAST END Market Weekend

SHOPPING | CULTURE | MARKETS

The East End of London has always been famous for its markets, and these three between Brick Lane and Hackney are among the best of the modern incarnations. Within walking distance of each other, they're a great way to spend a weekend, buying everything from 'cheap as chips' plants to vintage clothing and lunching in some of the best ethnic foodie markets in London.

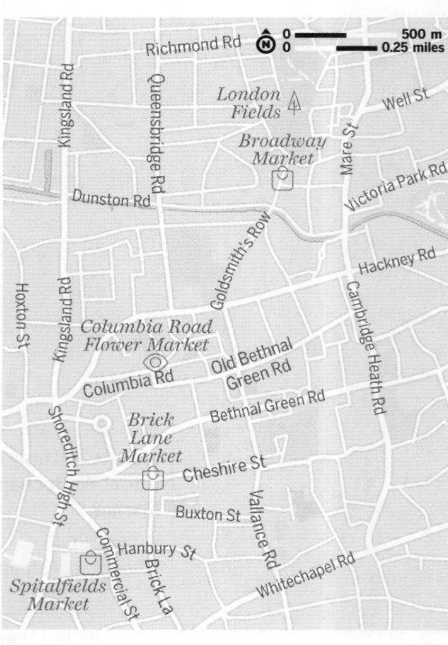

How to

Getting there Shoreditch High Street Overground Station or buses 8, 26, 78 or 149 for the Sunday markets. For Broadway Market, take bus 394.

When to go Broadway Market: 9am–5pm Saturday; Brick Lane's Sunday Market 10am–3pm Sunday; Columbia Road Flower Market: 8am–2pm Sunday

Rainy days Head for the nearby covered Spitalfields Market (open daily), which is also laden with quirky stalls and food trucks.

Saturday There is a buzzing atmosphere about cute little 'Victorian-era' **Broadway Market**. Start by browsing the vintage racks near the southern end then pause for Vietnamese coffee and to listen to the busker in the middle. Next grab some artisan bread and olives for home and a delicious Indian thali or vegan falafel wrap for your lunch, as you make your way out and across to **London Fields** where you can join the others who bought their picnic in the market.

Top right Bread stall at Broadway Market **Right** Antique stall at Brick Lane's Sunday Market

ALEX SEGRE/SHUTTERSTOCK ©

TONY BAGGETT/SHUTTERSTOCK ©

Brick Lane Beigels

No visit to Brick Lane is complete without stepping into the famous **Beigel Bake**, which serves easily the best and most reasonably priced salt beef beigel in all of East London, as well as a selection of scrumptiously fresh cakes. You'll know which one it is when you see the queue.

Sunday Once a flea market for locals selling unwanted goods, **Brick Lane's Sunday Market** is now one of the hippest Sunday spots in London. As well as being home to the largest halal foodie market in the East End, folk come here for quirky art, antiques, leather goods, vintage clothes and everything else we expect a modern market to offer before following the traffic north to **Columbia Road Flower Market**. Here you should first wander the hidden alleyways and courtyards, before elbowing through the crowds in search of that large potted plant at a knock-down price. Columbia Road traders have retained their ol' East End market charm, so expect to hear them yelling their wares long before you see them. Once you've got that plant, splash out on a designer pot to put it in from one of the surrounding shops.

25 Hackney's Wick-ed BREWS

DRINKING | WATERSIDE | BREWING

Nowhere in East London has as many hipsters downing pints of craft ale by the water. There are more microbreweries in the old canal-side warehouses here than you can shake a freshly fermented can of local brew at. It used to be a hidden patch only the cool kids knew about; not anymore – expect crowds at the weekends.

KATHARINE ROSE/ALAMY STOCK PHOTO ©

How to

Getting there Hackney Wick Overground Station is walking distance from all the action.

When to go There's a real party atmosphere along the waterside during the warmer months when revellers stay late into the night at canal-side terraces or take their beers onto the grassy slopes.

Non-alcoholic brews Look out for the Kompassion Kombucha bicycle bar if you'd rather something locally fermented (Chinese tea) that isn't alcoholic.

CKTRAVELS.COM/SHUTTERSTOCK ©

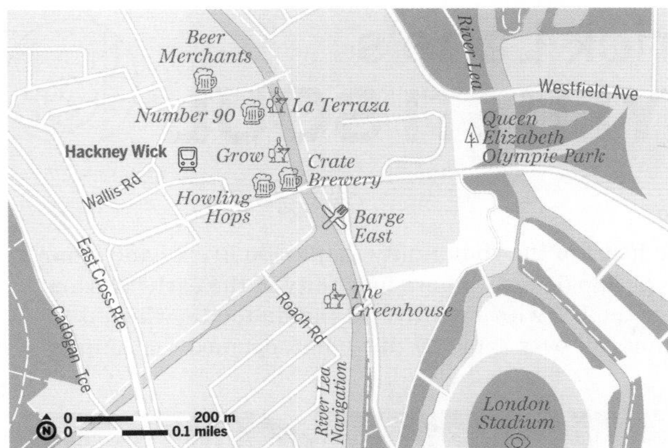

Canal-side drinking Hugely popular **Grow** is a canal-side community cafe by day, party central by night; lights flash and a bassline bounces off the water as the Wick's cool crowd arrive to dance the night away. This place gets busy. Equally popular and just a few doors down is pub stroke restaurant stroke art gallery, **Number 90**, home of great live music, and **La Terraza**, a scenic canal-side garden where you can drink outdoors year-round.

For more laid-back watering holes, **The Greenhouse** is intimate and great for live DJs at the weekends. Meanwhile, the **Beer Merchants Tap** is very chilled, serves excellent Belgian craft beer and has a food truck rock up outside serving delicious gourmet burgers.

The Wick's microbrewers Crate Brewery overlooks the canal, has its own brewery and serves deliciously creative pizzas to soak up all that alcohol you will no doubt drink here. **Howling Hops Brewery & Tank Bar** is legendary around these parts for its range of 'generously hopped' beers that are brewed on-site; the most popular being the Tropical Deluxe Pale Ale and the House IPA. Also here is the Tank Bar, which claims to be the 'UK's first dedicated Tank Bar'. Here the on-site brewed beer is poured directly out of 10 huge tanks – yes, you read that right.

Left Gow **Bottom left** Howling Hops Brewery & Tank Bar

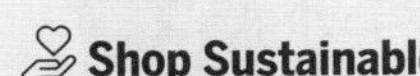

Shop Sustainable

Every weekend from 10am to 3pm the area around **Barge East Restaurant** turns into a small sustainable local market selling gourmet cheese, artisan bread baked by the Wick's very own Building Four Micro Bakery and, of course, beer from one of the numerous microbreweries.

26 Brick Lane's SYLHETI SOUL

CULTURE | FOOD | HERITAGE

This trail gets to the heart of the community that made Brick Lane famous for its curries, the Sylhetis of Bangladesh, whose ingenuity in the early '60s and '70s led to them taking over the UK with their hybrid Indian food - which is today served up in restaurants all over - and, at one point, deemed the country's national cuisine.

NIGELSPIERS/SHUTTERSTOCK ©

How to

Getting there The nearest Tube and Overground are Aldgate East and Shoreditch High Street. Popular buses serving the area include the 25 and 8.

When to go Sunday to combine with a wander through Brick Lane's lively food and vintage market.

Bangladeshi bazaar Stocked with desi produce just like an early-morning bazaar in Sylhet, Taj Stores is where you'll find that strange vegetable you ate in Graam Bangla.

Language of the Lane

It is a little-known fact that the Sylhetis of Bangladesh speak their own distinct language and not Bengali. Known as Sylheti Naghori, it is very much an oral language now, as it is no longer written down or read, though attempts are being made to revive it.

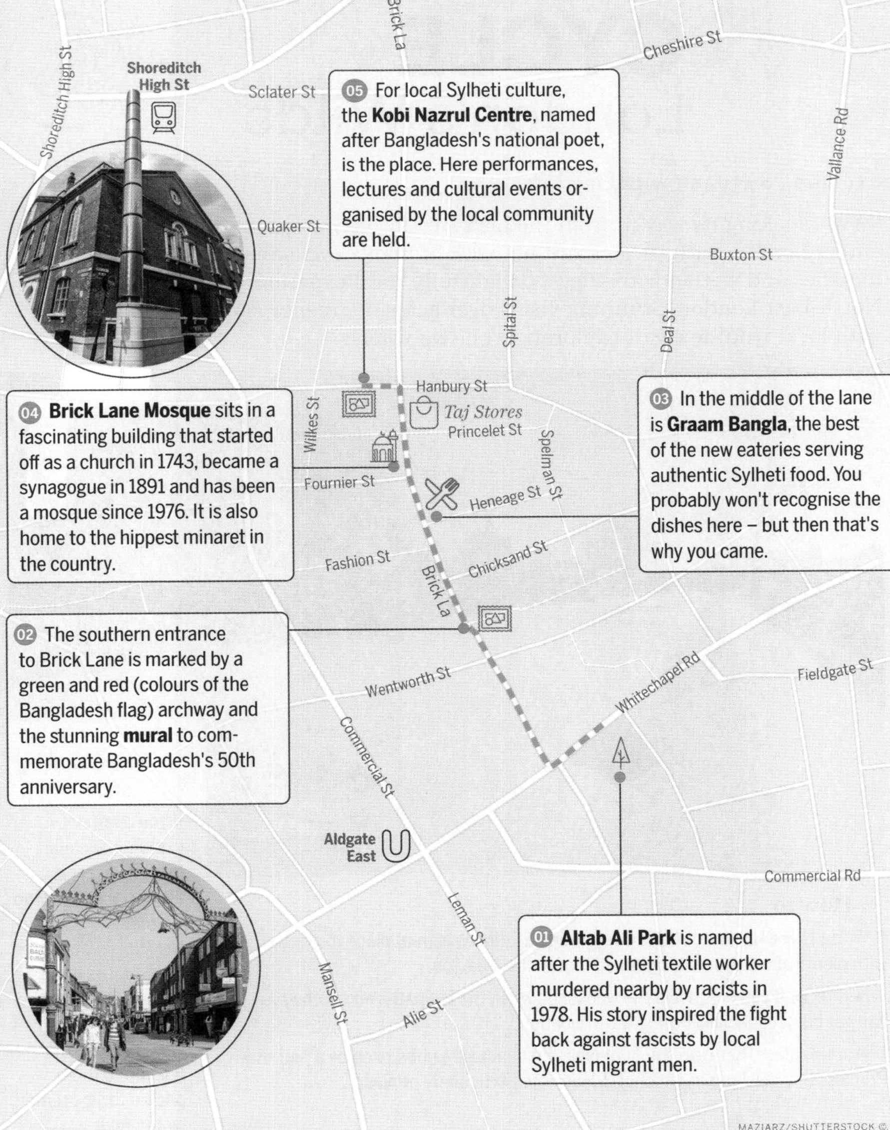

Brick La
Cheshire St
Shoreditch High St
Shoreditch High St
Sclater St
Vallance Rd
05 For local Sylheti culture, the **Kobi Nazrul Centre**, named after Bangladesh's national poet, is the place. Here performances, lectures and cultural events organised by the local community are held.
Quaker St
Buxton St
Spital St
Deal St
Hanbury St
Taj Stores
Princelet St
Wilkes St
Spelman St
Fournier St
Heneage St
04 **Brick Lane Mosque** sits in a fascinating building that started off as a church in 1743, became a synagogue in 1891 and has been a mosque since 1976. It is also home to the hippest minaret in the country.
03 In the middle of the lane is **Graam Bangla**, the best of the new eateries serving authentic Sylheti food. You probably won't recognise the dishes here – but then that's why you came.
Fashion St
Chicksand St
Brick La
02 The southern entrance to Brick Lane is marked by a green and red (colours of the Bangladesh flag) archway and the stunning **mural** to commemorate Bangladesh's 50th anniversary.
Wentworth St
Whitechapel Rd
Fieldgate St
Commercial St
Aldgate East
Commercial Rd
Leman St
Mansell St
Alie St
01 **Altab Ali Park** is named after the Sylheti textile worker murdered nearby by racists in 1978. His story inspired the fight back against fascists by local Sylheti migrant men.
0 200 m
0 0.1 miles
MAZIARZ/SHUTTERSTOCK ©, CHRIS LAWRENCE TRAVEL/SHUTTERSTOCK ©

27 CYCLE London's Wilds

CYCLING | NATURE | WILDLIFE

Snaking its way in from the lush Hertfordshire countryside, the Lea Valley enters London with its pleasant network of highly cycle-able canal towpaths, marshes and wetlands to offer a delightfully rural experience in the heart of North-East London. Stunning vistas over acres of greenery and water brimming with local wildlife await exploration on two wheels.

How to

Getting there Hackney Wick's Overground Station is a great place to start, with plenty of refreshment options around this area, too.

When to go If you can, avoid the weekends when the towpaths and pathways can get busy, especially during warm weather.

Waterside pint There are a host of pleasant canal-side pubs to enjoy a pint; the Princess of Wales and the Anchor & Hope are particularly popular.

The Canal by Canoe

If you'd rather explore the canal by drifting gently along the water, **Moo Canoes**, based at the Milk Float, sits on the canal as it passes under White Post Lane in Hackney Wick. Canoes that hold up to three people can be rented by the hour.

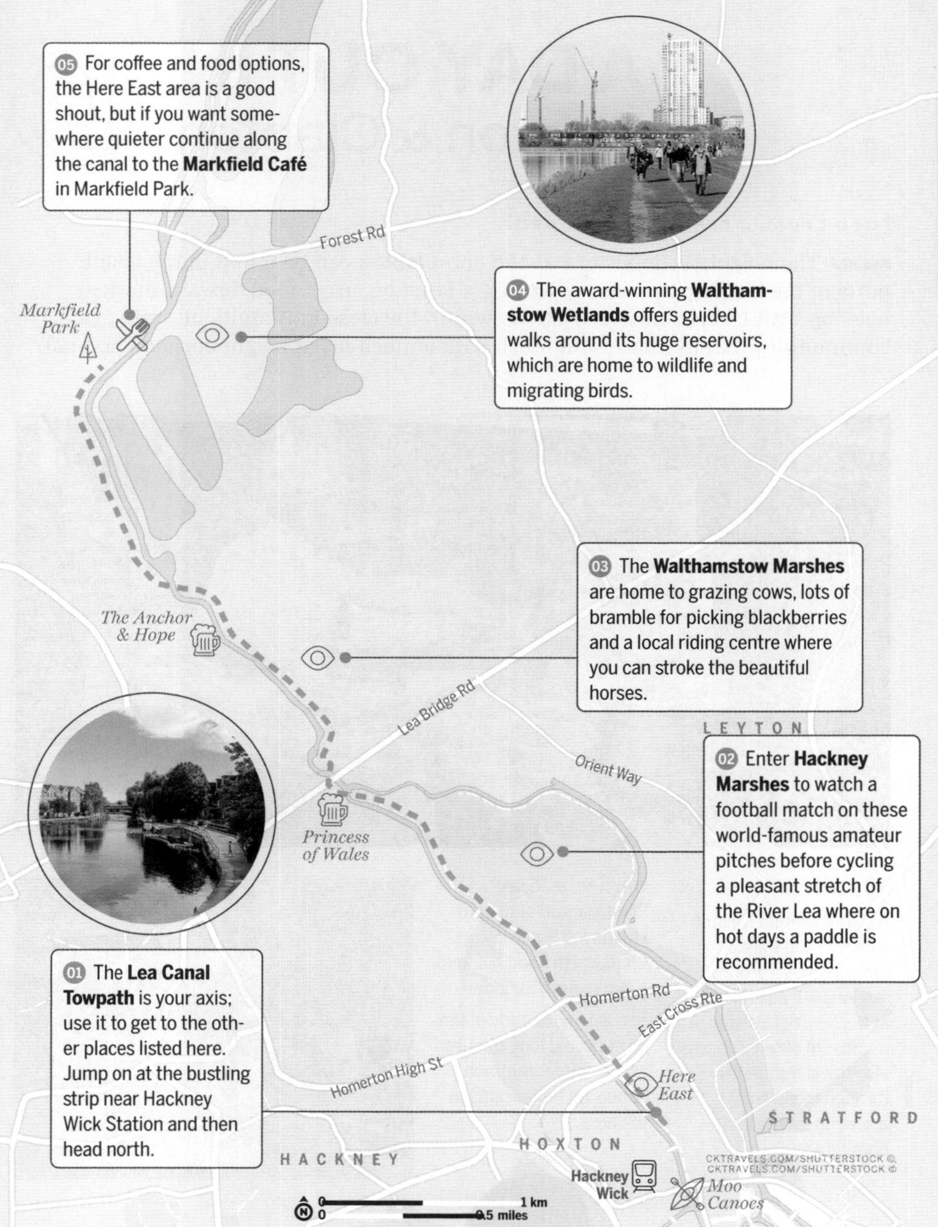

05 For coffee and food options, the Here East area is a good shout, but if you want somewhere quieter continue along the canal to the **Markfield Café** in Markfield Park.
04 The award-winning **Walthamstow Wetlands** offers guided walks around its huge reservoirs, which are home to wildlife and migrating birds.
03 The **Walthamstow Marshes** are home to grazing cows, lots of bramble for picking blackberries and a local riding centre where you can stroke the beautiful horses.
02 Enter **Hackney Marshes** to watch a football match on these world-famous amateur pitches before cycling a pleasant stretch of the River Lea where on hot days a paddle is recommended.
01 The **Lea Canal Towpath** is your axis; use it to get to the other places listed here. Jump on at the bustling strip near Hackney Wick Station and then head north.
Forest Rd
Markfield Park
The Anchor & Hope
Lea Bridge Rd
Orient Way
LEYTON
Princess of Wales
Homerton Rd
East Cross Rte
Homerton High St
Here East
STRATFORD
HOXTON
HACKNEY
Hackney Wick
Moo Canoes
0 1 km
0 0.5 miles

28 A DAY OUT IN Dalston & Clapton

FOOD | PUBLIC SPACES | OUTDOORS

The neighbourhoods of Dalston and Clapton can be found in the smallest parts of the buzzing borough of Hackney. Feast on street food, browse markets heaving with locals, immerse yourself within the close-knit multicultural communities that live here, and finish with a much-loved neighbourhood jazz bar.

G TORRES/SHUTTERSTOCK ©

How to

Getting around Dalston Junction and Dalston Kingsland Overground stations will position you at the heart of Dalston. A number of different buses also travel frequently through these areas and connect the two boroughs.

When to go Ridley Road Market: until 4pm Monday to Saturday; Chatsworth Road Market: 10am to 4pm Sunday

Top tip Arrive early in the day to avoid long queues which can be common at pop-up restaurants in the area.

PADMAYOGINI/SHUTTERSTOCK ©

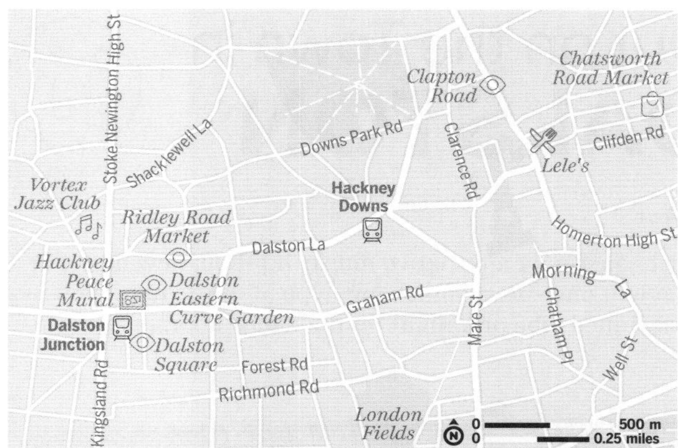

You haven't really been to Dalston until you've been to **Ridley Road Market**. If you're not greeted by blasting reggae and dancehall music when you arrive, then you need to keep walking all the way through, passing by Sierra Leonean and Ghanaian stores, stalls loaded with fresh produce bursting with colour, and sellers repeating over and over: 'A pound a bowl!' If you're hungry, then stop for a Indian and Middle Eastern snack. The market comes to life from the crack of dawn, when sellers set up shop; at night, the stalls are packed away and the open area is left to local roller skaters.

The **Chatsworth Road Market** in Lower Clapton was revived in 2010 after a 20-something-year hiatus; today you can find everything from food stalls, fresh produce, bakery goods and cheese, to crafts and clothing. From the market it's just a short work to Millsfields Park, Hackney Marshes and the River Lea. Also nearby is **Clapton Road**, once known as 'murder mile' due to a spike in crime in the late '90s and early 2000s. Today its reputation has been revived and it's a busy street, where you can get a haircut by a pro, try vegan cake at **Lele's**, and buy a bottle of wine at **Mr Singh's** (Just Drinks, 58 Lower Clapton Rd), a well-known name on Clapton Rd, with UK rap music playing to entertain passers-by.

Left Ridley Road Market **Bottom left** Dalston Eastern Curve

Top Open-Air Experiences

Dalston Eastern Curve Garden Founded in 2010 to provide more green space for the local community, this lush garden is free to visit and has a cafe serving drinks and homemade cakes.

Street art As you leave the Eastern Curve Garden, take a look at the **Hackney Peace Mural**, where people with different ethnicities, cultures and backgrounds surround each other to form a colourful carnival. The mural was originally painted in 1985 by Ray Walker but has since been restored.

Gillette Square You'll find many Dalston locals hanging out here, and just around the corner is the one and only **Vortex Jazz Club**, where great vibes are guaranteed. The jazz bar welcomes countless music lovers every week; you'll even find random pairs dancing on the square on a warm summer's evening.

29 Out on the Town in DALSTON

SOUL | DIVERSITY | VIBRANCE

If your music playlist consists of alternative music, hip-hop, new music or a bit of everything, Dalston will offer pretty much any type of music night you're looking for, whether it be a chilled vibe or a night on the dance floor.

WAYNE TIPPETTS/ ALAMY STOCK PHOTO ©

How to

Getting here Dalston Kingsland Overground Station is at the centre of things.

When to go Summertime brings a brighter energy and buzz, but you're guaranteed to catch a vibe regardless of the season.

Tip You won't be turned away from a Dalston or Clapton bar or club due to your dress code. Trainers, flip-flops, pyjamas – Dalston nightlife has seen it all!

More Night-time Options

Voodoo Ray's More than just a scrumptious pizza spot, this is also a popular hang-out for creatives to chat and mingle.

Brilliant Corners A cosy Japanese bar with wines and spirits imported from Japan. Some nights feature DJs playing soothing tunes to ease you into the weekend, a time when this bar really comes to life.

Untitled Bar With an Asian-inspired menu filled with scrumptious treats and a creative cocktail menu, you'll want to sample everything.

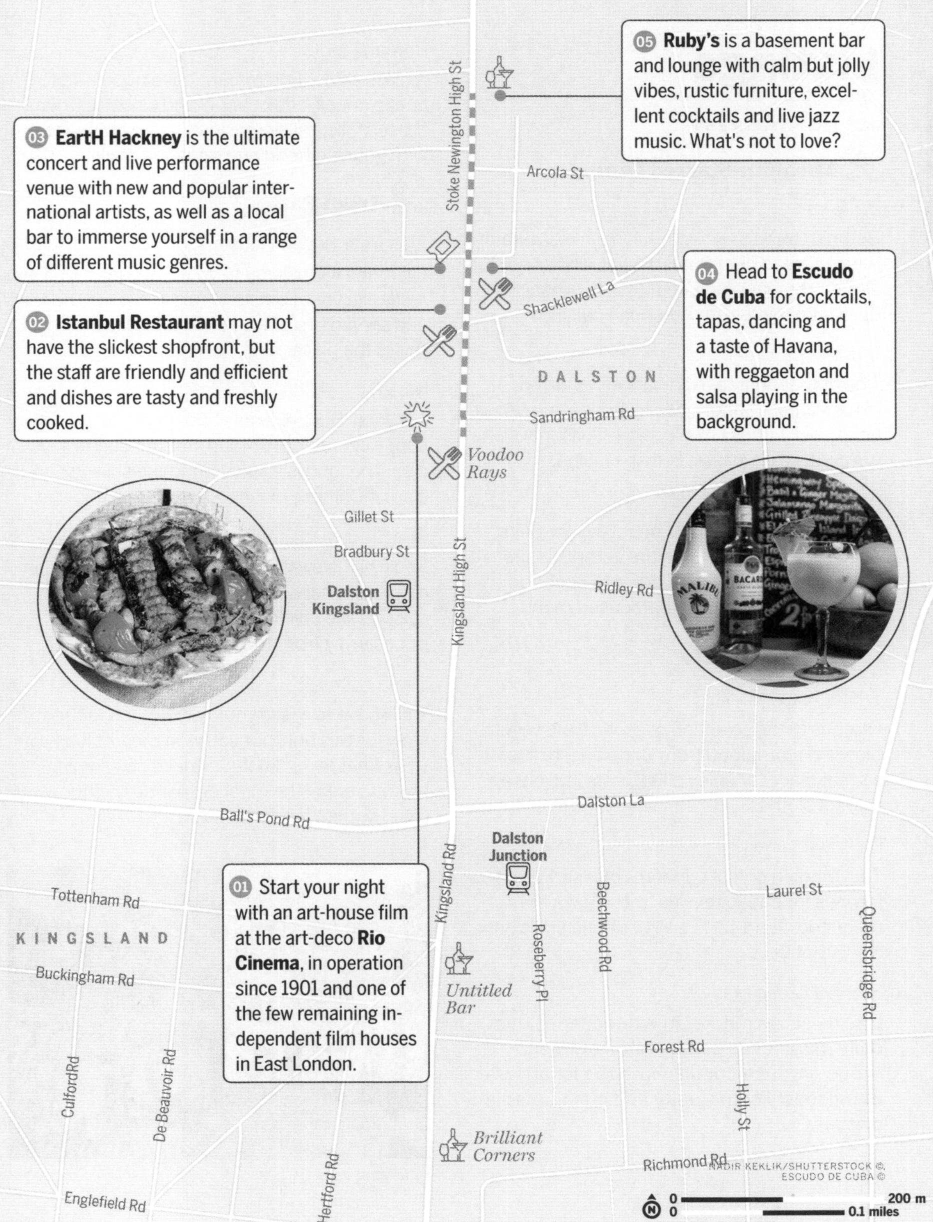
01 Start your night with an art-house film at the art-deco **Rio Cinema**, in operation since 1901 and one of the few remaining independent film houses in East London.
02 **Istanbul Restaurant** may not have the slickest shopfront, but the staff are friendly and efficient and dishes are tasty and freshly cooked.
03 **EartH Hackney** is the ultimate concert and live performance venue with new and popular international artists, as well as a local bar to immerse yourself in a range of different music genres.
04 Head to **Escudo de Cuba** for cocktails, tapas, dancing and a taste of Havana, with reggaeton and salsa playing in the background.
05 **Ruby's** is a basement bar and lounge with calm but jolly vibes, rustic furniture, excellent cocktails and live jazz music. What's not to love?
Stoke Newington High St
Arcola St
Shacklewell La
DALSTON
Sandringham Rd
Voodoo Rays
Gillet St
Bradbury St
Dalston Kingsland
Kingsland High St
Ridley Rd
Dalston La
Ball's Pond Rd
Dalston Junction
Kingsland Rd
Tottenham Rd
Laurel St
KINGSLAND
Buckingham Rd
Untitled Bar
Roseberry Pl
Beechwood Rd
Queensbridge Rd
Forest Rd
Culford Rd
De Beauvoir Rd
Holly St
Brilliant Corners
Richmond Rd
Englefield Rd
Hertford Rd
0 200 m
0 0.1 miles
N
MALIBU
BACARDI
NADIR KEKLIK/SHUTTERSTOCK ©, ESCUDO DE CUBA ©

Listings

BEST OF THE REST

Michelin-Starred Dining

Da Terra £££

Bethnal Green's two-star Michelin restaurant is led by head chef Rafael Cagali who serves up a pricey but stunning tasting menu inspired by European and South American cuisines.

Lyle's £££

One of the most relaxed Michelin-starred restaurants around, close to Brick Lane, where head chef James Lowe's micro-seasonal dishes are centred on classic British cuisine.

Behind £££

Hackney's Behind made headlines for being open for only 20 days before getting its first Michelin star, and it is all down to chef Andy Beynon's sustainable fish-focused menu.

Local Markets

Whitechapel Market

Famous for its selection of exotic fruit, vegetables and street food from Bangladesh, this is a great place for spicy cheap eats and cheap market clothes.

Petticoat Lane

This market, one of London's oldest, was once famous for cheap textiles; these days the ubiquitous food carts and boutique stalls have also crept in.

Bethnal Green Market

Like its sister market in Whitechapel, this daily market is a combination of fresh, exotic produce popular with the local Bangladeshi community and cheap market clothes.

Roman Market

A classic East End market once popular for cheap knock-offs of big-brand clothing. Today those stalls are increasingly vying for space with gourmet food and boutique stalls.

Asian Eats

Shalamar Kebab House £

Everyone will tell you to go to Tayyabs, but if you *really* like your Pakistani food authentic, no frills and served in a place still frequented by locals, this is the place.

Kar Woo £

The local Bangladeshis have kept this takeaway spot a secret for too long, but the queue says it all. The food is a spicy Bangladeshi twist on classic Chinese dishes – trust us on this one.

Red Chilli £

Red Chilli is every bit the classic British-Indian restaurant serving high-quality Anglo-Indian classics like chicken tikka masala at great prices away from the tourist traps.

Etles Uyghur £

You'll have to make your way out to Walthamstow for this one, but you won't regret it as you sit in what feels like the owner's cosy dining room to enjoy the most authentic Uyghur (Sino-Turkic) food in London.

Petticoat Lane

Shinwari £

It's quite the trek out east, but this is our favourite Afghan spot in East London. Sit cross-legged on a raised platform and await your steaming mound of *kabuli pulaw* and delicately spiced mince meat dish, *keema palak*.

Nakhon Thai £

In a stunning location overlooking the royal docks, Nakhon offers authentic Thai dishes including massaman curry and sticky mango rice, making it a tasty and potentially romantic dining experience.

Vintage Vibes

Beyond Retro

One of the earliest and original vintage stores in the East End, Beyond Retro hit the headlines because of alleged celebrity patronage. Housed in a huge warehouse off the main Brick Lane strip, there's a lot of choice here.

East End Thrift Store

Directly opposite student accommodation, down a Victorian alleyway, the Thrift Store is popular with young people for the £5 and £10 'fill a bag' deals they frequently offer.

Brick Lane Vintage Market

A great array of stalls and shops in a concentrated area, where crowds swell every Sunday and so do the prices; so while it's not the best for a bargain, it does have a great buzz about it.

Backyard Market

Browse this market for handmade jewellery, vintage items and creative gifts. All stalls are held by independent traders who assemble here every weekend.

Museums & Galleries

Museum of the Home

Housed in 300-year-old alms houses and recently renamed to distance itself from a

YAU MING LOW/SHUTTERSTOCK ©

Backyard Market

historic donor's links to transatlantic slavery, the Museum of the Home looks at the ways we engage with our own homes.

Museum of London Docklands

In a former Georgian-era sugar storehouse, this museum has a wonderful exhibition about the trade and industry of the docks as well as a particularly good interactive children's area.

Ragged School Museum

A cute little museum in a former 'ragged school' overlooking the Regent's Canal that tells the story of how London's poor were educated in these philanthropic institutes.

Whitechapel Gallery

The East End's original gallery, which has proudly premiered the likes of Mexican artist Frida Kahlo through to German photographer Thomas Struth, remains at the forefront of the area's contemporary art scene.

Chisenhale Galleries

For artists by artists, this is the gallery to see work by marginalised and overlooked artists. Previous exhibit titles include *Essential Black Art* and *Yellow Peril: New World Asians*.

Scan to find more things to do in East London online

HAMPSTEAD & NORTH LONDON

HISTORY | NATURE | DRINKING

Experience Hampstead & North London online

www.galtonflowers.com
The shop & Academy
L'OCCITANE

HAMPSTEAD & NORTH LONDON

Trip Builder

TAKE YOUR PICK OF MUST-SEES AND HIDDEN GEMS

Only central London has more blue plaques and celebrity residents than wealthy Hampstead and Highgate, where huge townhouses and the famous Heath are home to resident ghouls, antique and boutique shops and markets. Meanwhile, vibrant, multicultural Islington and Stoke Newington offer Ottoman-style mosques, the finest Anatolian cuisine and hidden rural escapes.

Neighbourhood Notes

Best for Experiencing the rural in London and multicultural heritage.

How long Give yourself four to five days.

Getting around The Overground conveniently moves across the north of London.

Tip Hampstead and Highgate are expensive; for cheap eats try the areas around Camden and Kentish Town.

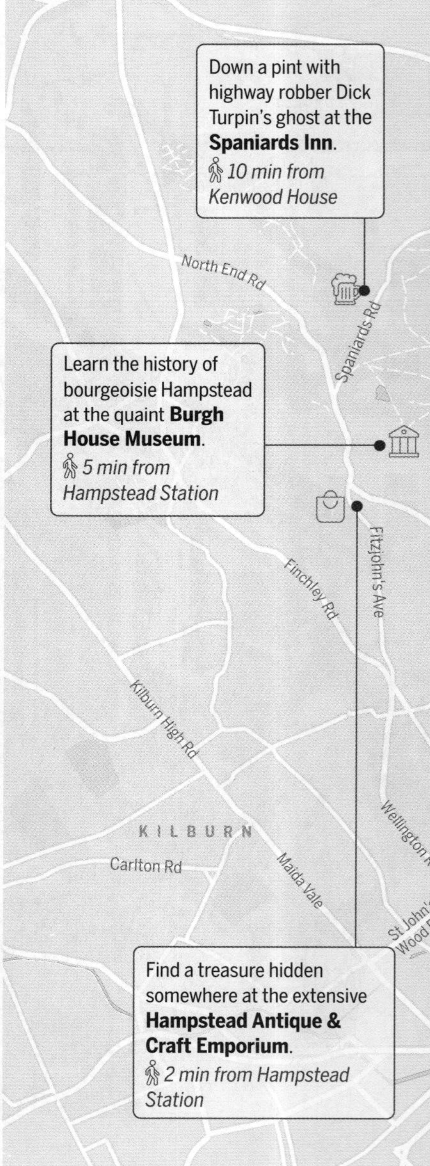

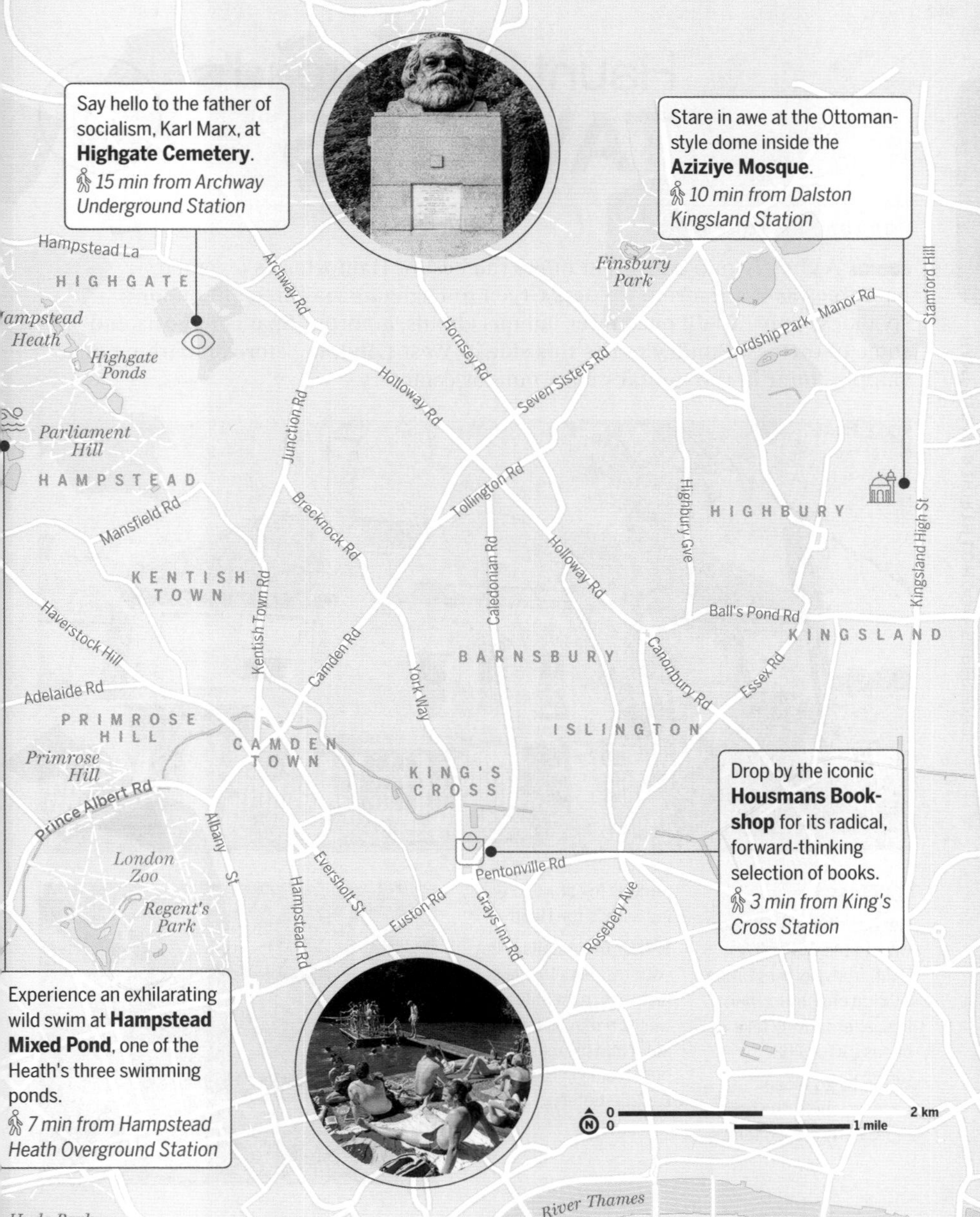

Say hello to the father of socialism, Karl Marx, at **Highgate Cemetery**.
15 min from Archway Underground Station
Stare in awe at the Ottoman-style dome inside the **Aziziye Mosque**.
10 min from Dalston Kingsland Station
Drop by the iconic **Housmans Bookshop** for its radical, forward-thinking selection of books.
3 min from King's Cross Station
Experience an exhilarating wild swim at **Hampstead Mixed Pond**, one of the Heath's three swimming ponds.
7 min from Hampstead Heath Overground Station
Hampstead La
HIGHGATE
Hampstead Heath
Highgate Ponds
Parliament Hill
HAMPSTEAD
Mansfield Rd
KENTISH TOWN
Haverstock Hill
Adelaide Rd
PRIMROSE HILL
Primrose Hill
Prince Albert Rd
London Zoo
Regent's Park
Hyde Park
Archway Rd
Junction Rd
Brecknock Rd
Kentish Town Rd
Camden Rd
CAMDEN TOWN
Albany St
Hampstead Rd
Eversholt St
Euston Rd
York Way
KING'S CROSS
Pentonville Rd
Grays Inn Rd
Hornsey Rd
Holloway Rd
Seven Sisters Rd
Tollington Rd
Caledonian Rd
BARNSBURY
Finsbury Park
Lordship Park
Manor Rd
Stamford Hill
Highbury Gve
HIGHBURY
Kingsland High St
Ball's Pond Rd
KINGSLAND
Canonbury Rd
Essex Rd
ISLINGTON
Rosebery Ave
River Thames
0 2 km
0 1 mile

30 Haunt Hampstead's TAVERNS

HORROR | HISTORY | PUBS

A ghostly pub crawl that offers the best of Hampstead's legendary hauntings as it goes from Golders Green to Highgate via three of London's spookiest pubs. You'll encounter famous ghouls, amorous Spanish ghosts and some of the best Sunday roasts this side of West London, before embarking on a vampire hunt in the capital's most famous cemetery.

VICKY JIRAYU/SHUTTERSTOCK ©

How to

Getting there It's a short walk to the Old Bull & Bush from Golders Green Station on the Northern line; alternatively take buses 210 or 268.

When to go When the days are short, the light fades early and London's famous fog starts creeping across the Heath.

Father of socialism Pay your respects to one of history's most influential western thinkers; Karl Marx and his marvellous bust reside in Highgate's East Cemetery.

OLIVIER GUIBERTEAU/SHUTTERSTOCK ©

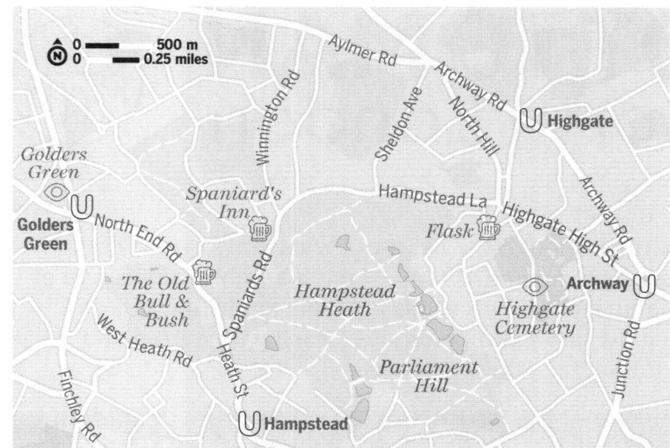

Start at **the Old Bull & Bush**, where a skeleton surrounded by surgical equipment was found behind a wall in 1987 and locals often report seeing a shrouded Victorian figure sat at the bar. Then head east to one of London's oldest pubs, **the Spaniards Inn**, where you'll meet the first of Hampstead's amorous Spanish ghouls: the inn's 17th-century landlord, Juan Porero, killed by his brother in a duel over a woman. In all likelihood, though, it's the inn's most famous ghastly resident, highway robber Dick Turpin, you're really here to meet. On the eastern edge of the Heath, another Iberian spook resides at **the Flask** – the former love-struck barmaid who hung herself in the cellar. But she's not alone. As you sit in one of the cosy corners of this 17th-century pub, beware her spooky co-worker who is often seen disappearing into pillars dressed in a Cavalier's uniform!

Finally it's London's most famous graveyard, **Highgate Cemetery**. Take your pick from a dark shrouded figure, a floating nun or a raging grey-haired woman. Or if you're really brave, go hunt the legendary Highgate Vampire, first spotted rising from graves here in the 1960s to attack locals. Soon after police were told about dumped carcasses of animals drained of their blood, and in the 1970s actual vampire hunts took place at the cemetery.

Left The Old Bull & Bush
Bottom left Highgate Cemetery

Hunting Dracula

The hunt for Highgate's vampire was led by 'magician' David Farrant and Bishop of the 'Old Catholic Church', Sean Manchester. On Friday 13th February 1970 both went on TV saying they would destroy the creature. This inspired a mob, wielding home-made stakes, to turn up at the cemetery within hours of the report being aired. Many entered the cemetery and desecrated a number of graves. The whole saga only came to an end in 1973 when Manchester claimed he had driven a stake through the heart of the vampire in a house dubbed 'House of Dracula'.

31 OTTOMAN North London

HISTORY | CULTURE | RELIGION

North London's A10 runs through the heart of the capital's large Turkic community, which is the place for Anatolian food – be it a humble *lahmachun* or a delicately spiced *guvec* (lamb stew). However, few people know that it is also home to three of London's most fascinating mosques – each with a little nod to the community's imperial forefathers, the Ottomans.

DAN KITWOOD/GETTY IMAGES ©

How to

Getting there Buses 149 and 243 pass all three mosques; Overground stations Dalston Junction and Dalston Kingsland are in the middle.

When to go Check listings for the five daily prayer times and avoid these when visiting the mosques.

Ottoman baths
Turkish baths were once extremely popular in London and then they suddenly disappeared. Now they're back! Try Turkish Bath Hammam close to Ramadan Mosque on the Crossway.

CKTRAVELS.COM/SHUTTERSTOCK ©

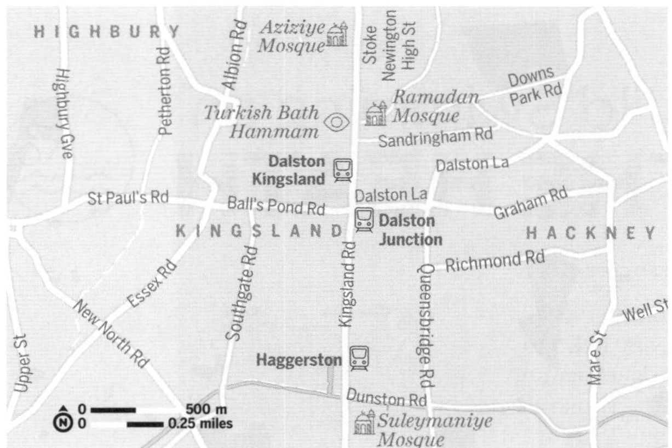

Everything about the **Suleymaniye Mosque** screams classically Ottoman. Named after the Empire's flagship mosque, the Suleymaniye in Istanbul – built by its greatest architect for its greatest Sultan – it has a classically Ottoman dome and a 66m-high minaret plucked straight from the Istanbul skyline (reportedly the tallest in the UK). Founded in 1994, it can hold 3000 people in an interior as spectacular as the exterior.

The **Ramadan Mosque** was set up in 1977 to serve the local Turkish-Cypriot community and sits inside the old Stoke Newington Synagogue. The fascinating building's design is 'Andalusian'; inside the standout feature is an Ottoman-era imperial insignia decorating the impressive stone mimbar. The mosque also has a nice on-site cafe and is known for hosting cultural events that encourage inter-community harmony.

Finally, and easily the prettiest of all, is the **Aziziye Mosque**, which until 1983 was a cinema showing martial arts and soft-core porn movies. Although structurally the building remains unchanged, it has been transformed by the addition of two ubiquitous Ottoman-style gold domes and the covering of the entire building in the famous blue Ottoman Iznik tiles – reportedly imported from Turkey. The blue continues inside, where a luxuriously thick blue carpet sits beneath a stunning central dome, decorated with exquisite Arabic calligraphy, red and blue patterns, and a central hanging chandelier.

Left Suleymaniye Mosque
Bottom left Aziziye Mosque

Mosque Etiquette

When visiting the mosques remember the etiquette: avoid visiting during the five daily prayer times and be sure to wear modest clothing that covers your shoulders and falls below the knee. Women should wear a headscarf and everyone should remove their shoes on entry. Some mosques will only allow men into the main prayer hall and women will have to use the balcony.

32 Wild Swimming on THE HEATH

SWIMMING | NATURE | OUTDOORS

Dive into open water, just as a swan takes off beside you, say hello to curious ducks while gently performing the breaststroke, and feel the brush of a water reed as you complete a lap in London's most exhilarating bathing spot. Welcome to Hampstead Heath's swimming ponds, the only place in the capital where you can go 'wild swimming'.

How to

Getting there Bus 214 passes close to the segregated ponds; Hampstead Heath Overground is a short walk from the mixed pond.

When to go The segregated ponds are open year-round; the mixed only between April and October. All charge a small fee.

Outdoor pool For those that want to swim outdoors but in an actual pool, Parliament Hill Lido is in the southeastern corner of the Heath.

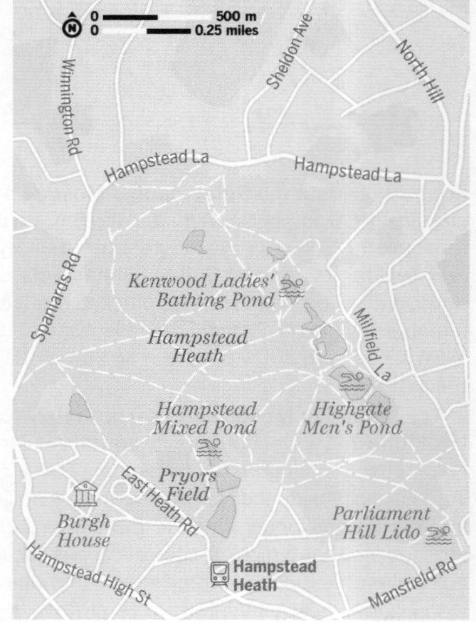

Locals have been dipping into the refreshing waters of Hampstead Heath's swimming ponds since the 1800s, when the three ponds – originally part of a series of reservoirs supplying London with water – became open-air swim spots.

The **Highgate Men's Pond** by the Heath's Millfield Lane entrance is the largest and boasts an impressive diving platform. This huge body of water has banks of green, grassy slopes with a number of mature trees and thick reed bushes at the edges; bathing in it genuinely

Top riight Hampstead Mixed Pond **Right** Duck on Hampstead Heath pond

JEREMY HOARE/ALAMY STOCK PHOTO ©

Brunch & the Burgh

Not far from Hampstead Mixed Pond is **Burgh House Museum**, an early-18th-century house that is a dynamic space for art, events and history and home to a great permanent exhibition about Hampstead through the ages. It's also home to a delightful cafe serving hearty brunches.

feels like a wild swim despite being in the heart of modern, urban London. This is particularly true during the colder months when only a handful of hardened locals come for a dip, creating an unmatched serenity about the place. Something that is also true about the **Kenwood Ladies' Pond**, just a short walk north. Much smaller and surrounded by thick bushy trees with low-lying branches that hover just above the water, the ladies-only pond has an almost medieval feel about it. Little wonder that regulars speak of swimming in either one as being a 'spiritual' experience. Finally, there's **Hampstead Mixed Pond**, on the other side of the Heath next to Pryors Field. In warm weather it's always the busiest of the three ponds, but it's closed to the public during the winter months.

ELIZAK/SHUTTERSTOCK ©

HIGH-END
Hampstead

01 Crêpes
You'll have to queue, but the French pancakes, especially the savoury ones, at La Crêperie de Hampstead are well worth the wait.

02 Antiques and collectables
Hampstead is filled with antique shops and markets such as the extensive Hampstead Antique & Craft Emporium.

03 Sigmund Freud Statue
He was one of Hampstead's most famous residents and fittingly, a statue with a great likeness to the father of psychoanalysis sits outside the world famous Tavistock College.

04 The Gallery
Enjoy the whisky, jazz nights and live DJ sets at this sleek bar, where much of what you drink will have been sourced from local breweries, distilleries and wineries.

04

05

06

05 Ham

Sophisticated and relaxed, Ham – taken from the old English for 'home' – offers luxurious, simple food like saddleback pork with roasted onions and cucumber.

06 Kenwood House

Imagine what it's like to be a Lord of the Manor and wander through the stunning rooms of this 17th-century country house on the famous Heath.

33 Tour Abandoned Tube STATIONS

UNDERGROUND | GHOST STATIONS | HISTORY

The Tube is more than just a way to get around: it's an iconic part of London life. See a different side of the system by discovering its disused stations hiding in plain sight all over the city.

NICK HARRISON/ALAMY STOCK PHOTO ©

How to

Getting around Kentish Town Underground Station is on the Northern line. Touch on and off the Tube with your Oyster card.

When to go Year-round

Photo-op Take a picture of the replica 'red' roundel on the eastbound platform of Covent Garden.

Detour For lunch make a detour to the London Transport Museum (Covent Garden Piazza), with its transport-themed cafe and shop.

This itinerary is by Geoff Marshall. Geoff is a Londoner, former Tube travelling World Record holder, 'Hidden London' guide, and in 2017 visited all 2563 National Rail stations in Great Britain. @geofftech

Closing South Kentish Town

Bizarrely, a strike at a power station meant that the station had to close due to lack of power. A decision was taken never to reopen it – even when the power was back up and running! You can get right up close to the building to study the tiles closely, or if you want to go inside, make use of one of the businesses now located in the former station.

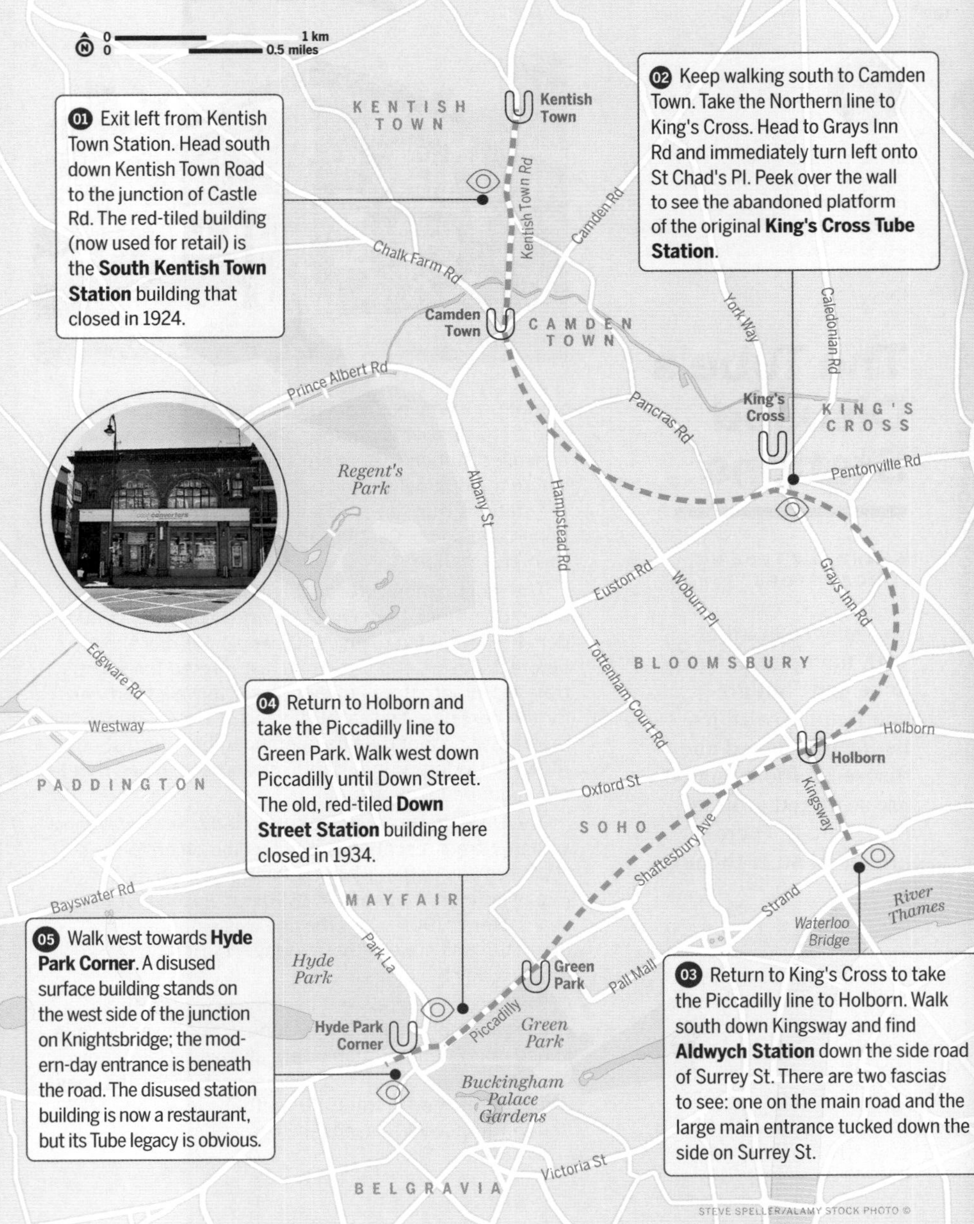
0 1 km
0 0.5 miles
KENTISH TOWN
Kentish Town
01 Exit left from Kentish Town Station. Head south down Kentish Town Road to the junction of Castle Rd. The red-tiled building (now used for retail) is the **South Kentish Town Station** building that closed in 1924.
02 Keep walking south to Camden Town. Take the Northern line to King's Cross. Head to Grays Inn Rd and immediately turn left onto St Chad's Pl. Peek over the wall to see the abandoned platform of the original **King's Cross Tube Station**.
Kentish Town Rd
Camden Rd
Chalk Farm Rd
York Way
Caledonian Rd
Camden Town
CAMDEN TOWN
Prince Albert Rd
Pancras Rd
King's Cross
KING'S CROSS
Regent's Park
Albany St
Hampstead Rd
Pentonville Rd
Euston Rd
Woburn Pl
Grays Inn Rd
Edgware Rd
Tottenham Court Rd
BLOOMSBURY
04 Return to Holborn and take the Piccadilly line to Green Park. Walk west down Piccadilly until Down Street. The old, red-tiled **Down Street Station** building here closed in 1934.
Westway
PADDINGTON
Holborn
Holborn
Oxford St
Kingsway
SOHO
Shaftesbury Ave
Bayswater Rd
MAYFAIR
Strand
River Thames
Waterloo Bridge
05 Walk west towards **Hyde Park Corner**. A disused surface building stands on the west side of the junction on Knightsbridge; the modern-day entrance is beneath the road. The disused station building is now a restaurant, but its Tube legacy is obvious.
Hyde Park
Park La
Green Park
Pall Mall
03 Return to King's Cross to take the Piccadilly line to Holborn. Walk south down Kingsway and find **Aldwych Station** down the side road of Surrey St. There are two fascias to see: one on the main road and the large main entrance tucked down the side on Surrey St.
Hyde Park Corner
Piccadilly
Green Park
Buckingham Palace Gardens
Victoria St
BELGRAVIA

By Geoff Marshall
Geoff is a Londoner, former Tube travelling World Record holder, 'Hidden London' guide, and in 2017 visited all 2563 National Rail stations in Great Britain.
@geofftech

The Tube's Disused Stations

WHERE THE TUBE NO LONGER STOPS

You may be familiar with the London Tube map, but are you familiar with its list of abandoned and disused stations that are scattered around the Capital? There are about 50 of them.

DRIMAFILM/SHUTTERSTOCK ©

Left Mornington Crescent Underground Station **Middle** Aldwych Underground Station **Right** Hidden London tour of Euston tunnels

'About 50'? Why not a definitive number? Good question... The answer is another question: how do you define a disused station? There are stations still open today where the original station building is disused, and there are stations that have moved so are technically abandoned and so on. Defining an abandoned station is open to interpretation.

The most famous is arguably Aldwych, an awkward one-stop branch from Holborn, whose passenger numbers had dwindled to just 450 people per day shortly before it closed, and if you had just missed the shuttle train at Holborn it was often quicker to walk than wait for the next one. And so, at the end of 1994 – due to the prohibitive cost of the lifts needing to be refurbished – Aldwych Underground Station closed and joined that list of abandoned stations.

The Underground's first abandoned station was King William Street. Located on what would be on today's Northern line right next to the Monument to the Great Fire of London, it opened in 1890 but closed just 10 years later in 1900 when the line was extended. The damp tunnels are still there today – buried beneath modern-day buildings.

Stations came and went over the years. The main cause was that originally the Underground was not one joined up system. Stations were all built by separate companies who competed against each other, but they were later unified in the 1930s with the creation of the London Transport Passenger Board.

RIGHTCLICKSTUDIOS/SHUTTERSTOCK ©

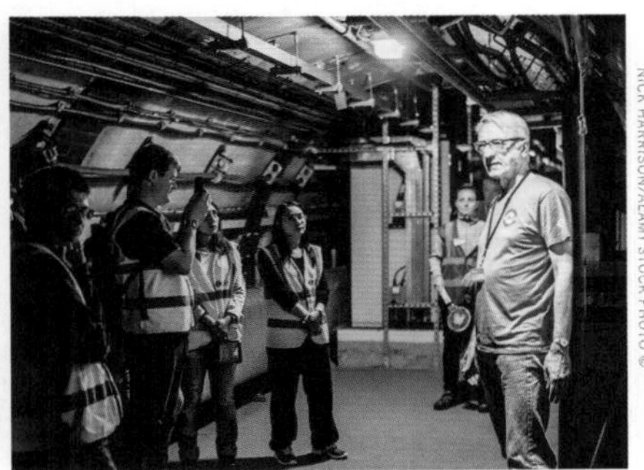
NICK HARRISON/ALAMY STOCK PHOTO ©

Two world wars played their part too with some stations closing during wartime and never reopening again afterwards. Others closed when it became clear that they were built too close to other stations and there was no need to duplicate. Others were rebuilt and moved – Osterley on the Piccadilly line was about 500m further up the line and was re-sited and rebuilt to be in a better location. Passengers going to/from Heathrow Airport whizz past the abandoned platforms that are still clearly visible, but many barely notice them.

> If you cannot get below ground, there are still many abandoned disused station buildings on the surface and they are a joy to spot.

It is possible to see some of the disused stations via Hidden London tours and other times when guides take you in for a tour inside and around the old stations. This is a must for Tube enthusiasts. If you cannot get below ground, there are still many abandoned disused station buildings on the surface and they are a joy to spot. My favourites are the ones featuring the deep 'oxblood' red coloured tiles created by designer Leslie Green.

Leslie Green & the Tube

Leslie Green is a renowned architect who designed several stations for the London Underground at the beginning of the 20th century. His distinct station style featured ox-blood red tiles as a frontage with a two-storey steel-framed building with semicircular 1st-floor windows and ornate tiled pattern interiors.

Several of his stations still exist and are in use today. They are instantly recognisable from a distance. Green's assistant Stanley Heaps carried on his work after he sadly died of tuberculosis in 1908 at the age of just 33. His legacy lives on in his beautifully designed station buildings.

Listings

BEST OF THE REST

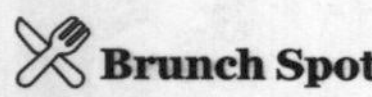

Brunch Spots

Roni's £

Head for Roni's on Swains Lane in Highgate for a North African brunch; the shakshuka is on point and always served with fresh, warm pitta bread.

Brew House £

This is all about the setting inside the 17th-century neoclassical Kenwood House overlooking the famous Heath; full English breakfasts are served until 11.30am on the weekend.

Breakfast Club £

This Islington institution gets busy on the weekend. That line of people in front of you are all going to order the Full Monty or its veg equivalent, the fantastically named Reggie the Veggie.

Museum Houses

Freud Museum

Enter the house of the father of psychotherapy to see many of his original items including the famous couch. This was also the home of his daughter, Anna Freud, and has a delightful garden area, too.

Keats House

This is where the renowned poet lived, and you can still glimpse many of his original poems and letters and sit in the very garden where he reportedly write his 'Ode to a Nightingale'.

Fenton House

This stunning 17th-century home has a collection of wonderful English post-impressionist art inside and a garden of carefully chosen flowers that are a blaze of colour in the spring.

William Morris Gallery

William Morris' prints and patterns are all the rage again. Step in to his family home and learn about the great entrepreneur and what inspired him.

Beautiful Books

New Beacon Books

A little bookshop close to Finsbury Park specialising in work by the hugely under-represented Black authors of the literary world as well as books about Black culture.

Black Gull Books

This brilliant secondhand bookshop has two branches; a small one in Camden and a bigger one in East Finchley, both with a particularly good range on social sciences.

Amnesty International Bookshop

Well organised, staffed by friendly people and supporting human rights – what's not to love about this great secondhand bookshop next to Kentish Town train station?

Stoke Newington Toys & Books

Part of the award-winning bookshop of the same name, this is a brilliant little spot to take

Keats House

the children and let them pick up a classic book or a book-related toy.

Housmans Bookshop

This iconic radical bookshop run by friendly staff near King's Cross specialises in feminist and LGBTIQ+ books, plus a good selection of titles on Black and progressive politics.

 Hampstead's Blue Plaques

Noor Inayat Khan

A female British-Indian secret agent sent into occupied France by Britain during WWII lived at 4 Taviton St.

Charles Darwin

The19th-century naturalist who popularised the theory of evolution lived in a house where the Biological Sciences Building at UCL stands.

Laurie Cunningham

The first Black footballer to represent England internationally and play for Real Madrid lived at 73 Lancaster Rd.

Anna Freud

The pioneer of child psychoanalysis lived at 20 Maresfield Gardens with her illustrious father Sigmund and their family.

George Orwell

The visionary 20th-century novelist and political essayist most famous for *1984* and *Animal Farm* lived at 50 Lawford Road.

Rabindranath Tagore

Tagore became one of the world's most famous men in the early 20th century after the Indian poet and mystic won the Nobel Prize for Literature in 1913. He briefly resided at 3 Villas on the Heath.

Ruth First

The South African anti-apartheid activist and scholar lived at 13 Lyme St with her husband Joe Slovo.

William Morris Gallery

 Antique Hunting

Hampstead Antique & Craft Emporium

A little cavern of different dealers that has been running since the late 1960s and includes stunning crafts by talented local artists.

Také Antiques

A proper old-fashioned antique shop that spills out onto the pavement and is run by a friendly, if somewhat eccentric, dealer.

Camden Passage

Turn up on Wednesday and Saturday and you'll have three adjoining markets to wander through in search of that elusive piece of antique silverware, porcelain or furniture.

Fleming Antiques

There are a few antique shops inside Camden's famous stables and Flemings is one of the better ones; pick up interesting furniture, porcelain or even a stuffed animal, if that's your thing!

Scan to find more things to do in Hampstead & North London online

NOTTING HILL & WEST LONDON

SHOPPING | PARKS | MARKETS

Experience Notting Hill & West London online

NOTTING HILL & WEST LONDON

Trip Builder

TAKE YOUR PICK OF MUST-SEES AND HIDDEN GEMS

Home to Europe's largest festival – Notting Hill Carnival – and the globe's most famous vintage market, this sprawled slice of the city is a mixed bag of quaint streets and parks, dense and diverse thoroughfares and marvellous fashion shops for a range of budgets.

Meighbourhood Notes

Best for Boutique shopping, vintage and antiques, parkland.

Transport Several stations, mainly within Zone 2, on the following lines: Overground, District, Circle, Hammersmith & City, Piccadilly, Central and Bakerloo.

Getting around Buses and trains for long distances, otherwise walking is recommended.

Tip Vintage shopping here isn't cheap, but you'll find plenty of quality and unique selections.

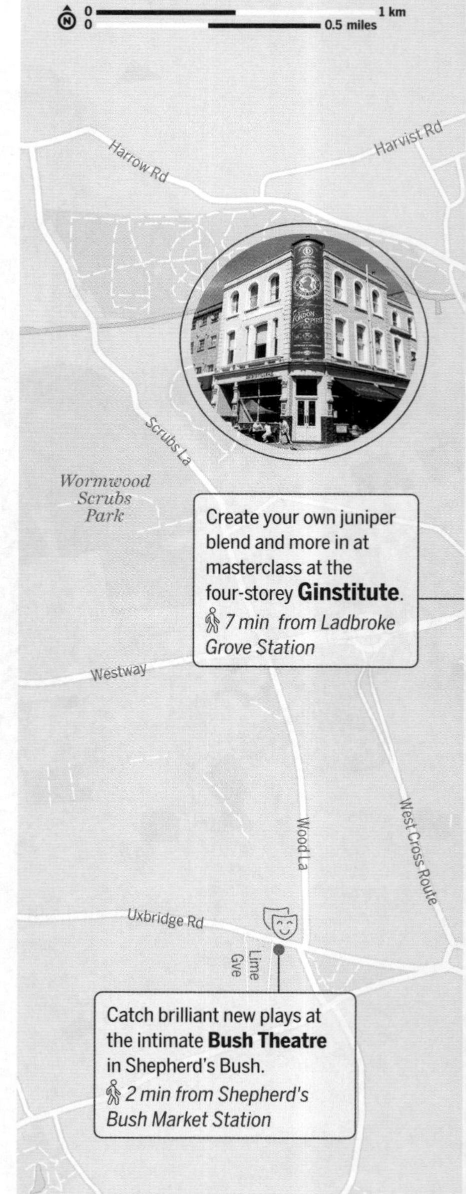

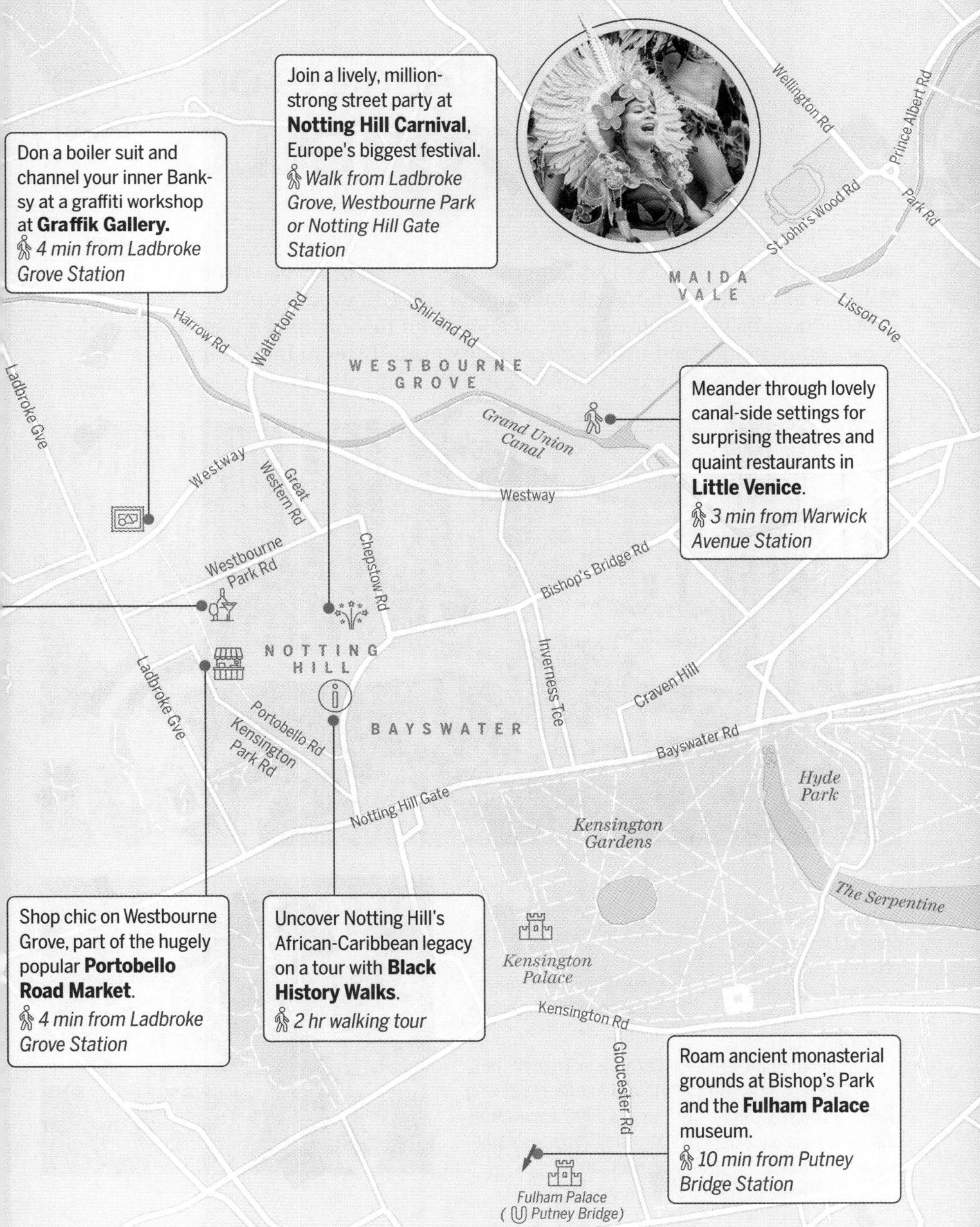

Join a lively, million-strong street party at **Notting Hill Carnival**, Europe's biggest festival.
Walk from Ladbroke Grove, Westbourne Park or Notting Hill Gate Station
Don a boiler suit and channel your inner Banksy at a graffiti workshop at **Graffik Gallery.**
4 min from Ladbroke Grove Station
Meander through lovely canal-side settings for surprising theatres and quaint restaurants in **Little Venice**.
3 min from Warwick Avenue Station
Shop chic on Westbourne Grove, part of the hugely popular **Portobello Road Market**.
4 min from Ladbroke Grove Station
Uncover Notting Hill's African-Caribbean legacy on a tour with **Black History Walks**.
2 hr walking tour
Roam ancient monasterial grounds at Bishop's Park and the **Fulham Palace** museum.
10 min from Putney Bridge Station
Wellington Rd
Prince Albert Rd
St John's Wood Rd
Park Rd
MAIDA VALE
Lisson Gve
Harrow Rd
Walterton Rd
Shirland Rd
WESTBOURNE GROVE
Ladbroke Gve
Grand Union Canal
Westway
Great Western Rd
Westbourne Park Rd
Chepstow Rd
Bishop's Bridge Rd
NOTTING HILL
Inverness Tce
Craven Hill
BAYSWATER
Portobello Rd
Kensington Park Rd
Bayswater Rd
Hyde Park
Notting Hill Gate
Kensington Gardens
The Serpentine
Kensington Palace
Kensington Rd
Gloucester Rd
Fulham Palace
(Putney Bridge)

34 Browse Markets on PORTOBELLO

SHOPPING | MARKETS | ANTIQUES

One of the world's most famous markets barely needs introduction. Millions of travellers and locals take to Notting Hill every year to navigate over 1000 stalls of antiques, assorted goods and food against a pastel-coloured backdrop of homes and brick-and-mortar shops. If you're into shopping and market culture, visiting this staple – especially on Saturday – is simply essential.

WILLY BARTON/SHUTTERSTOCK ©

How to

Getting there The closest Underground stations (on opposite ends of Portobello Rd) are Notting Hill Gate (Central, Circle and District lines) and Ladbroke Grove (Circle and Hammersmith & City lines). Several buses are available too.

When to go Saturday for the full heaving experience, followed by Friday; mornings are more manageable. Weekdays are quieter but with fewer open stalls.

Early riser Though the official Saturday opening time is 8am, a few jewellery stalls open as early as 5.30am.

GRACIELLADEMONNE/SHUTTERSTOCK ©

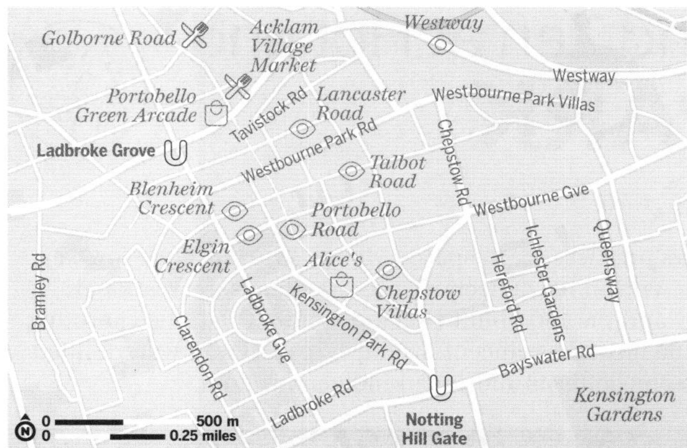

Left Portobello Road Market
Bottom left Street food in Portobello Road Market

A village of markets Portobello Road Market is not just one bustling market set along the eponymous corridor. Instead, it's a conglomerate of several markets (of varied offerings and trading hours) spread out through several Notting Hill streets, which surely helps offset the 100,000-plus visitors it receives on good-weather weekends. Antique-hunters should schedule for Saturday visits to Portobello Rd between Chepstow Villas and Elgin Cres streets, as the half-mile stretch contains the lion's share of vintage goods and collectables. For groceries and street eats, proceed to Elgin Cres to Talbot Rd for stalls serving everything from French crêpes to Caribbean jerk chicken, as well as take-home items such as fresh seafood and gourmet cheeses. The Westway area is a bit further out but is the hub for modern fashions and trendy vintage shops.

Hidden finds Take refuge from the Portobello Road Market rush and head into **Portobello Green Arcade** – the street's sole arcade – for a more relaxed browsing experience of upmarket, mainly contemporary indie shops. **Acklam Village Market**, tucked underneath Westway, is a vibrant weekends-only spot with global street food and a bar with free live music. Often overlooked by tourists is the market stretch along **Golborne Road**, which has a large Portuguese and Moroccan community, where a plethora of shops and stalls stand alongside vendors selling tasty *pastel de nata* (Portuguese custard tarts) and North African cuisine.

Market Like a Local

Arrive early

The market gets crowded later in the day, especially on Saturday. I recommend arriving around 9.30am or 10am on Saturday.

Don't forget the side streets

They're full of shops, cafes and colourful houses. My favourites are Lancaster Rd for its rainbow row of houses and Blenheim Cres for bookshops.

Explore inside the shops

Some have a labyrinth of rooms to discover beyond the storefront. Alice's, an antique store, is my favourite; going inside feels like stepping into a treasure trove, as vintage goods fill every space.

Tips by Julie Falconer, *local travel blogger, @aladyinlondon*

35 Find Zen at Holland PARK

NATURE | HISTORY | CULTURE

One of West London's prettiest green spaces, Holland Park is more low-key than London's larger parks. Within its 22 hectares are woodlands, recreational facilities, a stately orangery and the 1605-built Holland House. Of all the charming gardens, Kyoto Garden is the most magnificent, where carps swim in waterfall-fed koi ponds surrounded by stone lanterns and Japan-indigenous flora.

GS_S7/SHUTTERSTOCK ©

How to

Getting there Holland Park Station (Underground's Central line) is about a 10-minute walk.

When to go Summer months for optimal weather – and a chance to catch performances at the nine-week-only Opera Holland Park.

Star-spotting The Holland Park neighbourhood has several famous residents; maybe you'll see singer Elton John or the Beckams having a leisurely walk?

FB93/SHUTTERSTOCK ©

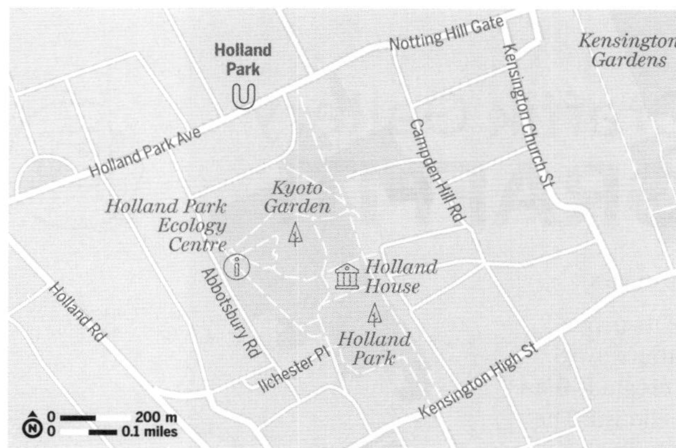

Left Kyoto Garden Bottom left A peacock in Kyoto Garden

From Japan, with love The **Kyoto Garden**, built in 1991, was a gift from the Chamber of Commerce of Kyoto to memorialise its lasting friendship with Great Britain. Ever since, Holland Park visitors have come to the picturesque area to see the koi pond and cascading waterfall, delight in the trees' vibrant colours in the springtime and autumn months...and spot meandering peacocks. There is an additional gifted Japanese garden, 2012's **Fukushima Memorial Garden**, from the Embassy of Japan, made as a 'thank you' for the British's helping hand after the devastating Fukushima earthquake and tsunami in 2011. Though the latter's origins are more sombre, both gardens offer fabulous respite in West London.

The wild side There's more to London's park wildlife beyond pigeons and squirrels – and, specifically to Holland Park, those colourful peacocks. A planned visit to the **Holland Park Ecology Centre** (rbkc.gov.uk/ecology) will provide an expert-led primer on the area's incredible biodiversity and ecosystem. Every season offers different activities. The autumn months, for instance, offer outings such as Fungi Foray, where groups search, identify and learn about the different fungi species in the park; and the Autumn Bat Walk, a torch-lit tour with bat experts who use special detectors to find the nocturnal creatures. In the summer, join tours for butterflies, amphibians and parakeets and partake in gardening workshops.

Top Holland Park Tips

See Kyoto Garden in the spring, when the cherry trees are in bloom and *koinobori* (Japanese carp streamers) are hung over the small waterfall and rippling koi pond.

Watch for peacocks, often found around Kyoto Garden. If you can't spy them, try looking up, as they can be spotted sleeping in the trees.

Catch an opera concert in the summer, when Holland House's romantic ruins are used as a backdrop for pop-up performances. Buy tickets early, as most performances sell out.

Enter via the south-western gate; it's off of Ilchester Pl, one of Britain's most expensive – and jaw-droppingly gorgeous – streets.

Tips by Nicole Trilivas, *local travel writer, @NicoleTrilivas*

36 Graffik Gallery GRAFFITI

STREET ART | GALLERIES | CULTURE

London is known for its urban art scene, and there's no better way to explore it, shop it and even create it than at Graffik Gallery on Portobello Rd. The city's pre-eminent space for high-end street art runs temporary exhibitions of emerging artists, has an impressive collection from luminaries such as Banksy and Bambi, and hosts family-friendly graffiti-making workshops.

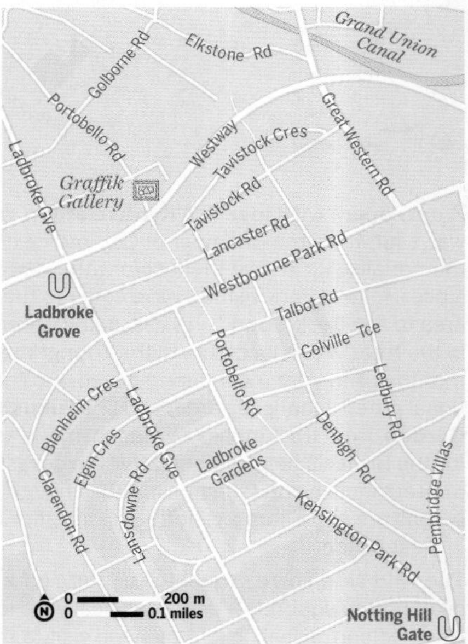

How to

Getting there Ladbroke Grove (Underground's Circle and Hammersmith & City lines) is a five-minute walk to the gallery.

When to go Weekend afternoons (closes at 6pm). Book well in advance for graffiti workshops and private classes.

Affordable art No budget for a £8000 original mixed-media collage? There are a few works (and art gifts) for sale under £150.

Not your average gallery

Graffik is one of the earliest (if not the first) commercial galleries dedicated to street art, representing some of the world's top urban art creators. Instead of Matisse-style paintings and Old World portraits, you'll find skateboard triptychs from Robin Coleman; spray-painted traffic signs from Tommy Gurr; and provocative limited-edition prints from Kunstrasen. While much of the art is relatively affordable, it's not uncommon to find original works selling for £17,500 or more. For serious collectors, the gallery can

Right Graffik Gallery
Below Graffiti process

ROBERTO HERRETT/ALAMY STOCK PHOTO ©

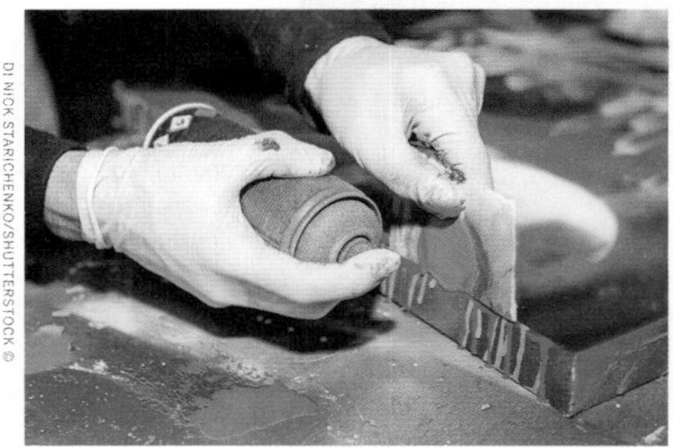

DI NICK STARICHENKO/SHUTTERSTOCK ©

Not for Sale

Even the building's a work of (street) art: it's easy to identify Graffik Gallery while walking along Portobello Rd, with Dotmaster's three-storey mural of a mischievous girl spray-painting the *Mona Lisa* on a blue brick exterior.

arrange appointment-only viewings of secondary market works of late art icons Andy Warhol and Jean-Michel Basquiat.

Make your own street art Far cooler than a typical art gallery, Graffik also runs a bevy of workshops and masterclasses for novice street artists. You'll don gloves, goggles and shiny blue boiler suits as expert instructors show you how to spray paint with stencils on canvas... or freestyle on the gallery's garden walls. Choose from open-to-all Weekend Graffiti Workshops (from £44 per adult) and private classes. If you're with older children, then it's an activity you can take the family to try, too. A dedicated two-hour Family Experience Graffiti Class caters for children aged eight and over; each person can create their graffiti piece individually, or work together on a larger canvas for a collective masterpiece.

37 Saunter through LITTLE VENICE

CANALS | FOOD & DRINK | THEATRES

Just north of thronging Paddington is Maida Vale's charming, colourful houseboat-dotted waterway where Regent's Canal and Grand Union Canal converge. Surrounding these canals are a few on-the-ground places to explore, including old-school pubs, quaint canal-side restaurants and wholly unique theatre venues.

How to

Getting there Warwick Avenue Station on the Underground's Bakerloo line is just two streets away.

When to go April to September, or any time the weather is dry and sunny.

Cruise the canal Take a relaxing 45-minute ride on a narrowboat along Regent's Canal from Little Venice to Camden Town (or vice versa) with London Waterbus Company (londonwaterbus.com).

Boat Bonanza

To see Little Venice at its liveliest, visit on the first May bank holiday to attend **Canalway Cavalcade**, an exciting waterside festival with more than 100 flamboyantly decorated narrowboats parading around the area. There are food and drinks stalls, attractions for children and live performances to complement the fun boat watching.

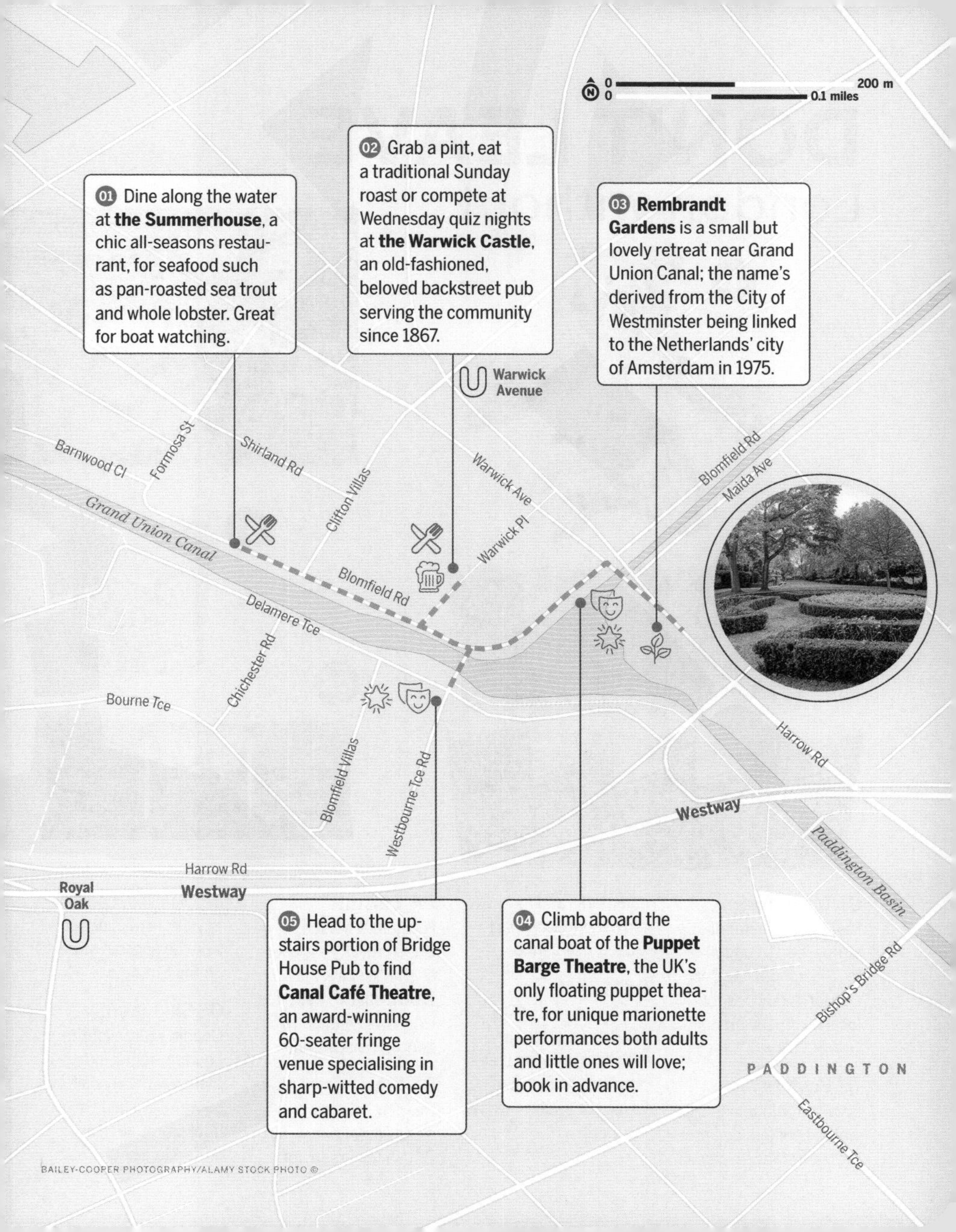

01 Dine along the water at **the Summerhouse**, a chic all-seasons restaurant, for seafood such as pan-roasted sea trout and whole lobster. Great for boat watching.

02 Grab a pint, eat a traditional Sunday roast or compete at Wednesday quiz nights at **the Warwick Castle**, an old-fashioned, beloved backstreet pub serving the community since 1867.

03 **Rembrandt Gardens** is a small but lovely retreat near Grand Union Canal; the name's derived from the City of Westminster being linked to the Netherlands' city of Amsterdam in 1975.

04 Climb aboard the canal boat of the **Puppet Barge Theatre**, the UK's only floating puppet theatre, for unique marionette performances both adults and little ones will love; book in advance.

05 Head to the upstairs portion of Bridge House Pub to find **Canal Café Theatre**, an award-winning 60-seater fringe venue specialising in sharp-witted comedy and cabaret.

DON'T LEAVE
London without...

01 Teddy bear
Head to department store Liberty London for the handmade Icon London teddy bear by local luxury toy brand Grin & Bear.

02 Posters
Browse for fabulous vintage posters depicting train stations, city landmarks and more in the London Transport Museum gift shop.

03 Mug
Transport yourself to London on every sip with the Quite Big London Mug, available at Oxford St's John Lewis & Partners.

04 Biscuits
Fortnum & Mason, British royalty's grocer of choice since the 1700s, offers a delicious, extensive selection of gourmet biscuit tins.

05 Tea
Head to Twinings, a quintessential British tea brand, for a triple-caddy London Skyline Tea Collection from its flagship store on the Strand.

06 Sketchbook
Doodle your favourite London sights and activities with Citysketch London, available at bookstores such as Waterstones.

07 Keychain
Take the famous well-travelled Paddington Bear wherever you go with a plush Classic Paddington Keychain from its eponymous store.

08 Bottle opener & corkscrew
For a utilitarian (and ubiquitous) London-themed gadget, grab a cheap red phone booth bottle opener and corkscrew.

09 Passport holder
Travel Hogwarts-style with a faux leather passport holder from the Harry Potter Shop at Platform 9¾ in King's Cross Station.

10 Tea towel
After a day exploring the Natural History Museum, hit the gift shop for a vibrant vintage butterfly diagram tea towel.

11 Gin
Visit Berry Bros & Rudd, England's oldest wine and spirits shop, for house-brand gin bottles and gift sets.

Listings

BEST OF THE REST

Historic Homes

Leighton House

Find stunning arabesque details and stuffed peacocks near the foot of Holland Park in the refurbished home of 19th-century artist Frederic Leighton.

Fulham Palace

The former summer residence of England's bishops from as early as 704 CE (set within Bishop's Park) is now a museum with guided history tours, garden walks and a courtyard cafe.

Sambourne House

Formerly known as 18 Stafford Tce, the renovated former abode of cartoonist Linley Sambourne is open year-round for a peek at Victorian-era living near Holland Park.

Design Museum

Source inspiration from the Holland Park–adjacent museum's enormous collection, striking exterior architecture and special exhibits.

Catch a Show

Lyric Hammersmith Theatre

A modern, multifaceted community space in the heart of Hammersmith with groundbreaking theatre programmes (at affordable prices) and an attractive roof garden.

Eventim Apollo

Hear the echoes of historic performances by David Bowie and the Beatles in this storied live entertainment venue in Hammersmith, with grand art-deco elements and an enormous pipe organ still intact.

Bush Theatre

An intimate and important London theatre in Shepherd's Bush that nurtures new playwright voices, many of which go on to take the famous West End circuit by storm.

African-Caribbean Culture

Notting Hill Carnival

Put on your dancing shoes for some Caribbean-flavoured bacchanalia at Europe's largest street festival, held every August bank holiday in Notting Hill and beyond. Expect steel drum-pounding paraders, live-music stages and more.

Black History Walks

There are several London areas covered by the award-winning Black History Walks, but the two-hour Notting Hill tour is one of the most essential and illuminating.

Cafes, Gastropubs & Grub

The Cheese Barge £

Take your taste for cheese up a notch inside a moored double-decker boat on the Paddington Basin. Find wallet-friendly cheeseboards, small plates and grown-up grilled cheese sandwiches.

Lowry & Baker £

Portobello Rd's cosy neighbourhood café. The mismatched crockery adds a dollop of fun eccentricity, while breakfast and brunch offerings such as ricotta-topped brioche and mushrooms on toast deliver the goods.

Fulham Palace

Antipode £

Get some reprieve from Hammersmith's bustle inside this Australian artisanal coffee shop. The kimchi and mature cheddar toastie is the star dish on the all-day menu.

Crab Tree ££

A classic if not upscale riverside pub in Fulham, with a strong dining menu. In warmer climes, the massive Orchard Beer Garden (and summer barbecues) is a local favourite.

The Cow ££

Gourmet pub staple in Notting Hill proudly offering up Guinness, oysters and seasonal seafood. Walls are adorned with quirky murals and cow portraits.

Harwood Arms £££

Gastropubs in London might be an ongoing trend, but the Harwood Arms – a Michelin-starred restaurant based in an unassuming residential street near Fulham Broadway – sets the bar.

Trailer Happiness £

A souped-up, rum-focused tiki bar on Portobello Rd of international acclaim. The potent island-themed drinks pair wonderfully with Caribbean dishes from Tetri Roti Shop, the bar's resident kitchen.

River Café £££

Far fancier than your average 'cafe', Hammersmith's Thames-hugging fine Italian restaurant has been a London institution since 1987. Anticipate daily changing menus and an all-Italian wine list.

Caractère £££

The haute French-Italian menu in this smart-casual Westbourne Park Rd restaurant reflects the heritage of wife-and-husband chefs Emily Roux (granddaughter of iconic French chef Michel Roux Jr) and Diego Ferrari.

Bush Theatre

The Ginstitute ££

Head to Portobello Rd's four-storey temple of gin for masterclasses and tastings, as well as regular restaurant and bar offerings (which serves other spirits, too).

For Shopaholics

Couverture & The Garbstore

Comprising two shops over three floors, Couverture (womenswear and home products) and The Garbstore (menswear) is a smart concept store in Notting Hill celebrating independent and international fashion brands.

Stuarts London

For over 50 years, this premier menswear store in Shepherd's Bush Market has been a force in British fashion trends. Find globally sourced designer duds and some vintage selections, too.

Found And Vision

You're likely to spot a celebrity on the hunt for marvellous preloved fashions at this Portobello Rd boutique, selling high-end finds from vintage Chanel hats to floral Kenzo dresses.

Scan to find more things to do in Notting Hill & West London online

BRIXTON, PECKHAM & SOUTH LONDON

CITY LIFE | CULTURE | PARKS

Experience Brixton, Peckham & South London online

Bonus Online Experience

▸ **See the New Elephant & Castle**

BRIXTON, PECKHAM & SOUTH LONDON
Trip Builder

TAKE YOUR PICK OF MUST-SEES AND HIDDEN GEMS

Once you've gotten your fill of central London's famous attractions, venture south of the River Thames for a more suburban side of the city. Some of London's most diverse and dynamic neighbourhoods are located here, along with a collection of exceptional (and less touristy) urban parks and food markets.

Neighbourhood Notes

Best for Affordable food and drinks, multicultural shops and charming green spaces.

Transport Victoria, Northern and Overground lines, plus National Rail trains.

Getting Around An extensive bus network will take you to hard-to-reach areas.

Tip The South is a sprawled collection of distinct neighbourhoods, so allot several days to explore.

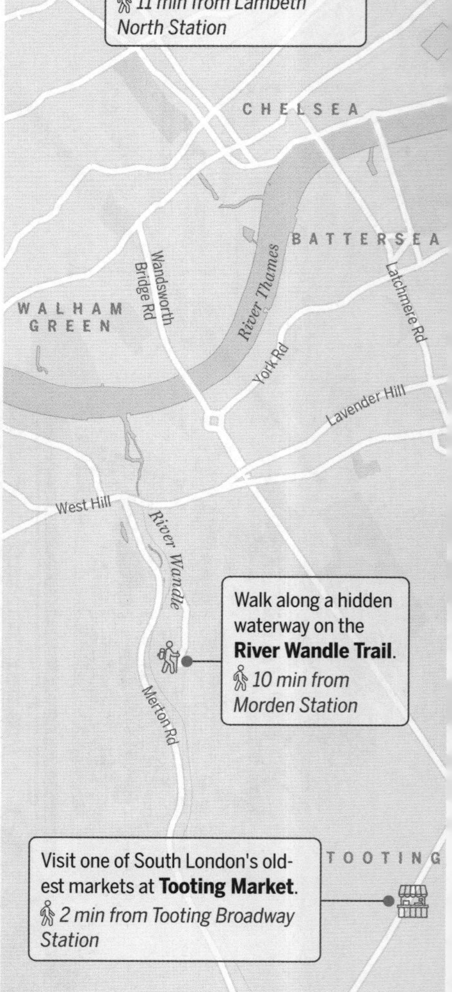

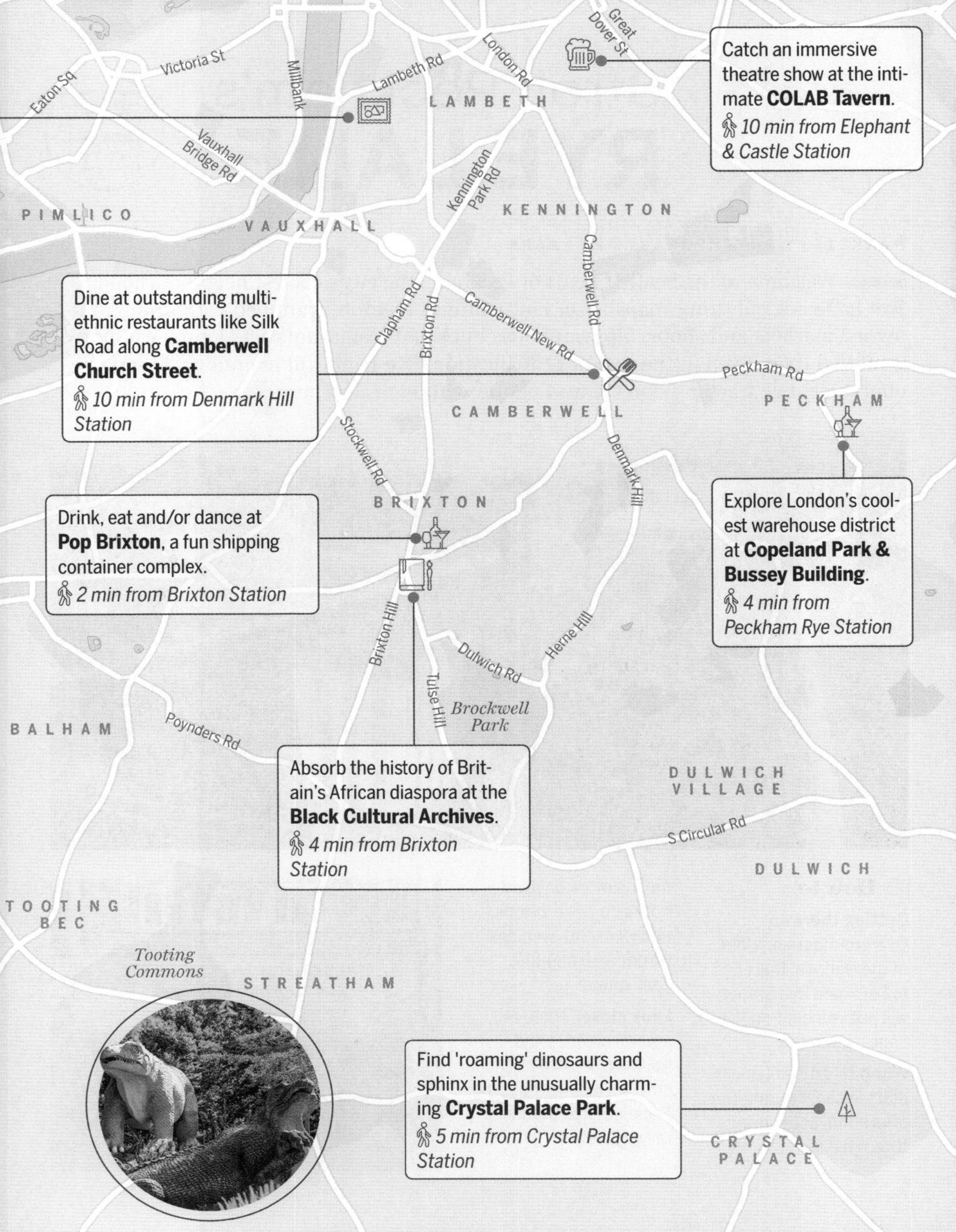
Catch an immersive theatre show at the intimate **COLAB Tavern**.
10 min from Elephant & Castle Station
Dine at outstanding multiethnic restaurants like Silk Road along **Camberwell Church Street**.
10 min from Denmark Hill Station
Drink, eat and/or dance at **Pop Brixton**, a fun shipping container complex.
2 min from Brixton Station
Explore London's coolest warehouse district at **Copeland Park & Bussey Building**.
4 min from Peckham Rye Station
Absorb the history of Britain's African diaspora at the **Black Cultural Archives**.
4 min from Brixton Station
Find 'roaming' dinosaurs and sphinx in the unusually charming **Crystal Palace Park**.
5 min from Crystal Palace Station
Great Dover St
London Rd
Lambeth Rd
Victoria St
Eaton Sq
Millbank
LAMBETH
Vauxhall Bridge Rd
Kennington Park Rd
KENNINGTON
PIMLICO
VAUXHALL
Camberwell Rd
Clapham Rd
Brixton Rd
Camberwell New Rd
Peckham Rd
PECKHAM
CAMBERWELL
Stockwell Rd
Denmark Hill
BRIXTON
Herne Hill
Brixton Hill
Dulwich Rd
Tulse Hill
Brockwell Park
BALHAM
Poynders Rd
DULWICH VILLAGE
S Circular Rd
DULWICH
TOOTING BEC
Tooting Commons
STREATHAM
CRYSTAL PALACE

38 Stroll Peckham's RYE LANE

MARKETS | CONTEMPORARY ART | BARS

Welcome to the beating heart of Peckham, the city's coolest neighbourhood. Rye Lane is a pulsating snapshot of multicultural London, crammed with immigrant-owned markets and shops, hip warehouse hubs and restaurants set along a winding graffitied road. Even in the face of gentrification, Rye Lane still maintains its scrappy, effervescent character – don't leave London without a stop here.

DAVID JENSEN/ALAMY STOCK PHOTO ©

How to

Getting there An Overground train or one of the National Rail lines to Peckham Rye Station will put you right on Rye Lane's doorstep.

When to go The Lane is at its liveliest during the afternoon. Late spring through early autumn means more daylight hours on the rooftops, and weekend evenings thrum with nightlife year-round.

Look closer There are several arcades and nooks to explore off the strip, including under the Peckham Rye Station railway arches.

PAT TUSON/ALAMY STOCK PHOTO ©

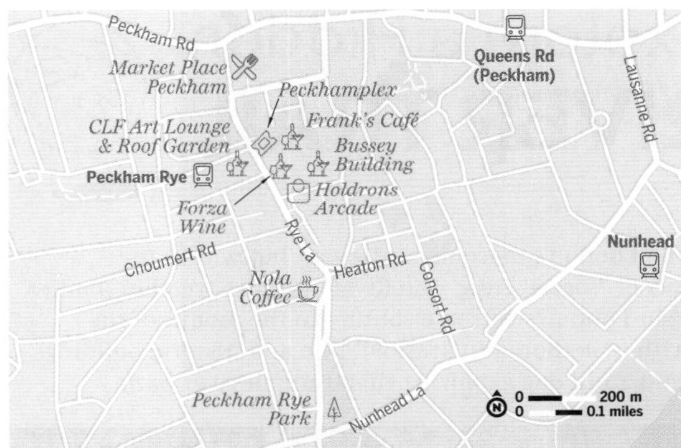

Left Rooftop cinema on the Bussey Building **Bottom left** Peckham Afro Foods Ltd

Rooftop-hopping Rye Lane might have London's tightest cluster of cool rooftop venues. The classic picks are based between two neighbouring warehouses-turned-multifaceted-hubs. The **Bussey Building** has a popular tropical-themed rooftop bar, and a separate rooftop cinema open in warmer months. Across the street, a car park's roof has become an essential hipster hang-out and arm of an arts organisation – **Frank's Café** – while affording the ultimate London skyline vista. The new kids down the block are **CLF Art Lounge & Roof Garden** – it might be inferior views-wise, but it's the most intimate and soulful of the bunch – and the fêted indoor-outdoor Italian bar **Forza Wine**, crowning a converted brick building with co-working spaces and a basement nightclub.

Small world From Nigerian cafes and Chinese grocers to Afghan bargain stores and vegan Caribbean joints, Rye Lane's multicultural character is second to none. People from across the globe – many of whom are of African and Caribbean descent – convene on the bustling lane which was once considered the 'Oxford St' of South London. The shops and ethnic food options are endless: whether you step inside the new **Market Place Peckham** for international food stalls and specialist boutique shops, order cheap but quality curry from **Asian Takeaway** or venture off-street to Choumert Rd's concentrated row of African restaurants and bars, you'll feel like you've travelled the world within a half-mile stretch.

Rye Lane's Essential Spots

Box Holdrons Arcade

A quirky little arcade with some really great stores. It's got vintage shops, its own radio station – it's a cool little melange of old and new Peckham.

Peckhamplex

A total neighbourhood classic. It's a cavernous cinema with super-cheap tickets (just £4.99 for standard showings and £5.99 for 3D releases) whenever you visit.

Nola Coffee

Some of the best coffee that you can get your hands on in South London. The venue is a nice, airy space to chill out, or you can take your coffee over to nearby Peckham Rye Park.

■ **Tips by Julianna Barnaby,** *editor of London x London, @londonxldn*

39 Explore a Hidden RIVER TRAIL

NATURE | HISTORY | TRAILS

The Thames might be London's marquee waterway, but within its tributary network lies a bucolic 'secret' river. The River Wandle stretches 9 miles northwest from Croydon – in London's extreme south – to the mouth of the Thames at Wandsworth, with a plethora of parks, wildlife and historic buildings in between. Prepare to spend a full day exploring this tranquil river path.

ABDUL SHAKOOR/GETTY IMAGES ©

How to

Getting there There are several options for trail access, depending on your preferred total walking distance. For a 6-mile route, start at Morden (via Northern Line's Morden Station) and walk your way up to Wandsworth where the Rivers Thames and Wandle meet.

When to go March to May for blooms; June to August for warm walks; and October to November for foliage.

Find your way A trail map is essential; visit the Wandle Valley Regional Park Trust (wandlevalleypark.co.uk/map) website for mobile- and print-friendly itineraries.

PAUL GAPPER/ALAMY STOCK PHOTO ©

Left River Wandle Trail
Bottom left Carshalton Water Tower

Nature and preservation The **River Wandle Trail** has an impressive network of parks and reserves on offer, led by the efforts of environmental charities. You might never guess on a stroll through the 4.5-hectare pastoral **Wandle Meadow Nature Park** – with tadpole-filled marsh ponds and abundant flora – that it was once a sewage plant. **Wilderness Island**, wrapped within the river's two arms, was an important industrial mill site and later a pleasure garden. Today the reserve is a trail highlight for wanderers exploring its ponds, wildflower meadows and woodlands. One of the newest River Wandle–adjacent parks to open is the lush **Watermeads Nature Reserve**, having been closed to the public for 100 years until 2015.

Walking through time Along the trail are relics of riverside life dating as far back as the 12th century. The **Merton Priory** – a once-significant English monastery founded in 1114 – became obsolete for centuries until archaeologists unearthed the foundations of its **Chapter House**, which is now a heritage museum. The **Carshalton Water Tower** was a lavish private estate pump house in the 18th century, and you can see its preserved saloon, orangery and a bath chamber with hand-painted Delft blue tiles on Sunday-only guided tours. To learn why the Wandle was once known as London's 'hardest-working river' (when it had 90 working mills on its banks), veer off-path along London Rd for the **Wandle Industrial Museum**.

Must-See Trail Sightings

Inside Morden Hall Park is the **Wetlands Boardwalk**, a series of wooden, accessible pathways that zigzag over the wetlands fed by the river.

Merton Abbey, once an important textile mill factory, has been transformed as a modern entertainment hub with a craft market, theatre and a restaurant.

Watch for sections with **fast-flowing streams**; that flow helped power over 90 mills to produce products such as gunpowder, paper, wheat and snuff in the area's heyday.

There's an old bell in **Wandsworth** that is chimed at high and low waters, and bears the inscription 'I AM RUNG BY THE TIDES'.

■ **Tips by David Fathers,** *local author and illustrator of several London guidebooks, @fathers_walks_london*

40 Meander Brixton Village MARKET

SHOPPING | MARKETS | CULTURE

Brixton Village Market (which includes the adjoining Market Row) is an essential stop when visiting the ever-busy Brixton neighbourhood. It's South London's premier international bazaar of affordable boutique shops, grocery goods, cocktail bars and a range of small restaurants – some of which are among London's finest – all underneath covered, colourful arcades.

ELENACHAYKINAPHOTOGRAPHY/SHUTTERSTOCK ©

How to

Getting there It's a short walk from the Victoria Line's Brixton Station or the separate National Rail Brixton Station.

When to go The market's mostly indoor layout provides year-round, all-weather appeal. Avoid Sunday and Monday as many shops are closed.

Bright idea Step out and peruse the lively Electric Avenue Market (closed Sunday), based on a pedestrianised strip famed as the world's first electricity lit market street in the late 1800s.

CKTRAVELS.COM/SHUTTERSTOCK ©

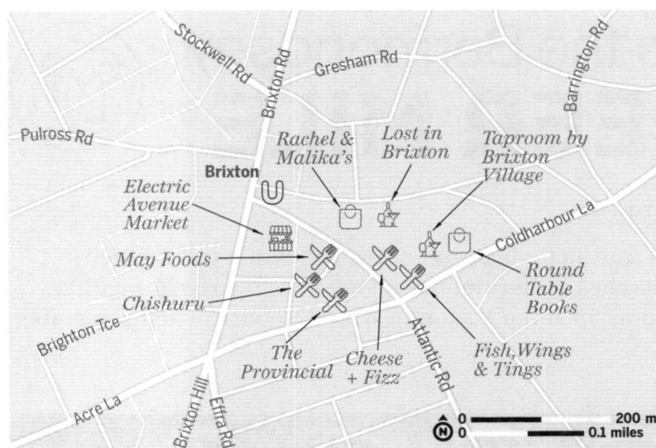

Left Brixton Village Market
Bottom left Taproom by Brixton Village

Happier hours The majority of the Village comprises restaurants or shops, but don't overlook its small but noteworthy bar and nightlife options. Head to **Taproom by Brixton Village** for craft beers sourced from independent South London breweries, or pair your champagne with gooey truffle raclette at **Cheese + Fizz**. The market's splashiest new hangout is **Lost in Brixton**, a casual, covered rooftop terrace bar discreetly tucked in a back corner (security guards manning the entrance give it away).

The Caribbean and African experience Brixton has had a strong Black British presence since the 20th century, and this market – formerly known as Glanville Arcade – was once a vibrant reflection of this. Today both the area and market have expanded into a more global, if not gentrified, profile, but there are still Caribbean and African market vendors from which to absorb Brixton's cultural legacy. For Caribbean food, start with an alfresco meal at **Fish, Wings & Tings** for Trinidadian-style fare, or head next door to **Eat of Eden** for all-vegan dishes like pumpkin and sweet potato curry. Hankering for African cuisine? **May Foods** serves authentic Ghanaian dishes, while **Chishuru** – from award-winning Nigerian chef Adejoké Bakare – dazzles with an elevated, inventive West African menu. For travellers with kids, the inclusion-driven **Round Table Books** is a delight, and avid shoppers should pop into **Rachel & Malika's** for gorgeous West African crafts and gifts.

Best Market Eats

The Provincial

Latin American cuisine meets Spanish tapas at this cosy restaurant. Try the Cali or Medellin brunch with a mimosa or fresh squeezed juice with ginger for the perfect morning or early afternoon start.

Senzala Crêperie

This Brixton staple serves up the best French crêpes and galettes with a Brazilian flair. Creative offerings like the King Prawn Cajun or the Rosa Squash crêpe are sure to make your taste buds dance.

Kaosarn

This award-winning Thai restaurant plays no games with its succulent offerings of gang keaw waan, chu chi, pad thai and more. Don't forget the sticky rice.

■ **Tips by Eulanda Shead Osagiede,** *Head of Content at Hey! Dip Your Toes In @dipyourtoesin*

41 Go the Bermondsey BEER MILE

BEER | WALKING TOUR | HISTORY

You can find London's ultimate beer bar crawl beneath a fragmented series of Victorian railway arches in Bermondsey. There are nearly 20 quality micro-breweries and taprooms within a 1.25-mile stretch to visit – just remember to pace yourself.

JESSICA LONG/ALAMY STOCK PHOTO ©

How to

Getting there It's a quick walk to the main strip from Bermondsey Station, on the Tube's Jubilee Line. The National Rail–serviced South Bermondsey Station awaits at the Mile's extreme end.

When to go Saturday is the best bet for open-to-the-public brewery hours, with Friday a close second.

Food fuel Before your beer quest, anchor your stomach with food from the nearby top-rated Maltby Street Market.

Tapped Out

Not into beer? There are a few alternatives. On the mile's western end are two gin houses – **Bermondsey Distillery** and **London Distillery** – and London's first-ever urban cidery, **Hawkes Cidery & Taproom**, where you can do flight tastings, take cider-making masterclasses or simply quaff a tasty pint or three.

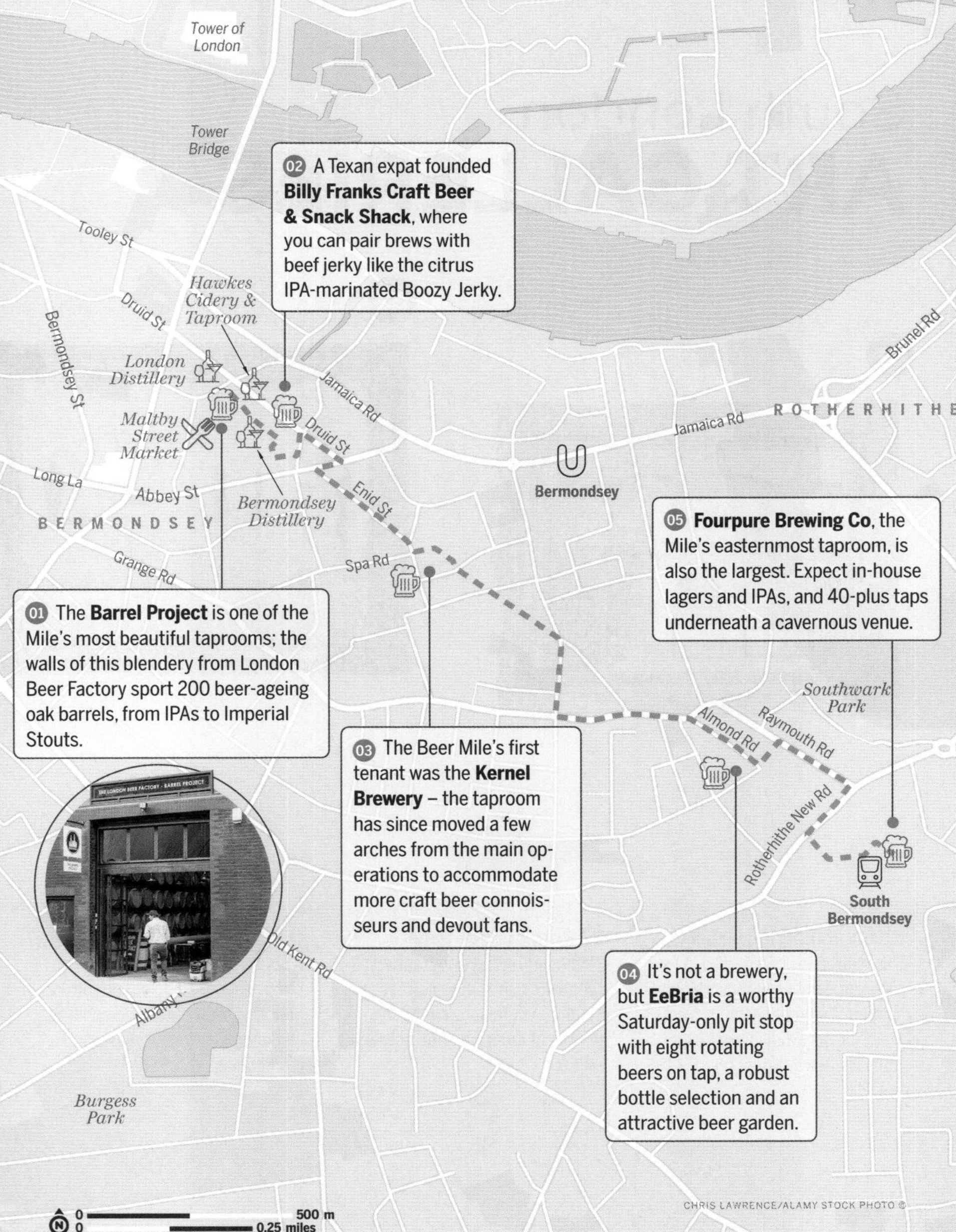
Tower of London
Tower Bridge
Tooley St
Druid St
Bermondsey St
Hawkes Cidery & Taproom
London Distillery
Maltby Street Market
Jamaica Rd
Druid St
Long La
Abbey St
BERMONDSEY
Bermondsey Distillery
Enid St
Grange Rd
Spa Rd
Bermondsey
Jamaica Rd
ROTHERHITHE
Brunel Rd
Southwark Park
Almond Rd
Raymouth Rd
Rotherhithe New Rd
South Bermondsey
Old Kent Rd
Albany
Burgess Park
02 A Texan expat founded **Billy Franks Craft Beer & Snack Shack**, where you can pair brews with beef jerky like the citrus IPA-marinated Boozy Jerky.
01 The **Barrel Project** is one of the Mile's most beautiful taprooms; the walls of this blendery from London Beer Factory sport 200 beer-ageing oak barrels, from IPAs to Imperial Stouts.
THE LONDON BEER FACTORY · BARREL PROJECT
03 The Beer Mile's first tenant was the **Kernel Brewery** – the taproom has since moved a few arches from the main operations to accommodate more craft beer connoisseurs and devout fans.
05 **Fourpure Brewing Co**, the Mile's easternmost taproom, is also the largest. Expect in-house lagers and IPAs, and 40-plus taps underneath a cavernous venue.
04 It's not a brewery, but **EeBria** is a worthy Saturday-only pit stop with eight rotating beers on tap, a robust bottle selection and an attractive beer garden.
0 500 m
0 0.25 miles
N
CHRIS LAWRENCE/ALAMY STOCK PHOTO ©

South London
ART GALLERIES

02

01

01 South London Gallery
This renowned philanthropy-driven gallery in Camberwell spearheads numerous community art projects while housing works from juggernauts like Tracey Emin.

02 Bermondsey Gallery
Find paintings, photography, sculptures and several other art mediums in this independent temple of emerging and esteemed artists.

03 Gasworks
A contemporary arts hub in Kennington focused on cross-cultural dialogue, with renowned exhibits, workshops, artist studios and residencies.

03

05

04 Newport Street Gallery
Art icon Damien Hirst opened this stunning industrial-style gallery in Vauxhall, putting his breadth of work (and his contemporaries) on grand display.

05 Dulwich Picture Gallery
Designed by English architect Sir John Soane, the world's first purpose-built public art gallery remains culturally significant some 200 years after its opening.

Listings

BEST OF THE REST

The Great Outdoors

Brockwell Park

This tranquil, sprawling park just south of Brixton has trails, playgrounds, duck ponds and the locally loved Brockwell Lido. Find a high point on the grassy terrain for sweeping London skyline views.

Battersea Park

A famous, family-friendly park straddling the Thames with a children's zoo and lake paddle boat rentals. Book via Go Ape *(goape.co.uk)* for ziplining and treetop thrills above the urban forest.

Dulwich Park

One of London's quaintest spaces since 1890 (Queen Mary was a fan). Explore woodlands and manicured gardens, rent a bicycle and enjoy sourdough pizza at the Dulwich Clock Café.

Burgess Park

Wedged between Camberwell and Peckham, this is the largest park in the Southwark borough. You'll find locals lake fishing, playing sports, grilling in dedicated barbecue areas or simply relaxing on the grass.

Crystal Palace Park

Deep in the South London suburbs is a noted park with maze garden, urban farm, boating lake, skating park, and beguiling 30-plus collection of Victorian-era dinosaur sculptures.

Top Meals

Tiwa N Tiwa £

It gets no more authentically Nigerian than this no-frills spot tucked off Peckham Rd. The *suya* (grilled, sliced beef crowned with fiery spices, onions and tomatoes) is a knockout dish.

Kudu ££

Head to Peckham's Queen's Rd for gourmet South African plates in a retro-glam dining room. Brunches are especially popular, with Bloody Mary jugs to pair with boerewors rolls and peri-peri chicken.

Trinity £££

Clapham's Michelin-starred restaurant shines with inventive Modern European dishes and a faultless service staff. The aptly named Upstairs at Trinity, one floor above, provides a more casual and wallet-friendly experience.

Silk Road £

A rare taste of Xinjiang (a northwest China province) at wildly affordable prices on Camberwell Church St. Sample dumplings, cumin-dusted lamb skewers and hearty noodle soups in an unpretentious, communal setting.

Restaurant Story £££

Block out several hours for chef Tom Sellers' Michelin-starred gastronomic theatre near Tower Bridge. It's a contemporary, no-menu tasting experience of up to 10 courses, so expect elements of surprise throughout.

For Theatre Buffs

Tara Theatre

Conceived after the racially motivated murder of a Sikh boy in London in 1977, this acclaimed Wandsworth theatre spotlights South Asian

CKTRAVELS.COM/SHUTTERSTOCK ©

Dulwich Park

thespian talent, tackling social issues through powerful performances.

Theatre Peckham

Star Wars' John Boyega got his start here: a noted programme focused on nurturing young, underrepresented talent. Catch a show in the modern 200-seater to spot the next big star.

Bread & Roses Theatre

An innovative fringe pub theatre in Clapham, showing a wide range of performances inside a 60-seat venue. Have post-theatre drinks downstairs at Bread & Roses' inviting beer garden.

COLAB Tavern

A dedicated immersive theatre company inside of a former pub near Elephant & Castle.

Markets & Hang-Outs

Mercato Metropolitano

Roam this trendy community market's endless maze of food and drink stalls at an abandoned paper factory site near Elephant & Castle; there's an on-site brewery and jazz club, too.

Prince of Peckham

An enormous 'Welcome to Peckham' sign lures Queen's Rd passers-by into this quirky Black-owned pub. Come for delicious Caribbean food, generous happy hours and a fun, diverse crowd.

Railway Tavern

Tucked underneath Tulse Hill Station is a friendly neighbourhood haunt with an enormous garden patio and eclectic events line-up, including reggae and soul DJ sets and quiz nights.

Pop Brixton

In the shadow of Brixton Village Market is a hip community initiative hosting indie food stalls and bars, shops and more in a lively stacked shipping container complex.

Maltby Street Market

Lined underneath a Victorian archway near London Bridge, this weekends-only market beloved by gourmands and trendsters hosts a wide range of eats, from gyoza and Spanish tapas to pâtisserie treats.

Pop Brixton

East Street Market

For an un-touristy market experience, ease your way inside Walworth's iconic and cramped stall corridor for fresh produce, assorted goods and mostly African clothing. Best for bargain hunters.

Tooting Market

A Tooting High St stalwart for over 90 years, with a global range of vendors. Eat at several food stations, shop around or sip gin cocktails from a micro-distillery.

Herne Hill Market

While away a Sunday afternoon at Herne Hill's top attraction. The pedestrianised strip just outside of Herne Hill Station features artisanal crafts, vintage items and gourmet bites.

Cultural Exhibits

Black Cultural Archives

One of the UK's foremost spaces highlighting the Black British experience. Based in the heart of Brixton, the national heritage centre has a revolving calendar of insightful (and free) exhibits.

Southwark Heritage Centre & Walworth Library

A spiffy new-for-2021 cultural centre near Elephant & Castle Station, with exhibitions and artefacts showcasing the local area's rich history.

Scan to find more things to do in Brixton, Peckham & South London online

DAY TRIPS

HERITAGE | CULTURE | FOOD

DAY TRIPS
Trip Builder

TAKE YOUR PICK OF MUST-SEES AND HIDDEN GEMS

In an hour or less, you can travel from London to fascinating historic cities such Oxford, Cambridge, Windsor or Canterbury, where you can marvel at two of the oldest universities in the English-speaking world, a 1000-year-old castle and an even older cathedral.

Trip Notes

Best for History, heritage, culture and food.

Transport Well connected from London with daily direct trains.

Getting around Easy to navigate on foot or bike. Local transport services are efficient and inexpensive.

Tip Leave early and return late to get the cheapest fares and make the best of your time.

Leicester

Visit the **Divinity School** and marvel at its Perpendicular Gothic architecture featured in *Harry Potter and The Philosopher's Stone*.
15 min walk from Oxford Station

Tour **Christ Church College** to see the real-life inspiration for *Alice in Wonderland* and *Harry Potter*.
20 min walk from Oxford Station

Oxford

Explore **Windsor Castle** and visit the vaults which hold the bodies of Henry VIII and his third wife Jane Seymour.
7 min walk from Windsor & Eton Riverside Station

Reading

Portsmouth

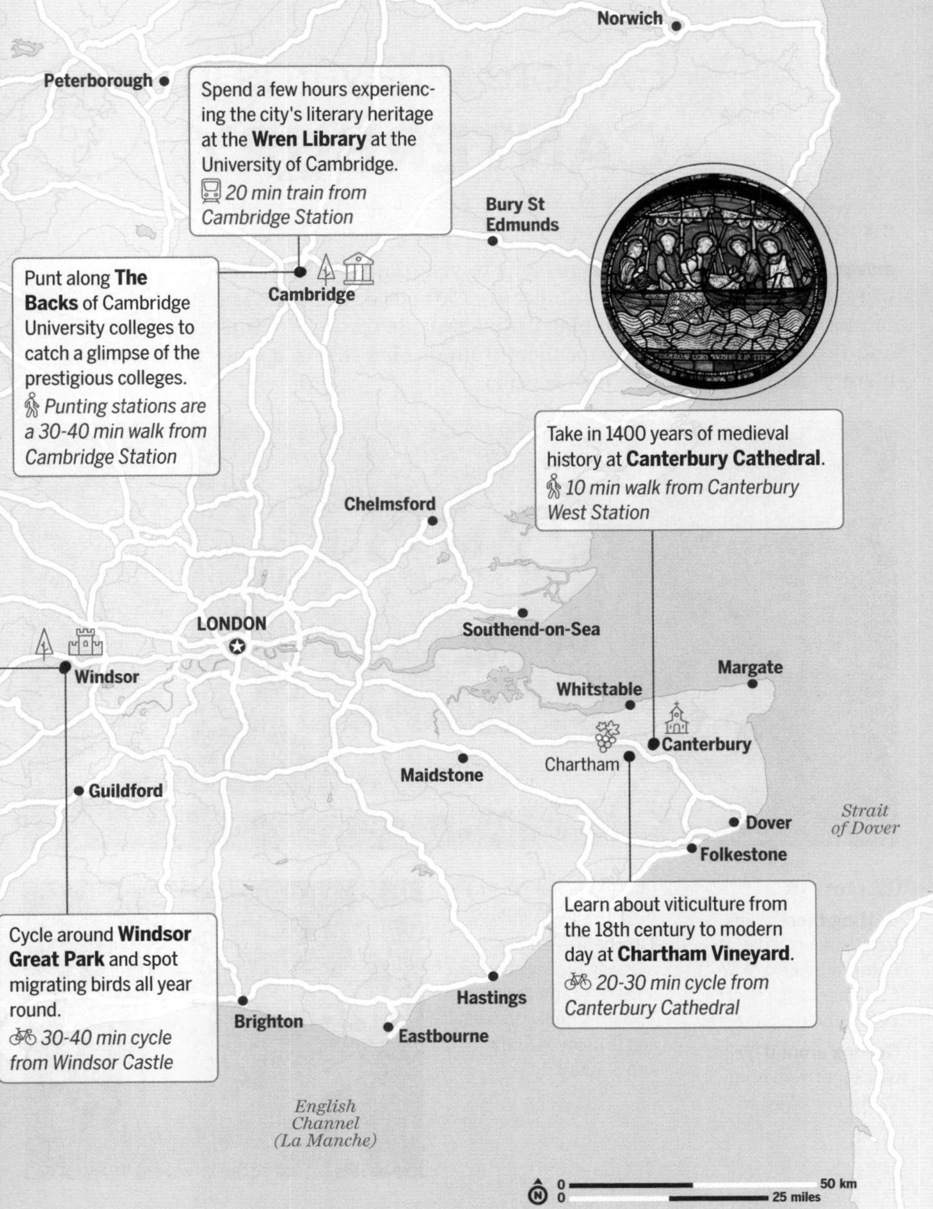

Norwich
Peterborough
Spend a few hours experiencing the city's literary heritage at the **Wren Library** at the University of Cambridge.
20 min train from Cambridge Station
Bury St Edmunds
Cambridge
Punt along **The Backs** of Cambridge University colleges to catch a glimpse of the prestigious colleges.
Punting stations are a 30-40 min walk from Cambridge Station
Take in 1400 years of medieval history at **Canterbury Cathedral**.
10 min walk from Canterbury West Station
Chelmsford
LONDON
Southend-on-Sea
Windsor
Margate
Whitstable
Canterbury
Chartham
Maidstone
Guildford
Strait of Dover
Dover
Folkestone
Cycle around **Windsor Great Park** and spot migrating birds all year round.
30-40 min cycle from Windsor Castle
Learn about viticulture from the 18th century to modern day at **Chartham Vineyard**.
20-30 min cycle from Canterbury Cathedral
Hastings
Brighton
Eastbourne
English Channel (La Manche)
0 50 km
0 25 miles

42 Explore Vineyards in CANTERBURY

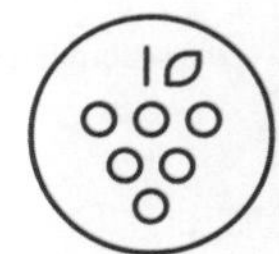

HISTORY I VINEYARDS I CYCLING

There are several good reasons to visit Canterbury in Kent: it's home to England's first cathedral, Canterbury Cathedral; the town is less than 30 minutes by car from the popular British seaside towns of Whitstable, Margate and Broadstairs; and it's just a short train or bike ride to a vineyard that has a history dating back to the 14th century.

JACOBS STOCK PHOTOGRAPHY LTD/GETTY IMAGES ©

How to

Getting there Trains from London arrive at Canterbury East or West Stations, both a short walk from the cathedral.

Getting around It's a quick train ride from Canterbury West to Chartham Station, where the vineyard is located.

Tip There is a daily morning prayer open to all at the cathedral at 7.30am Monday to Friday and 9.15am Saturday and Sunday.

INSPIRED BY MAPS/SHUTERSTOCK ©

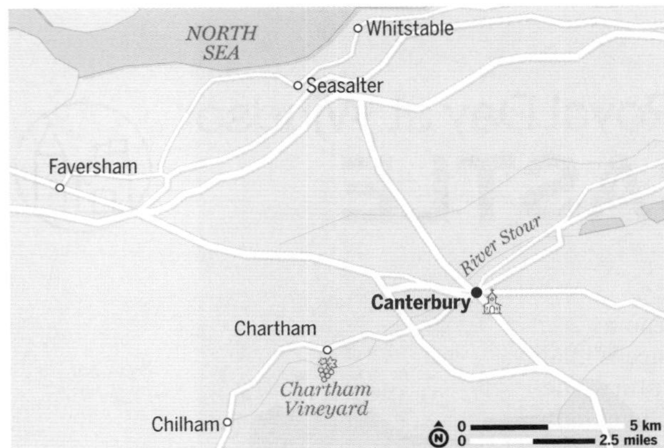

England's first cathedral It would be tough to visit Canterbury and miss the 1400-year-old, 72m-high **Canterbury Cathedral**. Sometimes referred to as 'England in stone'. it has magnificent Gothic architecture, stunning gardens and as many historically important artefacts – paintings, manuscripts, photographs and records – as you might expect from a World Heritage Site. This is one of the most visited places in the UK so expect a well-regulated crowd. Tours of the cathedral can be booked in advance via the website.

Enjoy English winemaking From the cathedral it's a scenic 6km, traffic-free bike ride along **River Stour** to Chartham and its vineyard. Kent has a long history of viticulture dating back to the Domesday Book which recorded a survey of England and Wales under the orders of William the Conqueror. **Chartham Vineyard** has records dating back to 1303 as well as buildings dating from the 18th century. Take a guided vineyard tour and learn about the traditional and modern approaches to viticulture and winemaking. Group tours and tastings are available at 11am and 2pm on Saturday only. Tours with tastings cost £15 per person and must be booked in advance via the website.

Left Variety of tasting wines
Bottom left Interior of Canterbury Cathedral

Chartham Vineyard's Best Wines

Blanc de Blancs (2018) A delicate sparkling with flavours of peach, citrus and a fine mousse made from 100% Chardonnay grapes hand-picked in late September 2018.

Pinot Noir (2018) A delicate yet firm, silky, rich red with Morello cherry notes made from 100% Pinot Noir grapes hand-picked in October 2018.

Bacchus (2019) A floral, aromatic white made from 100% Bacchus grapes hand-picked in September 2019.

Pinot Gris (2019) A high-quality dry white with gentle flavours and texture made from 100% Pinot Gris grapes hand-picked in October 2019.

Some wines may be replaced with later vintages.

Recommended by Roz and Richard Goodenough, *co-owners of Chartham Vineyard, charthamvineyard.co.uk*

43 A Royal Day at Windsor CASTLE

CASTLE | NATURE | HISTORY

Windsor Castle has been a residence to 39 monarchs since William the Conquerer in the 11th century. The town itself is a cosmopolitan hang-out with great shopping, restaurants and cafes, all with the oldest and largest occupied castle in the world as a backdrop. The Changing of the Guard ceremony is an unmissable highlight.

How to

Getting there Frequent daily trains from London's Waterloo and Paddington Stations run to stations in Windsor; the journey takes between 30 minutes and an hour.

Getting around See the sights on foot; there are also hop-on, hop-off buses around the town. Windsor Great Park is about 8km south of the castle; buses take around half an hour to get here or it's a quick ride in a taxi.

When to go Any time of year; on Tuesday, Thursday or Saturday to see the Changing of the Guard.

The **Changing of the Guard** ceremony is surely the highlight for any visitor to Windsor. The guards march through the town centre, in full regalia and accompanied by a band, from 10.45am and arrive at the castle at 11am. If you want to watch the rest of the ceremony, which happens within the castle, you will need to buy a ticket.

With an entry ticket, it is possible to visit the state apartments, the semi-state rooms and the Waterloo Chamber and see **Queen Mary's Dolls' House**, built by British architect Sir Edwin Lutyens with contributions

Top right The Royal Guard in Windsor **Right** St George's Chapel

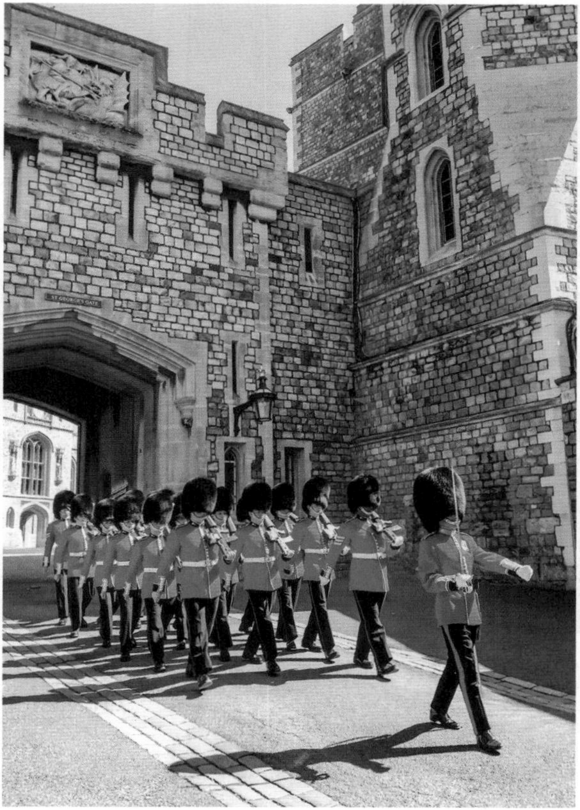

NUI7711/SHUTTERSTOCK ©

KIEV.VICTOR/SHUTTERSTOCK ©

Bird-Spotting at Windsor Great Park

January–April Fieldfare, kingfisher, redwing

May–August Chiffchaff, swift, ring-necked parakeet

September–December Goldfinch, common buzzard, great spotted woodpecker

■ **Tips by Flock Together**, *a birdwatching collective for people of colour, Instagram @flocktogether.world*

from over 1500 artists, craftspeople and manufacturers. You can also enter **St George's Chapel**, where King Henry VIII and third wife Jane Seymour rest.

From the castle, **Windsor Great Park** is a bus or taxi ride away. Places of particular interest within the park include the **Long Walk**, which is iconic for its view of Windsor Castle in the distance. You can also cycle through parts of the park; it's on National Cycle Route Network 4. The rest of the park is best enjoyed on foot. The **Savill Garden**, **Valley Gardens** and **Virginia Water** are truly enjoyable and **Queen Anne's Ride & Stag Meadow** is great for a picnic. Alternatively, the **Virginia Water Pavilion Cafe** makes for a good pit stop for lunch.

Windsor Great Park, large parts of which are designated as conservation areas, is also great for **bird-spotting** – carry your binoculars.

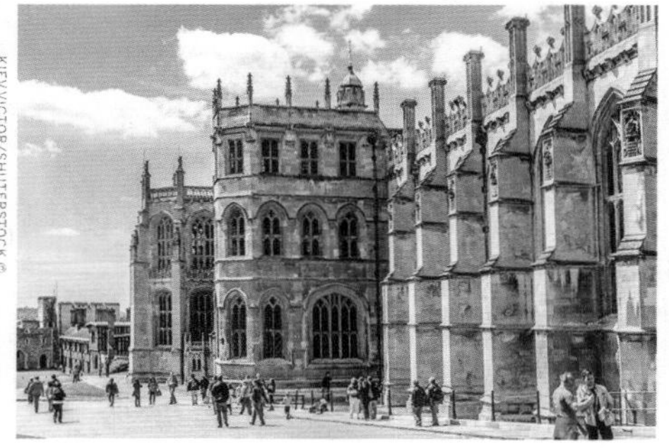

44 Follow the Cambridge FOOD TRAIL

FOOD I HERITAGE I CYCLING

Cambridge's local food scene is a thing of beauty that makes it possible to take the less-trodden path to points of interest. The city's diverse community has created a string of inventive eateries with each experience raising the game higher.

NATHANIEL NOIR/ALAMY STOCK PHOTO ©

How to

Getting there Frequent daily direct trains connect London to Cambridge from Liverpool Street, St Pancras International and King's Cross. The average journey time is one hour and 15 minutes.

When to go Anytime of the year. There is plenty to see and do from January to December.

How much Fares from London to Cambridge start from £8 one way. You can also hire a bike for the day from Rutland Cycling at Cambridge Station.

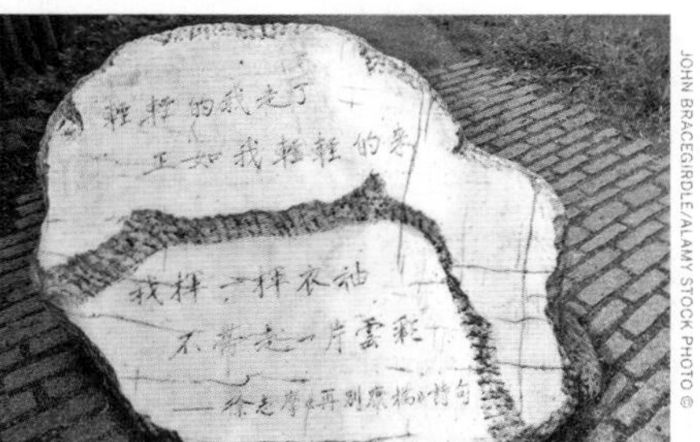

JOHN BRACEGIRDLE/ALAMY STOCK PHOTO ©

ROBERT EVANS/ALAMY STOCK PHOTO ©

Get to know Cambridge's literary side and enjoy a pint Plath, Hughes, Milne – they all walked the streets of Cambridge. Bring them to life with a visit to Trinity College's **Wren Library** at the University of Cambridge. Also worth visiting is **Sarah Key Books – The Haunted Bookshop** – it's not haunted! – to get your hands on rare children's books. Don't miss the **Cambridge University Press Bookshop**, which has been selling books since 1581. Finally, show off your literary genius at the **Pint Shop**, which was inspired by the beer houses of the 1800s, the birthplace of the modern pub. They sell bread, beer and meat – with style.

Experience student life and eat at Bread & Meat Who better to give an insight into Cambridge University life than a graduate

Punting Tour

Take a picnic punting tour with the Traditional Punting Company and raise a glass to honour the **Xu Zhimo Memorial Garden** at King's College as you pass. The famous Chinese poet studied and spent time here. The first and last lines from his poem 'Second Farewell to Cambridge' are carved on a stone in the garden.

Above left The Pint Shop **Above** Xu Zhimo Memorial Garden, King's College **Left** Sarah Key Books – The Haunted Bookshop

or alumni guide? Take a tour of the colleges with one, walk the gardens and be captivated by the long history of the university. Afterwards, head to **Bread & Meat** for wholesome food and homemade mayonnaise. The roast-meat sandwiches with poutine – the Canadian dish of French fries and cheese curds topped with gravy – is a speciality.

Hunt for vintage on Mill Rd. Spend a few hours at Mill Rd and find vintage homeware, vinyl and pre-loved clothing among the many independents which line this busy street. After a day of browsing, head across town to the rooftop of the **Varsity Hotel & Spa**. It was started by a group of Cambridge graduates and the roof terrace has the best view over the city. The hotel's own **River Bar Steakhouse & Grill** next door has a great steak and fish menu for dinner with a view.

Punt then tea at Fitzbillies Cambridge without punting is like fish without chips. Where to punt? **The Backs**. This area of

Ride & Eat at Guerilla Kitchen

Cycling is the best way to get around cycle-friendly Cambridge and you can hire a bike for the day pretty much anywhere. Follow the cycle route from Midsummer Common along the River Cam to the village of Waterbeach (10.5km one way). It's an easy scenic ride. Along the way look out for the **Guerilla Kitchen Bao Bus** (guerillakitchen.co.uk) serving buns filled with pork belly, chicken and halloumi. Pre-ordering online and collecting your baos from the bus is highly recommended as, in true guerilla style, it is never parked in the same place.

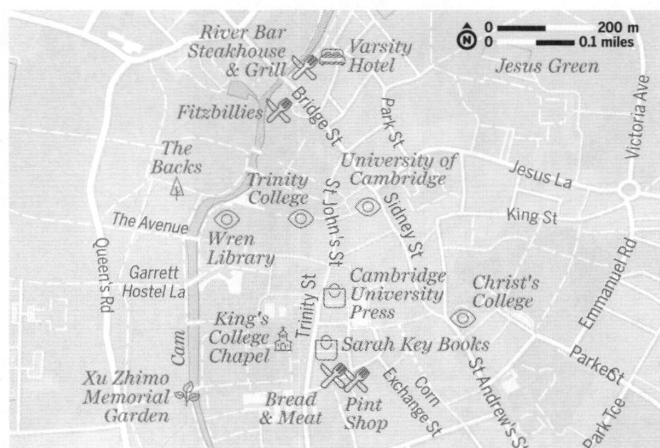

central Cambridge runs along the back of seven of Cambridge University's most prestigious colleges: Magdalene, St John's, Trinity, Trinity Hall, Clare, King's and Queen's. The land is privately owned by the colleges, so unless you're a student at Cambridge University, this is the only way to experience the romanticism of the Backs. Start at Mill Lane and head along the River Cam, passing beautiful grassy banks, low medieval bridges and the staggeringly beautiful architecture of the university's colleges. Finish with a pot of tea and a sticky bun at **Fitzbillies** (36 Bridge St), close to Magdalene Bridge punt station. This is the newer branch of the original bakery (51-52 Trumpington St), which is more than 100 years old.

Left Market square and St Mary's church. **Below** Chelsea buns in Fitzbillies

45 Literary Magic in OXFORD

FANTASY | LITERATURE | HISTORY

As you walk the streets of Oxford it's impossible to miss the presence of Harry Potter and Alice in Wonderland, who are immortalised by a connection to the University of Oxford's Christ Church College. Tour the city to see why Harry and Alice continue to draw legions of fans from around the world.

EXPOSE/SHUTTERSTOCK ©

How to

Getting there Frequent daily trains connect London's Marylebone and Paddington Stations to Oxford. The journey takes 44 to 67 minutes.

When to go Oxford is beautiful year-round. Visit in July when the city marks Alice's Day, a festival celebrating *Alice in Wonderland*.

Tip The Bodleian Library and Weston Library, which are part of the University of Oxford, are open daily to visitors.

SERG ZASTAVKIN/SHUTTERSTOCK ©

Take a tour of Christ Church College The **Great Hall** at Christ Church College has been in continuous use since the 16th century. Its rich detail inspired the Mad Tea Party in *Alice's Adventures in Wonderland* by Charles Dodgson, better known by his pen name Lewis Carroll, who lived and worked at the college for 47 years.

On the left wall of the hall you can see **Alice's Window**. The stained-glass window depicts the real-life inspiration of Alice (Alice Liddell) and the fictional Alice, wearing a blue dress, right below her. Carroll is to the right, with a dodo identifying him in the story. Portraits of Carroll and Alice's father Dean Liddell also hang in the Great Hall.

The fan vaulted staircase that leads to the Great Hall was featured in *Harry Potter* films

TERESA DAPP/PICTURE ALLIANCE/GETTY IMAGES ©

Row a Boat to Binsey

The story of *Alice's Adventures in Wonderland* started with a tale told on a boat ride on the Thames. On the boat were Charles Dodgson (Lewis Carroll), Reverend Duckworth, Alice Liddell and her sisters. Rent a rowboat at Folly Bridge and recreate their journey to the hamlet of Binsey (2.4km northwest of Oxford).

Above left The Great Hall, Christ Church College **Above right** Vaulted ceiling in the Bodley Tower **Left** Alice's Window in the Great Hall

as the entrance to Hogwarts; the Great Hall was recreated in its entirety in a studio for the films.

Bodleian Libraries & the Oxford Dodo

Even without Hollywood fame **The Bodleian Libraries** at the University of Oxford are must-visit places in Oxford. The principal library is the **Bodleian Old Library** which includes **Duke Humfrey's Library**, featured as the Hogwarts Library in the *Harry Potter* films. The **Divinity School**, unmissable for its architecture, was the Hogwarts Infirmary; the room was originally built as an exam room for the university. Both are covered by library walking tours.

Visit the **Oxford University Museum of Natural History** to see the Oxford dodo, which not only inspired the famous role in the story of Alice but is also the most complete remains of a dodo in the world. The museum houses other remarkable collections of palaeontology, art and architecture and hosts

The Perch Inn

Arrive in Binsey and enjoy British farmhouse food at the Perch Inn. This 800-year-old riverside pub, which is as old as the university, is where Lewis Carroll made his first public reading of *Alice's Adventures in Wonderland*. It has an extensive rustic garden for outdoor dining and a thatched roof. The food is a mix of traditional and modern British dishes and includes a vegan menu. The beer and wine list is impressive with a good selection of English wines. Keep an eye on the pub's social media as it host events to celebrate Alice's Day in Oxford.

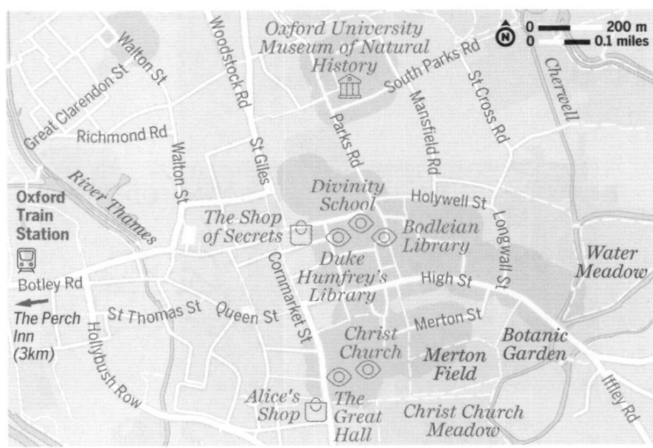

regular events. Entry is free but it's best to book tickets in advance.

Knock on Beguiling Doors There are many doors that beguile visitors to Oxford. The main door to the **Bodleian Old Library** dates back to 1602 and has the coats of arms of several of the university's colleges. The gate to the **Weston Library** is inscribed with '*Si bonus es intres, si nequam ne quaquam*' (If you are good, enter. If wicked, by no means). **Alice's Door** (not for public viewing) connects the Deanery garden at Christ Church, where Alice Liddell lived, to the cathedral garden – a gate she would have found firmly locked, much like her counterpart in Wonderland.

Shop with Alice & Harry The **Shop of Secrets** sells all things Harry Potter including clothing, jewellery and mugs. Get your hands on your own wand or Triwizard Cup. **Alice's Shop** is located inside the 15th-century building which inspired the illustrations of the Old Sheep's Shop in Lewis Carroll's sequel, *Through the Looking-Glass*. Alice Liddell and her sisters lived within walking distance of this Victorian shop of curiosities. The tiny shop now sells *Alice in Wonderland* memorabilia and has remained relatively unchanged from the outside.

Left Oxford University Museum of Natural History. **Below** A door at the Bodleian Libraries

Practicalities

Right A shop in Portobello Road Market (p160)

GRATEFUL DEAD
CONCERT
MADISON SQUARE GARDEN
NEW YORK CITY
OCTOBER 13-15-17-19
1994
FOREST HILLS MUSIC FESTIVAL
ALICE IN CHAINS
CONCERT
LIVE AT THE CONCERT HALL
TORONTO, ONTARIO, CANADA
NOVEMBER 29
THE KINKS
PLUS SPECIAL GUEST STARS
SUNDAY EVENING, MAY 12
8 PM, ROBERTSON GYM, UCSB
FLEETWOOD MAC
TUSK TOUR
UNKNOWN PLEASURES
HERE COME THE BEATLES
SAN FRANCISCO 1965
MOODY BLUES
NIGHTS IN WHITE SATIN
ROBERT PLANT
SARCASM
DAILY
KEEP CALM
20x30 cm SIGNS
1 x 14.95
2 x 24.95
3 x 34.50
ABBEY ROAD NW8
CITY OF WESTMINSTER
BAKER STREET W1
LONDON · ENGLAND
NOTTING HILL GATE
PORTOBELLO ROAD
WHISKEY
Coca-Cola 5¢
GET YOUR KICKS ON
HIGHBURY STADIUM N5
ARSENAL FOOTBALL CLUB
ST JAMES' PARK NE1
NEWCASTLE UNITED F.C.
WHITE HART LANE N17
TOTTENHAM HOTSPUR
GOODISON PARK
EVERTON
IN THE
MIND THE GAP
DRUG FREE ZONE
UNDERGROUND
LONDON
NO SMOKING
TOILET
WAY OUT
CAMDEN HIGH STREET NW1
ABBEY ROAD NW8
PORTOBELLO ROAD W11
NOTTING HILL GATE W11
PICCADILLY CIRCUS W1
BAKER STREET
ISLE OF MAN T.T. RACES
SUPERMAN
FANTASTIC FOUR
CAPTAIN AMERICA
WONDER WOMAN
Cocktail Lounge
DANGLES
the Notting Hill shopping bag:

EASY STEPS FROM THE AIRPORT TO THE CITY CENTRE

Most visitors to London arrive by air. Long-haul and business passengers normally land at Heathrow or London City, both of which are served by London's transport system and are the closest to the city centre. Southend, Gatwick, Luton and Stansted, which are located 25 to 40 miles outside of the city centre, are mostly used for shorter flights run by budget airlines like Ryanair and easyJet.

AT THE AIRPORT

ATMs
Linked to all the major bank systems (Visa, Mastercard, Maestro etc), they are in all the airports and many dispense both euros and GBP (the British Pound Sterling).

SIM Cards
Easily acquired at almost all the airports either in a WHSmith, via a SIM vending machine or Sim Local stores. These shops are open until around 10pm while the machines are accessible 24/7.

ALEXANDRE ROTENBERG/SHUTTERSTOCK ©

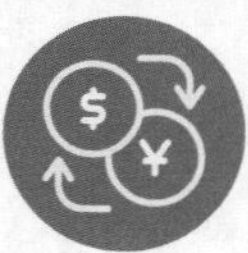

INTERNATIONAL CURRENCY EXCHANGE Outlets can be found in every airport, though rates will always be better at banks in the city.

WI-FI Free and easy to access in every airport serving London.

CHARGING STATIONS Now available in all the airports except the smaller Southend one; sometimes these are embedded into the seating.

CUSTOMS REGULATIONS

Duty-free You can bring in up to 200 cigarettes, 18L of wine or 4L of spirits from outside the UK under your personal allowance.

GETTING TO THE CITY CENTRE

Express train Express trains serve all airports except London City, which is close to central London and on the Docklands Light Railway (DLR) line. Depending on the airport, express trains take passengers to either London Liverpool St, London Victoria, King's Cross or Paddington; tickets start from £9.70 one way.

Coach There are National Express coaches from Stansted, Luton and Gatwick to central London from £5. These go to major transport hubs like Stratford, London Victoria and King's Cross and have several stops in between.

Public transport Heathrow airport is on the Underground's Piccadilly line in Zone 6 and is also served by buses into central London (5am–midnight). London City Airport is on the DLR train line that goes to central London.

HOW MUCH FOR A...

£10 for a 2 mile or 10 minute journey

£1.55 for any bus ride with a **£4.65** daily cap

£6 Heathrow to central London

Taxi There are signposted pick-up points at all the airports and taxis all accept card payments. Ride share and taxi apps usually collect customers from the drop-off zones.

Plan your journey Use the Google Maps public transport option to plan your journeys to/from the airport; the TfL Go app is useful for navigating London's public transport system.

Visitor Oyster cards Oysters are used to pay for individual trips on all TfL services and on special services like the Emirates Air Line cable car. Consider purchasing one in advance, as contactless card and phone payments are accepted but may incur bank charges. Topped-up Oyster cards can be purchased from the British Tourist Board (visitbritainshop.com) or at all airport train stations. They can be topped up at any station, ticket machines, local stores and online, or via the TfL Oyster app for those who have a UK address.

OTHER POINTS OF ENTRY

Eurostar An increasing number of international visitors arrive via Eurostar's high-speed passenger rail service, which links London St Pancras International train station with Paris, Brussels, Amsterdam and Marseilles. Fares can vary greatly, from £46 for a one-way standard-class ticket to Paris to around £276 for a fully flexible business premier ticket.

Boat-and-train combo Sail and rail options are available from Dublin and Belfast to London Euston starting from £50 for a one-way ticket. The service is provided through Transport for Wales (buytickets.tfwrail.wales). Stena Line offers something similar from London Liverpool St to any station in Holland, with prices starting at around £49 for a one-way ticket to Amsterdam with an option to purchase a cabin for the overnight ferry.

Bus Probably the cheapest way international visitors enter London is by coach. National Express offers services from Dublin, Paris, Amsterdam and Brussels to London Victoria Coach Station, with tickets starting at £10 one way. Euroline also runs routes from across Europe into London Victoria Coach Station, with single tickets starting around £36 one way from Paris.

TRANSPORT TIPS TO HELP YOU GET AROUND

TfL
Transport for London runs the city's public transport and its website (www.tfl.gov.uk) and app (TfL Go) are the best for journey planning.

UNDERGROUND
The Tube (London Underground) is the easiest way of getting around. It runs from approximately 5.30am to 12.30am, and 24 hours across five lines on Friday and Saturday.

WALKING
London is highly walkable and this is the best way to explore its historic centre, where many key sights are close to each other.

BUS
The London bus network is very extensive and efficient, although in heavy traffic it can be quicker to walk. A single adult journey costs £1.55.

OVERGROUND & DLR
Linked to the Tube are the Docklands Light Railway (DLR) and Overground lines. These connect central London to parts further afield, like Enfield in the north and Peckham in the south, or in the case of the DLR, to a specific zone like the Docklands.

CYCLING
Santander Cycles are a great way to cover shorter journeys around central London, especially now London has developed an extensive network of cycle lanes. Download the app to hire a bike. There is no expectation for cyclists to wear helmets.

THAMES CLIPPERS

One of the most pleasant ways to get around is by using the Thames Clippers boats along the River Thames where the stops are close to several of London's most significant sites, such as Big Ben, Shakespeare's Globe Theatre and Tower Bridge. The Clippers run daily between Putney in the west and Woolwich in the east, with the service spread across three zones (west, central and east). An unlimited daily ticket costs £18.40/9.20 per adult/child.

TAXIS

London's ubiquitous black cabs are available around the clock, and while they're not cheap, you can hardly leave without getting in one. It's all for the experience. You can hail one on the street or order one on a number of different apps, the most popular being Gett and Freenow.

Increasingly, Londoner's are using taxi apps to get around which are generally a lot cheaper. Uber and Bolt are the most popular in the city.

Right London Underground map **Far right** TfL Go app and Oyster card

ACCESSIBILITY

Accessibility isn't great on London's train network so plan carefully. Look for the blue and white wheelchair signs on maps for each station. Blue means step-free access from street to train and white means step-free access only to the platform; ask staff for assistance boarding the train when necessary. London's buses have limited wheelchair space and during busy periods it can be difficult to board.

PUBLIC TRANSPORT ESSENTIALS

Navigating the chaos that is London's train network.

Transport lines Include the Underground, TfL rail, Docklands Light Railway (DLR), Overground, trams (South London only) and the Emirates Air Line cable car (across the River Thames).

Colours and names London's lines have their own colours and names. The two most important for exploring the city centre are the Circle Line (yellow) and the Central Line (red).

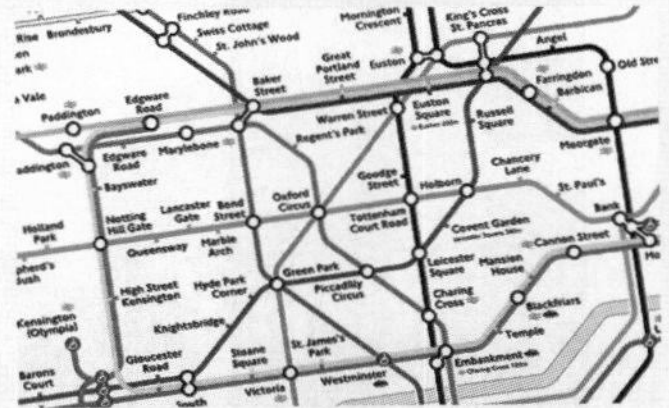

Fares London's train fares are ridiculously complex and dependent on several variables: how you pay (cash, contactless or Oyster card); the time of day you travel; the zones you travel through; and how many journeys you make. The easiest thing to do is to put your journey into the TfL website or TfL Go app and let that work out the cost. The cheapest option for lots of journeys is to load a daily or weekly travelcard onto an Oyster card either at a station ticket machine, local newsagents, online or via the Oyster app.

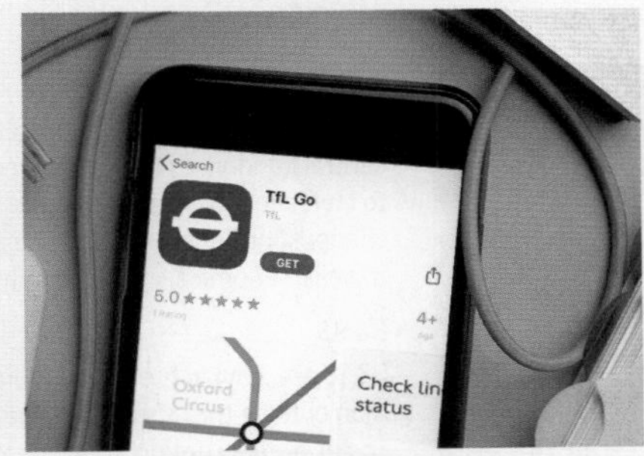

Oyster v Contactless There is no price difference in the pay-as-you-go fare when using an Oyster card or contactless options (with card or phone). But if your contactless option is via a foreign bank, then you may by charged for this and should consider a Visitors Oyster. It will also be cheaper to a load a travelcard onto that as opposed to the more expensive paper travelcard.

Transfers Line changes can be made at a number of larger stations across the network; some of the biggest include Liverpool St, Bank, Oxford Circus and King's Cross.

Maps and apps There are transport maps in every station, on every platform and on every train. You can also download PDF versions from the TfL website, or access it through the TfL Go app.

UNIQUE & LOCAL WAYS TO STAY

London is notoriously expensive for accommodation, with the cheapest options being the few hostels that remain. Try cosier, independently run B&Bs away from the centre for a warmer welcome, or a luxurious, serviced, aparthotel for the more glamorous London experience, complete with your very own concierge.

Find a place to stay in London

HOSTELS

There are fewer and fewer hostels in central London, as rental rates continue to increase. However, they remain the cheapest options, especially for solo travellers. Some also have family rooms.

B&BS

B&Bs are a dying breed and more common outside the city centre. They offer a cosier, homely option at reasonable rates and usually with a hearty breakfast.

HOTELS

The main form of traditional tourist accommodation found all over London. Those in the centre and close to the Thames will be the most expensive.

PRIVATE RENTAL & AIRBNB

The trend of offering up one's London flat for private rental is ever popular; there are many options but they will not come cheap.

APARTHOTEL

A cross between an apartment and hotel, these are usually more upmarket, situated in highly convenient and desirable locations, with a concierge and cleaner.

BOOKING

Some independent hotels offer better rates if you book directly with them, but in most cases, using one of the big apps will usually get you the best price. The busy periods are the summer holidays (July and August) and around Christmas and the New Year.

Booking.com Extremely popular accommodation site offering discounts for loyalty.

Hostelworld (hostelworld.com) Cheap hostels often aimed at backpackers and solo travellers.

Luxury Serviced Apartments (luxuryservicedapartments.com) Great site for upmarket serviced aparthotels in popular districts.

WHERE TO STAY, IF YOU LOVE...

History, architecture & secret gardens City of London (p54) Oodles of history and impressive skyscrapers within walking distance; surprisingly quiet at night and not cheap.

Theatre, dancing & shopping The West End (p32) Expensive but exciting. Lots of late-night entertainment and it's great for a shopping spree, but there's not much quiet here.

↓ Parks, luxury & museums Kensington & Hyde Park (p90) Refined and elegant with several world-class museums, though cheap accommodation is difficult to come by and it's a 25-minute commute from central London.

Markets, boutique shopping & gastropubs Notting Hill & West London (p156) The famous market is here, as is the carnival, but it's tough getting reasonably priced accommodation.

↗ Culture, art & food markets South Bank (p74) Enjoy world-class art and theatre, all within close proximity of one another, and affordable sleeping options away from the river.

Bars, live music & shopping Clerkenwell, Shoreditch & Spitalfields (p106) Plenty of bars and restaurants, but don't expect any peace and quiet. Plenty of accommodation options and close to the City.

Culture, local markets & food East London (p120) Edgy Michelin-starred and ethnic food galore. The best local markets and reasonably priced accommodation and it's surprisingly close to central London.

Boutique shops, green space & Anatolian food Hampstead & North London (p138) Home to the famous Heath and favoured by the wealthy. Pleasantly quiet and convenient, but it's pricey and a 20- to 30-minute commute to the city centre.

Local culture, food & microbreweries Brixton, Peckham & South London (p172) Exciting and vibrant spots with a very local feel; it's the furthest of all from the centre and, therefore, has the cheapest accommodation.

Facing page Ritz Hotel **Left** Hampstead Heath (p146)
Above Butcher at Borough Market (p80)

SAFE TRAVEL

London is safe for its size, but use common sense. Occasional terror attacks do happen, but the risk to individuals is low. Keep an eye on handbags, wallets and phones in bars and nightclubs and on public transport.

MEDICAL SERVICES

EU nationals can obtain free emergency treatment on presentation of a European Health Insurance Card (EHIC). Reciprocal arrangements with the UK allow Australians, New Zealanders and residents and nationals of several other countries to receive free emergency medical treatment and subsidised dental care through the National Health Service.

EDGY NEIGHBOURHOODS

There's a reason they're edgy; when exploring these areas, stick to the main tourist strips and do not go exploring solo into unfamiliar parts, especially at night as muggings and pickpocketing, though rare, are not unheard of.

CROSSING ROADS

As well as making sure you look the right way when crossing roads, there are now a series of cycle lanes between the pavement and the road so be careful when crossing these.

I WEI HUANG/SHUTTERSTOCK ©

PHARMACIES

Pharmacies are common all over London and many are open seven days a week; there are also a number that are open 24 hours.

UNLICESED TAXIS

Don't ever use an unlicensed taxi. Always stick to either black taxis or those ordered through an established taxi or ride-share app.

QUICK TIPS TO HELP YOU MANAGE YOUR MONEY

CREDIT & DEBIT CARDS

The growing popularity of contactless payments (card/phone) was further accelerated by the Covid-19 pandemic so now even market stallholders will have a machine to tap and pay on. Card transactions are subject to additional charges for foreign cardholders. American Express and Diners Club are far less widely accepted than Visa and Mastercard.

CHANGING MONEY

If possible change money at a local post office as commission is not charged here. Other options include banks, some travel agencies and the bureaux de change across the city.

ATMS

ATMs are everywhere in London. Bank ATMs are free to use, whereas private ones charge a small fee. ATMs in entry ports (air and rail) also dispense euros.

CURRENCY

British Pound

HOW MUCH FOR A...

coffee
£2.70

pint of beer
£5.00

dinner for two at Gauchos
£11.00
(not including drinks)

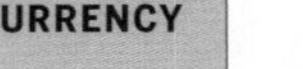

SPLITTING THE BILL

Most restaurants are happy to split bills for you and take payments from individual diners. However, who pays what will need to be worked out by diners unless separate bills are requested at the start.

TIPPING

Londoners tip 10% in restaurants or 15% if impressed with the service. Some establishments bill with a service charge already included. For most other services, like taxis or bartending, tipping is optional.

DISCOUNTS & SAVINGS

All sites, activities and transport offer discounts for students, seniors, children and families. There are also a number of city passes that allow visitors to save on entrance fees to major sites. The most popular is the London Pass, which starts at £56 for adults and £37 for children.

CASHLESS SOCIETY

Cash usage continues to decline in London, and for services like taxis ordered via apps, there is no cash option. However, most restaurants, bars, and tourist services will normally accept cash.

RESPONSIBLE TRAVEL

Positive, sustainable and feel-good experiences around the city.

CHOOSE SUSTAINABLE VENUES

Shop at pioneering ethical shops. Karavan Eco, for example, has been banging this drum since 1995 and is the ideal place to grab your bamboo socks and T-shirts. @karavan_eco

Watch a play at London's carbon-neutral theatre the Arcola Theatre in Dalston, where carbon emissions have been reduced by 25%, solar panels installed, locally brewed beer is served and on Tuesday you 'pay what you can'. @arcolatheatre

Eat from a waste-reducing menu. St John in Smithfields uses all those parts – tongues, trotters and bones – often thrown away by butchers these days to make delicious food. @st.john.restaurant

Go on an Unseen tour (unseen-tours.org.uk) which allows the formerly homeless and socially excluded people to earn a living by guiding you through their city.

Above Volunteering with GoodGym
Right Bags at Portobello Road Market (p160)

GOODGYM ©, OLESEA VETRILA/SHUTTERSTOCK ©

GIVE BACK

Get fit and give back with the Goodgym (goodgym.org), where you run, walk or cycle to do good; help a vulnerable member of society, visit a lonely elder or take part in a community project, all while getting fit.

Volunteer at the Food Cycle (foodcycle.org.uk) and feed hundreds of vulnerable Londoners by turning surplus food into wholesome, nutritious meals and generating a sense of community.

Clean up London's canals with London Boaters and Moo Canoes (moocanoes.com). Float along the city's beautiful waterways in a canoe and exchange your trash for treats at these weekly and monthly events.

SUPPORT LOCAL

Visit real London markets and buy from stalls run by locals for locals.

Eat and shop locally. Purchase a leather handbag from Paradise Row (paradiserow-london.com) made by a local artisan helping to revive East London's lost leather trade; eat dinner cooked with locally sourced ingredients at the Barge East Restaurant (@bargeeast).

Raise a glass to independent brewers. Drink from locally owned microbreweries like the Crate Brewery (@cratebrewery) in Hackney and the Kernel Brewery (@thekernelbrewery) at Bermondsey.

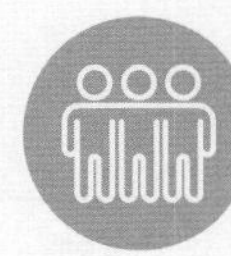

LEARN MORE

Attend a cultural festival and learn about British-Bangladeshis at the Boishakhi Mela (p9, p23).

Visit London's diverse neighbourhoods like Anatolian North London, African-Caribbean South London and Bangladeshi East London.

Educate yourself about the history of London's residents at little-known institutes like the Kobi Nazrul Centre (p129)and the Black Cultural Archives (p187).

LEAVE A SMALL FOOTPRINT

Shop at zero-waste grocery stores that let you bring your own container.

Take your own mug along to coffee shops.

Always keep your reusable shopping bag handy.

Cycle or walk as much as you can when moving around the city.

Buy clothes and gifts at the flea markets and vintage stores.

CLIMATE CHANGE & TRAVEL

It's impossible to ignore the impact we have when travelling, and the importance of making changes where we can. Lonely Planet urges all travellers to engage with their travel carbon footprint. There are many carbon calculators online that allow travellers to estimate the carbon emissions generated by their journey; try resurgence.org/resources/carbon-calculator.html. Many airlines and booking sites offer travellers the option of offsetting the impact of greenhouse gas emissions by contributing to climate-friendly initiatives around the world. We continue to offset the carbon footprint of all Lonely Planet staff travel, while recognising this is a mitigation more than a solution.

RESOURCES

handsonlondon.org.uk
wildlondon.org.uk
socialenterprise.org.uk
safh.org.uk
londonyouth.org

ESSENTIAL NUTS-&-BOLTS

POSTCODES

Work out which part of London a place is in by the letter the postcode begins with; E for East, W for West etc.

WI-FI

Wi-fi is available for free in most cafes, bars and some streets too.

FAST FACTS

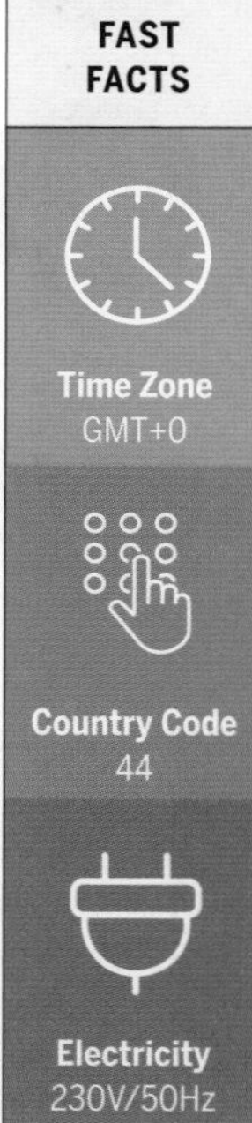

Time Zone
GMT+0

Country Code
44

Electricity
230V/50Hz

GOOD TO KNOW

Free newspapers and magazines like the *Evening Standard*, *Metro* and *Time Out* are good for listings.

Visitors from several nations like Australia, Canada, US and New Zealand can stay up to six months without a visa.

The legal age for buying and drinking alcohol is 18.

You can bargain for goods (except food) in markets but not in shops.

Escalator etiquette means standing on the right and walking on the left.

ACCESSIBLE TRAVEL

Larger, new hotels are far more accessible than older ones, so try to book these in advance.

Transport transfer. Check carefully before going from one accessible train or tube station to another if you need to switch lines; sometimes the station where you switch may not be step-free.

Most major sights like the British Museum or Tower Bridge have an audio guide or hearing loop facility. Sadly guides in Braille remain rare.

Parking bays reserved for visitors requiring assisted access are common across London.

Black taxis are all wheelchair accessible and new ones also have induction loops and intercoms fitted for hearing-aid users.

Buses are much easier to access outside of peak travel times: they can all be lowered to street level; wheelchair users travel free and have priority over pushchairs for the wheelchair spaces on buses.

Guide dogs are welcome everywhere.

Visit Transport for London's accessibility page (tfl.gov.uk/transport-accessibility) to better plan your journeys on London's transport system.

AccessAble (accessable.co.uk) is an excellent resource that provides detailed information about accessibility to many of London's major sights.

Download Lonely Planet's free Accessible Travel guides from shop.lonelyplanet.com/products/accessible-travel-online-resources

APOLOGISING
Londoners, like all Brits, apologise all the time. It's a cultural thing.

GREETING
When meeting someone formally for the first time, shake their hands.

SMOKING & VAPING
Banned indoors and near many buildings, but there are designated smoking areas.

FAMILY TRAVEL

Free travel on buses and trains for children aged 10 and under.

Pushchair space is limited on public transport, especially at peak times when some buses won't even let them on.

Changing facilities for babies are most common in larger chain cafes in central London.

Family eating is easy at chains like Nandos, Wagamama and Giraffe, which have high chairs and kids menus, as do some family-friendly pubs in more residential neighbourhoods.

Admission at all tourist sights is considerably cheaper for children.

WEIGHTS & MEASURES
The UK has a wonderfully confusing mix of both metric and imperial systems for measuring and weighing things.

TOILETS

- Most eating establishments and pubs let you use their toilets if you walk in and ask.
- Some train stations require you to pay to enter.
- Several chain cafes/restaurants have a coded entry with codes printed on the receipt.
- Some larger parks still have public toilets.

MARIO-GALAS/SHUTTERSTOCK ©

LGBTIQ+ TRAVELLERS

Outright discrimination is very rare in London, especially in the centre of town, though it is not unheard of in more conservative and local neighbourhoods.

British culture is still not wholly comfortable with open or extended public displays of affection.

Soho's gay village is the best place for a concentration of venues guaranteed to feel welcoming.

Time Out London LGBT (timeout.com/london/lgbt) remains one of the best sites for LGBTQI+ listings in the capital.

Index

E

F

G

H

I

J

K

L

M

N

000 Map pages

000 Map pages

DEMI PERERA

Demi was born in Sri Lanka and grew up in London. She loves the energy and diversity of the city. Demi's favourite way of exploring any destination is on foot; best for catching things you'd not notice any other way.

@girl_travelsworld

My favourite experience is dinner in Exmouth Market. Eating outside with friends on a summer evening and talking away the hours, long after eating.

QIN XIE

Qin Xie is a London-based journalist and editor specialising in food and travel. When not away on assignment, she loves to check out London's new restaurants, go paddleboarding on the Thames and see quirky shows at smaller theatres.

@qinxiesays

My favourite experience is seeing an evening show at Shakespeare's Globe. The stories are familiar but it feels like a different experience every time.

THIS BOOK

Design development
Lauren Egan, Tina García, Fergal Condon

Content development
Anne Mason

Cartography development
Wayne Murphy, Katerina Pavkova

Production development
Mario D'Arco, Dan Moore, Sandie Kestell, Virginia Moreno, Juan Winata

Series development leadership
Liz Heynes, Darren O'Connell, Piers Pickard, Chris Zeiher

Commissioning Editor
Sandie Kestell

Product Editor
Alison Killilea

Cartographer
Mark Griffiths

Book Designer
Virginia Moreno

Assisting Editors
Gabrielle Innes

Cover Researcher
Lauren Egan

Thanks
Ronan Abayawickrema, Jess Boland, Gwen Cotter, Joel Cotterell, Andrea Dobbin, Gabrielle Stefanos, John Taufa

Our Writers

HANNAH AJALA

British-Nigerian Hannah shares a lot of her local and global adventures mostly online and through her work as an international journalist, from West African travel to being a proud Londoner. She's currently producing and presenting podcasts for the BBC.

@hannah_ajala

My favourite experience is taking an overhead train through my colourful, buzzing borough of Hackney, which is filled with a mix of pop-up stores and galleries, as well as a taste of any continent's cuisine.

LINDA KONDE

Linda is a Congolese-born journalist and editor from Sweden and a former Los Angeles resident. She is passionate about travel, culture and food, and runs VacayStories, a colourful blog about London, food and travels.

@lyndakonde

My favourite experience is dinner in Soho or the Shoreditch area, enjoying a drink with a nice view with friends, or hanging in a park on a warm summer day.

THARIK HUSSAIN

London-based Tharik is author of the acclaimed book *Minarets in the Mountains; A Journey into Muslim Europe,* and knows a thing or two about Muslim heritage and travel. He's also authored Lonely Planet guides to Thailand, Bahrain and Saudi Arabia.

@tharik_hussain _tharikhussain

My favourite experience is a lazy Sunday afternoon in Brick Lane indulging in culinary adventures, antiques, vintage and culture, before heading to Columbia Road Flower Market.

TRAVIS LEVIUS

Travis is a Brooklyn-born multimedia journalist and content creator straddling the Atlantic between Atlanta and London. He runs workshops on freelance travel writing and is in the early stages of penning a book bridging self-help and travel.

@misterlevius

My favourite experience is gazing at the London skyline during early sunset, with a cider in hand, atop Frank's Café in Peckham.